Deeper

LifeStyle

Insights
For
Spirit-Filled
Christians

JIM H.YOHE

ISBN 0-9670603-1-1
Library of Congress Catalogue Card Number: 00-090450

First Printing...Winter 2000

For information contact:
FAITHCHILD COMMUNICATIONS
P. O. Box 5, Independence, LA 70443-0005

Acknowledgments

I'd like to dedicate this book to my pastor and wife, Bro. John & Sis. Londa Cupit of New Orleans, Louisiana. They have been my friends through the high times and the valleys. Their example of faithfulness and trust in God is an inspiration to all who know them.

Thanks to an old friend and soon-to-be Ph.D, Sarah Logan for checking the manuscript for punctuation and grammar. Also a big thank you to Brian Banashak & crew at Genesis Communications in Mobile, Alabama for the great cover!

A special thanks to three very special families who have become a home-away-from-home in my ministerial travels. In Indiana, my great friend and cousin, the Rev. Thomas & Linda Simison. In Illinois, Uncle Jimmy & Aunt Shirley Howe. In Florida, Rev. George & Kay Robbins who have fed me many a meal. Without friends and supporters like these, I would have returned to radio many years ago. Of course, the many pastors and editors across America that create opportunities for both pulpit and writing ministry. From the bottom of our hearts, Marilee and I thank you.

Books By Jim H.Yohe

Confronting Racism
Putting God's Grace Over Race
Does the Bible teach that blacks are cursed? Were American blacks put into slavery as a punishment for idolatry? Learn how the red blood of Jesus covers white indifference and black rage! Racial myths are examined in the light of God's word!

Deeper LifeStyle
Insights For Spirit-Filled Christians
Prayer is important, but is it enough? How important is submission, witnessing, study or faith? What about spiritual heroes, respect or having the right attitude? You will be challenged to dig deeper into God's love!

Table Of Contents

Foreword

deeper *(dep'ur)* 1. strongly felt *(deeper* love) 2. hard to understand; abstruse *(deeper* book) 3. extremely grave or serious 4. intellectually profound 5. sunk in or absorbed by: with *(deeper* in thought*)* 6. great in degree; intense *(deeper* joy) ***adv.*** in a deeper way or to a deeper extent

lifestyle *(lif'stil')* ***n.*** the consistent, integrated way of life of an individual as typified by his or her manner, attitudes, possessions,etc.

-Webster's New World Dictionary

Foreword

The Psalmist David said, *"Deep cries unto deep . . .",* those in search of mining in the richer veins of Jesus will quickly drill into Jim Yohe's latest book, *Deeper LifeStyle.* Though the book is named, *"Deeper...",* the shallow who hunger for more depth will readily comprehend the Biblical affirmations of this work.

Through its page you will come to understand that one Christian cannot perform all of the functions of the entire church. *"The individual talents and abilities that God has given you are a good indicator of the type of role He wants you to perform."* Jim further wisely observes, *"If you want to become someone's friend, you find what you have in common with that person and then discuss those subjects or participate in those activities in the friendship's infancy. No one builds a friendship by focusing on differences of opinion."* He goes on to say, *"As the relationship matures, you can then begin to walk where angels fear to tread."* Yes, *"He that winneth souls is wise."*

The observations on attitudes that are dealt with in this book are vital for the church in the 21st century. Yes, you can attract more flies with sugar than vinegar. Jim Yohe gives some fresh insights into apostolic Christian living in the contemporary society of this 21st century. The chapters on "Goals", "Submission", "Respect", "Holiness", "Purity" are worth not only reading but anointed thinking and comprehension.

I commend my friend for again giving himself to this insightful work. Read *"Deeper LifeStyle"* and let it do just what the title infers- take you deeper into the fathomless love of our Lord Jesus Christ. Salvation is free but discipleship will cost you everything.

T.F. Tenney

Chapter One
" *Great Expectations* "
" These signs shall follow them that believe . . ." (Mark 16:16)
- Personal Goals -

What a relief! It lifted such a heavy load from my mind when I realized that the *Acts of the Apostles* were written over several decades! The dynamic exploits of the disciples recorded in the book of Acts were the *highlights* of the early church. They were like the fruitful Ethiopian crusades led by the Rev.Billy Cole. The *Acts* were the apostles' spiritual high times that were recorded and retold to encourage the early church and to glorify God! For years I had mistakenly thought that these supernatural demonstrations were everyday occurrences! That the entire book of Acts probably happened in one week! My understanding of the apostolic lifestyle had served as a great source of discouragement to me. If God wasn't a respecter of persons and I had received the *same* Holy Ghost, then why wasn't God working through me in the *same* way?

I had carefully obeyed the injunction of Peter to *" Repent: and be baptized every one of you in the name of Jesus Christ: for the remission of sins: and ye shall receive the gift of the Holy Ghost"(Acts 2:38).* I, too, spoke in other tongues when I received the Holy Ghost. But the external evidences of my apostolic experience seemed to end there. There had been no Gate Beautiful demonstrations of healing. I hadn't been cast into jail by jealous religious and governmental authorities because of any supernatural event. What was wrong with me? I thought that I had become an apostolic Christian.

As the years passed, I did become involved in what I thought were apostolic-type ministry outreaches. In late 1973, I was thrown off the stage of a Trinitarian youth convention in Stockton, California. Over 5,000 saw me take over the microphone and condemn them as apostates. To say the least, I didn't make my college president, Bro.

Kenneth Haney very proud. In early 1974, I was arrested and thrown into jail for preaching on Houston's Market Square. That early Sunday morning, at 2 a.m., Bro. James Kilgore paid my bail of $22 and took me home.

It was readily apparent that no one was being saved or healed as the result of my *apostolic* efforts. I put increasing pressure upon myself to be more *apostolic*. Instead of being encouraged by anointed sermons which glorified the miraculous works of God, they would instead plunge me into the depths of depression. *I simply missed the fact that only God can perform the miraculous!*

As I entered into marriage, parenting, and the responsibilities of earning a living, my spiritual self-image continued it's downward spiral. My image of being a contemporary Christian was to live a life of victory, to enjoy a glorious mountaintop-to-mountaintop lifestyle. Though faith had been carefully drilled into me by the church, even the remotest possibility of failure had never been addressed. My concept of Christianity was made up of great expectations or great rejections. Being raised in the church, I knew that the flip-side to acceptance *of* the body of Christ was rejection *by* the body of Christ. Going through *immediate*, extreme changes in character and lifestyle were considered the normal response to salvation. It seems that time was never given for a Christian to grow into the image of Christ. Everything is supposed to happen immediately or it's deemed a reflection of the shallow depth of your conversion experience.

If asked about my spiritual life, in an honest moment I would have answered, " I've been encouraged to adopt the quick pictures of healing and deliverance in the New Testament as my role model. The advice of Paul to a young minister, Timothy, to *' Be instant in season, and out of season;'* (II Tim 4:2) has become the self-defeating paradigm of my spiritual life. Being a debater, I am very much aware of the inconsistency of my testimony. Like many spirit-filled Christians, I boast of my belief in the gifts of the Spirit, and I am quick to point to the gifts of utterance, i.e. tongues, interpretation of tongues and prophecy that are in operation in our local church, along with the fervent belief that the word of knowledge, the word of wisdom, and the discerning of spirits are active in the preaching of the Word.

But often I feel compelled to come up with elaborate reasons why there are no physical evidences of the gifts of healing, the working of miracles and the gift of faith! My hollow affirmations make me feel dirty, dishonest and afraid that something is wrong with my spiritual walk. The unyielding standard of normal apostolic life that is constantly placed before me makes me doubt my own salvation." What a sad state of affairs! Consequently, I ended up leaving the church for eleven long years of disillusionment and heartache.

We must all realize that one Christian cannot perform all of the functions of the entire church! The individual talents and abilities that God has given you are a good indicator of the type of role he wants you to perform. Just like the gardener who is watering his plants has nothing to do with how the water benefits the plants, he is simply directing the flow of water. Likewise, as a Christian you can allow the Spirit to flow through you, but you cannot mandate just how the Spirit is working! Initially, God wants you to share your personal testimony. Don't feel pressured to be Peter, James or John! Simply be a witness of what God has done in your life. As you grow in Christ, you may evolve into an apostle, prophet, pastor, teacher, evangelist or you might continue to grow as a soulwinner and discipler. I've noticed that the most fruitful Christians are those that have learned to relax and simply let God use them.

I allowed that same paradigm of apostolic example to hang over me in the early years of my pulpit ministry. I longed for God to take over the service and baptize dozens with the Holy Ghost. I would hear of well-known ministries that evidenced such mighty moves of God. Ever the student of apostolic demonstration, I would travel to be in their meetings. When the service was over, dozens were filled with the Spirit, mighty healings would occur, I would still go home frustrated. I'd ask my wife, " *Tell me, just what did he say tonight? He just screamed a bunch of cliches and told a Bible story! And fifteen get the Holy Ghost! Can you believe it?* " In my puzzlement, I had missed the obvious. Walking in a deeper lifestyle than my own, the successful preacher had learned not to put pressure on himself to provide the salvation experience or healing miracle. Obviously, it was beyond his own abilities! He had simply learned to promote an atmosphere of faith and then *let God do the work!*

If your back is itching, it's just a natural reflex for your fingers to curl up, your arm to reach back over your shoulder and commence to scratching! All of this activity occurring in response to instinctive commands from the brain. Tell me, what would happen if your elbow popped out of joint just because it *never* got to do any scratching? Huh? Why do we allow ourselves to get out of joint when God doesn't use us in the way that we think He should? Christ is the head of the church which is His Body. It is just as natural for Jesus to instruct the appropriate members of His church to do the work they were created to do, just as it is for your brain to order your back to get scratched by the fingernails of your hand! A deeper lifestyle is one that is totally submitted to the Master!

Don't allow yourself to be beaten down by unrealistic expectations. Have the great expectations of *God!* Take comfort in the fact that the same Jesus who set the believer's standard , *"Go ye into all the world and preach the gospel to every creature . . .and these signs shall follow them that believe; In my name shall they cast out devils, they shall speak with new tongues; They shall take up serpents; and if they drink any deadly thing, it shall not hurt them; they shall lay hands on the sick, and they shall recover"(Mark 16:16-18),* on a previous occasion had quietly affirmed, " *My sheep hear my voice, and I know them, and they follow me: And I give unto them eternal life; and they shall never perish, neither shall any man pluck them out of my hand. My Father, which gave them me, is greater than all; and no man is able to pluck them out of my Father's hand. I and my Father are one." (John 10:27-30)* To obtain a deeper lifestyle in the Spirit, we must learn to seek His Kingdom and rest in the assurance that His will is being done in our lives!

Our great expectations must be in His abilities, not in our own!

Chapter Two
" Secrets Of Soulwinning "
" He that winneth souls is wise" (Proverbs 11:30)
-Soulwinning -

I confess that I've made many mistakes in my witnessing efforts to reach the lost. I grew up with the mind-set that people who didn't share my religious convictions were going straight to Hell! It didn't matter whether they were atheist or agnostic, Baptist preacher, Catholic pope, Episcopal priest or any other minister or church member from the other branches of Christianity; they were all in the same boat headed south. I was convinced that all the other Christian denominations *really* knew that we spirit-filled Christians were right, but because they didn't want to *"pay the price"* of being different from everyone else, they deliberately taught false doctrine. In other words, I believed everyone was being dishonest about God except me and my little group. So, consequently, I didn't respect the religious experience of anyone else.

Religious or atheistic, they were all fair game to me. Instead of seeking out any common ground of belief, I immediately went for the differences in doctrine that were sure to ignite a heated debate. After watching me street witness, one of my friends commented dryly, *"Jim, it's a good thing you're 6'3 and weigh 240 pounds! Otherwise, he would have decked you!"* Motivated by deep convictions and religious zeal, I invaded the outreach crusades of other Christian groups, took over their microphones, and was once arrested and jailed. All the time thinking that I was on the side of truth fighting man's false religious tradition. I always had this Old Testament model of a prophet calling down judgment in my mind!

That was almost thirty years ago. I was taken aback recently when I learned that the pastor of one of the largest churches that we had consistently attacked, now teaches my doctrinal position to his congregation. Why did he finally change? Because some other spirit-filled Christian took a different approach than I did. He approached him as a friend who had common ground in believing that the Bible is the Word of God. Observing that *"You catch more flies with honey than vinegar!"* he was able to accomplish what our *"bold"* methods couldn't. As time passed, this denominational pastor was convinced of the spirit-filled experience along with many of his church members!

As Christians, we must learn to respect truth, nothing but the truth, and acknowledge truth no matter who affirms it! Scientist Carl Sagan once contrasted the varying degrees of commitment that science and the church world have regarding truth. *" This is one of the reasons that organized religions do not inspire me with confidence. Which leaders of the major faiths acknowledge that their beliefs might be incomplete or erroneous and establish institutions to uncover possible doctrinal deficiencies? Science is forever whispering in our ears, ' Remember, you're very new at this. You might be mistaken. You've been wrong before.' Despite all the talk of humility, show me something comparable in religion!"* More truth is what we all seek even if we discover it outside of our own current religious experience! One religious sage proclaimed, *" If a thousand old beliefs are shattered in our march towards truth, we must still march on!"*

Think about it; if you want to be someone's friend, you find what you have in common with that person and then discuss those subjects or participate in those activities in the friendship's infancy. No one builds a friendship by focusing on differences of opinion! As the relationship matures, you can then begin to walk where *"angels fear to tread."* King Solomon knew what he was talking about when he commented, *" He that winneth souls is wise!"(Proverbs 11:30)* Successful soulwinners know that an investment of time is required. Soulwinning is rarely a hit and run operation. At the first contact, very few people are going to immediately fall at your feet and begin to repent!

No one responds to a know-it-all. When witnessing to traditional Christians, learn to show a little respect for their personal experience with God. Didn't you feel the presence of God at repentance? Well, so did they! If you are hungry for more truth from God, you may very well learn something from them that may strengthen *your* walk with God. Believe it or not, God is not through revealing truth to mankind!

You happen to be spirit-filled, but have you *really* experienced everything you believe? Do you demonstrate healing? Deliverance? Can't you find room to grow spiritually yourself? In adjusting your attitude, put yourself in your friend's place. Understand that you are trying to help a fellow believer *grow* in Christ. Share what you have without ridiculing or condemning what they have. Why focus on what they have wrong when God just wants you to share what you have right?

With the attitude of a fellow believer, realize that everyone is at a different stage of spiritual growth. I mean Baptist, Church of God, Disciples of Christ, etc. as well as both Trinitarian and Apostolic Pentecostals! Before you judge others, first review your own salvational status. Are you saved? Granted, you're saved from your old sins, but are you eternally saved? As spirit-filled Christians, we are s-a-f-e, but no one is really s-a-v-e-d until the pearly gates smack us on the backside! We may consider ourselves further along than other professed Christians, but we're still striving to make Heaven our home! Please realize that most spirit-filled and mainstream Christians agree on basic Christian doctrines such as the inerrancy of the Bible, the blood, the family, morality, seeking to live a holy life, the need for salvation, the work accomplished by Jesus at Calvary, etc. It's in the application of these shared truths that divide Christian believers. Often it's our superior attitude that drives people away, not our Pentecostal beliefs!

We can accept that a grade schooler is not as knowledgeable as a junior high student. And likewise, a high-schooler is not as educated as a college senior about to graduate. If you are an upper classman, is it fair to be contemptuous at the lack of knowledge displayed by students who haven't attained your level of education? Of course not!

You should try to relate to them on the level of what they *have* been taught. In the area of religious experience, we should not display an arrogant attitude towards those who have only experienced what they've been taught. But for the grace of God, we wouldn't know the deeper lifestyle enjoyed by spirit-filled Christians ourselves. The golden rule of *" Do unto others as you'd have them do unto you"* should be the first rule of successful soulwinning Mutual respect is the basis of all friendship or fellowship.

Can you imagine how it grieves the heart of God when some of us unwise soulwinners stand during the church service and testify ,
" Well, I tried to witness to them today, but they just couldn't stomach the truth! Brothers and sisters, the world just doesn't want holiness!"
The actual truth is they couldn't stomach your nasty, disrespectful attitude towards them and what they have from God. They didn't see Christ in you! They didn't see anything in you that they would want in their own lives. Despite your self-serving testimony at church, they didn't reject *truth*, they rejected *you*. Tell me, should our soulwinning efforts fill up Hell or Heaven? Personally, I choose the latter.

The mythical Atlas once stated, *" Give me a place to stand and I can move the world!"* All Christians have the common ground of the written Word of God. Acknowledge that common belief, stand together upon it, and then do as Jesus did; point them to Jerusalem to Pentecost! As fellow believers, they should be made aware that *" Ye shall receive power after that the Holy Ghost is come upon you!"(Acts 1:8)*. I rejoice that in my Christian walk I have won many to the Lord. It is my sorrow that I know that in foolish zeal I have driven many away. I think it's worthy of note that in the nine gifts of the Spirit, God provided the word of wisdom that would operate hand-in-hand with the word of knowledge. Because knowledge without wisdom can destroy! So God provides us not only a word of knowledge but also the wisdom in how to use it. In our soulwinning we should also seek wisdom in how-to-use the knowledge of God's word to save and not destroy! If he that winneth souls is wise, then he that loseth souls is foolish.

God given wisdom is the soulwinner's secret.

Chapter Three
" Supernatural Documents "
" My word . . .shall not return unto me void" - Isaiah 55:11
- Tract-Passing -

One new convert with a burning desire to win souls. One slip of paper put into the hands of a visiting African journalist. The One True God whose printed word turned that paper into a supernatural document that resulted in tens of thousands of African souls being born into the Kingdom. What was this supernatural document? A small gospel tract! The result? The birth of a new missionary work in Ghana!

It happened in the mid-60's, sometime between the assassinations of John and Bobby Kennedy. A new convert at our church in Bloomington, Illinois got this great idea about handing out tracts every Saturday. Soon all of us pre-teen church boys were drafted into Bro.Richard Harp's tract-passing team. Each week we'd meet at the church, first to methodically indulge in the dullest activity ever devised, i.e. stamping tracts, and then we'd all head downtown!

What livened things up every weekend was the fact that Bloomington's African-American citizens were civil-rights marching around the courthouse square! Bored from days of repetitious marching, the participants willingly accepted our tracts. After shifting their placards to one side, they would read the tract while continuing to sing and march. So, with such a large crowd gathered downtown, we always ran out of tracts quickly! Which meant it was time to enjoy the ten-cent bottle of ice-cold Orange Crush that Bro.Richard always bought us!

One day, my Dad, the late J.H.Yohe, Sr., received an unexpected letter from Africa. It was from a friend of an African journalist who had flown down from Chicago to Bloomington to cover the demonstrations. While standing on the town square, he had received a tract from one of us kids. Several weeks later while flying home to

Africa, he pulled the tract out of his coat pocket and began to read. Immediately he noticed a similarity in belief to views held by one of his religious friends. Arriving in Africa, he contacted this friend who also read the tract, who then turned it over to read: *" First Pentecostal Church, 601 N. East St., Bloomington, Illinois 61701, J.H. Yohe, Sr. Pastor, Phone: 967-8053, "* **You see, it does pay to stamp tracts!** Quickly he fired off this letter to my father in Illinois asking him to come to Africa and share the spiritual insights mentioned in the tract.

Within the text of his letter, he related that in the early 1900's, a group of Africans that had been partially evangelized began praying and seeking for the Holy Ghost. One day a cloud of fire appeared over the prayer hut and burned brightly day and night for several weeks! Whoever entered the prayer hut was instantly baptized with the Holy Ghost and began to speak with other tongues! His letter inquired about baptism in Jesus Name and the Oneness of the Godhead, two subjects of the tract that greatly interested him.

Dad's excitement was only exceeded by his great pride in Bro.Richard's little group of tract-passers! As the months passed he made travel plans, raised funds for his upcoming trip, and accepted a traveling companion, a fellow pastor, Rev.Robert Rodenbush, who was the editor of the Illinois District News whose anticipated role was to report the activities that would occur. What actually happened? Well, you'll probably read it in great detail someday whenever Bro.Rodenbush decides to write his own book, but in a nutshell, this is what took place.

Upon arriving in Ghana, they began teaching and debating the various truths of the Word. Their efforts resulted in the baptizing of seventy-two Nazarene pastors who then joined Bro.Rodenbush and Dad in baptizing their own congregations. Over 1066 were immediately baptized in Jesus Name, a number that quickly mushroomed into over three thousand! In fact, those original seventy-two churches became the nucleus for the thriving missionary force in Ghana that still exists today!

Returning to the United States, both men amazed audiences as they told of the mighty move of God taking place in West Africa! Eventually, Bro.Rodenbush resigned his church and returned to Ghana as a resident missionary to disciple and establish the work. This great harvest of souls was due to a small group of little Pentecostal boys handing out religious tracts! Today tens of thousands of African souls are thankful that one determined soulwinner, Bro.Richard Harp, didn't feel that handing out tracts was a waste of time!

The Word declares, *" So shall my word be that goeth forth out of my mouth: it shall not return unto me void, it shall accomplish that which I please, **and it shall prosper in the thing whereto I sent it.** "* *(Isaiah 55:11)* In this age of mass communication and the Internet, don't ever think that the buying and distributing of religious tracts is ineffective! When the Living Word is printed with a few drops of ink on paper, that paper is transformed into a supernatural document that can change lives and save a nation! Only in Africa? Absolutely not!

In the seventies, a lone tract was blowing down a tree-lined street of New Orleans when a young man, Danny Brown picked it up and read it. Interested, he turned it over and read the stamped imprint, *First Pentecostal Church, 122 N. Dorgenois St., New Orleans, LA, John R. Cupit, Pastor, 822-0668.* He immediately headed to the church and inquired of the pastor about how-to-be-saved. The rest is history. Bro.Danny Brown was saved and later when he was called into the ministry, *First Church* helped him start the now legendary *Apostolic Outreach Center* which recently moved into a new 1200-seat sanctuary in New Orleans East. Now also pastored by Bro.John Cupit, who assumed the pastorate after Bro. Brown's untimely death, *Apostolic Outreach Center* stands as a testament to the power of one religious tract!

Today the tract ministry is still going strong! The written Word turns a religious tract into a supernatural document! The church stamp directs the tract reader to a flesh-and-blood soulwinner! Because of some humble tract-stamper, thousands of people in both Ghana and New Orleans have been saved.

Think about it . . .what if those tracts hadn't been stamped?

Chapter Four

" Just A Wal-Mart Cashier . . . "

" Ye are our epistle . . .known and read of all men: " II Cor.3:2

- Attitude -

She knew I was a Pentecostal preacher. I knew she had a Pentecostal background. She was dining at the next table at the *McDonald's* restaurant inside the local *Wal-Mart* store. A group of holiness Christian women who knew me passed us by while nodding at me and furtively staring at her. Sitting at the table with her dyed-blond hair, a full complement of rings and things, and also wearing dark pants that blended with her blue *Wal-Mart* smock, it was obvious that I was talking to an attractive woman who didn't follow the accepted standards of holiness churches.

Noticing the stares of the church ladies, my guest commented to me, *" You wouldn't believe how rude these Pentecostal women are!"*

" Really?" I responded in surprise.

" A few years ago when I hired on at ' Lane Bryant,' the plus-size ladies store at the mall, and during my orientation, even the manager warned me about the Pentecostals!" she volunteered. Though small in resident population, our town has over ten spirit-filled holiness churches within driving distance of the local *Wal-Mart*. The dress standards of the churches run the gamut, everything from forbidding the wearing of neck ties and store-bought clothes to the more widely-accepted standards of the organized churches of the world-wide holiness movement.

Shocked, I retorted *" Warned you? About us?"*

Nodding, she answered *" Here's what she said, ' I need to warn you about the Pentecostal women. They're unfriendly and rude, in fact, they are the most demanding customers we have. But they do spend money. They get angry because we don't carry jean skirts year round, but they do spend money! And she was absolutely right! "*

Embarrassed by what she had just shared with me, I blurted out, *" But surely you have other customers who aren't as polite as they should be?"*

She nodded, *" Yes, but by their hair and dress, holiness women are announcing to the world that they're holier than everybody else!"* she countered. *" Here at Wal-Mart, they walk in with their stringy-hair and baggy jean skirts with the longest faces you've ever seen! We joke in the break room how unhappy and grouchy these holiness women are! None of us would ever want to be like them! If there's an item mis-priced, they always demand to see the manager or demand a discount for their trouble! No forgiveness or understanding! And the women that know my own Pentecostal background avoid talking to me by deliberately not getting in my line! It's almost like they resent the fact that I don't attend church regularly! It's like they're angry at me for not being like them!"*

Humbled by what she was divulging to me, I immediately thought of the old adage, *" You attract more flies with honey than vinegar".* As Christians, we must realize that our lives are constantly being watched by others. True, they may be looking for one of our faults to surface so they can attempt to justify their own weaknesses, but we must still seek to example Christ at all times. We want the world to want what we have! Getting desperate, I protested, *" You probably don't have any more problems with Pentecostals than anyone else! You just probably notice it more because of our ladies distinctive dress and hairstyles!"*

She nodded her head, and then thoughtfully replied, *" I guess because they're Christians you notice it more. You just don't expect that kind of behavior from a Christian."* What could I say? Do we only save our smiles and polite behavior for our own brothers and sisters at church? Though we preach *" With joy we draw water from the wells of salvation! The joy of the Lord is our strength!"* can the world that reads our lives as *" living epistles"* see the joy bubbling from within us? Should we even bother to listen to a report from this unknown individual who takes our money at the store?

After all, she's just a *Wal-Mart* cashier.

Who has a soul.

Chapter Five
" Playing Possum "
" You are dead, and your life is hid with Christ in God" - Col.3:3
- Submission -

Back in the '60's, I once had the whole gang over for a sleep-over on a Friday night. After my folks sent us up to the bedroom, the inevitable slumber-party pillow fight broke out! And after yelling at us several times, my Dad finally sent my Aunt Lucille Courtney up to check on us. When she reached the bedroom door, she looked in on us and then called back down the stairs, *" Jim, these little guys are all playing possum!"* Possum? Though frozen in fear-of-a-whipping, we breathlessly looked at each other in amazement! What was playing possum?

The next morning the first thing we did was look up Uncle Fuss (which is what we called Aunt Lucille's husband, Russell, because he was always fussing about something!) *" Uncle Fuss, what did Aunt Lucille mean when she said we were playing possum? "* With a grin, he kicked back in his easy chair and immediately began spinning one of his tall tales. This one was about being fooled by ten cat-napping opossums back in the Great Depression days when he and his father trapped skins to sell. After several twists and turns, he eventually concluded by saying *" Jimmie, Jr., my Dad grabbed the bag, looked in it and then pulled out the only remaining possum that hadn't run off. Knowing I was scared, having lost nine possum, he said,*
' Russell, I'm not going to whip you, it was my fault. I should have made sure they were really dead. The reason they're gone, Russell, is they weren't really dead, the possum's were just playing possum. Acting like they were dead when they really weren't!"

In the letter to the church at Colosse, Paul wrote to people who claimed to be dead to the temptations of the world, but who really weren't! *" Wherefore IF ye be dead with Christ from the rudiments of the world, why, as though living in the world, are ye subject to ordinances? (Touch not; taste not; handle not; Which all are to perish with the using;) after the commandments and doctrines of men . . .If ye then be risen with Christ, seek those things which are above, . . .Set your affection on things above, not on things on the earth. FOR YE ARE DEAD, and your life is hid with Christ in God. When Christ, who is our life, shall appear, then shall ye also appear with him in glory!" (Col.2:20-22, 3:1-4).* That particular spiritual problem wasn't unique with Epaphras' converts in the church he founded at Colosse. Even today *"playing possum"* is too often practiced by modern day Christians! Acting as though we are dead to the world, but in truth, our carnal desires are very much alive!

If you have *given* your life to Jesus, then your life is no longer yours, but His. When people think of us, all they should see is Christ in us. They may never know my name, but they must be aware that I am a Christian. Essentially Paul is asking, *" If you are dead, how come you act like you're still alive? How come you still seek the approval of the world by trying to live by the fashions and opinions of the world?"* Tough questions! The fact is that many of us *are not* dead to the world, we're just playing possum. It's easy to let Christ shine through us while singing, shouting and worshipping Him in the church house. It's easy to give Him preeminence while surrounded by fellow believers, but we *haven't* learned to love spiritual things more than everyday things.

Once a wise sage remarked, *" If we Christians ever got to the point where we didn't care WHO got the credit, we could win the world to Christ!"* In a nutshell, if we could die to our own egos, God could work through us to reconcile the world to Himself. We must not let the human desires for new cars, the bigger house, the finer vacations, the classier wardrobe be the driving force of our lives. Our need for recognition or prominence must not be given precedence over the cause of Christ. Our personal wants and identity must be lost in another who lives His life through us!

Paul sums it up, " *When Christ, who is our life, shall appear, THEN shall ye also appear with Him in glory!*" In other words, hang in there, your time is coming. You are dead to your own desires and ego so that Christ can work through you to win the lost and dying of the world. Christ is literally YOUR life. Your life is Christ's life. However, when he shall appear, You, too, will appear with Him in glory. Your next personal appearance isn't slated until the Rapture of the Church! So, we must honor our commitment to give our life to Him and not continuously wrestle Him for control of it. He's Lord of all or not Lord at all! Have you ever heard of a dead person suing for control from beyond the grave? Of course not! Because the dead have no rights! We are quick to give Jesus our wrongs, but Paul demands that we give Him our rights as well.

For Christ's sake, let's quit playing possum!

Chapter Six
" The Little Red Stapler "
Along with his Bible, Bill Drost always carried one.
- Commitment -

In late 1964, my father, the late J.H.Yohe, Sr was invited to preach a missionary conference in Palmira, Columbia. Other invited speakers included Oscar Vouga, O.W.Williams, Bro.Staires from Canada, Bill Drost of Peru, as well as Bro. & Sis. Thompson, Morley and Larson, who were the resident missionaries. After an explosive conference which yielded several physical miracles, my Dad, Bill Drost and I were flying on an *Avianca* plane to minister at Santa Rosa, Columbia.

Santa Rosa was a beautiful Columbian village nestled in the mountains. It was known for it's spectacular falls and therapeutic hot springs. Bro.Drost was scheduled to preach at a small church there. Arriving at the airport, Bro.Drost negotiated the cab fare with a local driver to deliver us to Santa Rosa's downtown area. The colorful, talkative cab driver conversed excitedly with Bro.Drost in Spanish all the way to town! Not understanding a word of it, my father and I took in the breathtaking scenery. It was when we got out of the cab onto the picturesque town square that I noticed the towering Catholic cathedral. Being the perfect host, Bro.Drost was informing us about the sights we were seeing when all of a sudden a Catholic priest stepped out of the church and spoke sharply to Bro.Drost in Spanish. The sight of another Protestant missionary in town was not a welcome sight! Nodding politely to the priest, Bro.Drost quickly answered him. Pulling my father aside, Bro.Drost spoke quietly to my father in a way that I couldn't hear what was being said.

Abruptly, Bro.Drost turned to me, *" Jimmie, Jr.! Are you hungry? Let's head for the cafe!"* Both men grabbed one of my hands and began walking at a furious pace, literally dragging me toward the corner restaurant. Once we entered the establishment and sat down, Bro.Drost ordered for us and began his dining ritual that as a ten-year old I found fascinating. He carefully began biting his fingernails, and when our drinks arrived, he invariably always poured salt into his *Coca-Cola* which made it fizz! Reaching into his front pants pocket, he spilled the contents on the table to sort out a few coins for a newspaper. Along with the coins he dropped a little red tot-stapler on the table. Wide-eyed with amazement, I asked,*" Why do you carry a little red stapler in your pocket, Bro.Drost? I've never heard of that!"*

In askance, Bro.Drost looked at my father. Without speaking a word, Dad nodded his permission. Taking my right hand, and carefully placing the stapler in it, Bro.Drost answered the question. *" Little Jim, when I leave to preach in areas that do not love the true gospel of Jesus Christ, not only do I pack my Bible, but also this little stapler. Did you notice that priest that was angry with me, a few minutes ago?"* I nodded in the affirmative. *" Well, about three weeks ago, I was preaching in front of his church on that same town square we walked across. The priests in this area frown on Protestant missionary activity. While I was preaching, the priest led a large group of men armed with ball bats and clubs to attack the worshippers and myself. Though we tried to resist, they soon prevailed. And I was beaten into unconsciousness."*

Stopping to take a drink of salty *Coke*, Bro.Drost continued, *" After several hours I woke up in a dark jail cell. I was covered with blood, bruises and in extreme pain. My clothes had been ripped into shreds, they left me there with no food, with only water for three days. All of a sudden, the cell door opened and they commanded me to leave. Grabbing the remaining shreds of my clothes in the pitch-black cell, I followed them until all of a sudden I was blinded by the bright light of the sun, when they pushed me, completely naked out into the town square where a group of people were gathered to jeer and make fun of me. Little Jim, being naked, I was embarrassed, I dropped to the ground and attempted to cover myself. Then after awhile, the crowd went away."*

I interrupted him, *" But Bro.Drost, what about the little red stapler? Was it from the priest? You found it in the jail cell?"* The restaurant chatter had silenced as other American tourists were listening to this incredible story.

Bro.Drost finished, *" Then I reached into my shredded pants pocket, pulled out my little red stapler and carefully stapled my clothes back together so I could walk to the airport fully clothed. That's why I always carry a stapler with me, in case I am stripped and beaten."*

Though I was only ten years old, I felt the presence of God that day in a way that I have rarely felt Him even as an adult. Later in life, when I read Paul's writing, *" You are dead, and your life is hid with Christ in God!"* (Col.3:3) *" I am crucified with Christ: nevertheless I live, yet not I, but Christ liveth in me!"*(Gal.2:20) *" Likewise reckon ye also yourselves to be dead indeed unto sin, but alive unto God through Jesus Christ our Lord!"*(Romans 6:11) I realized that I had seen this type of commitment in action in the life of Pentecostal missionary Bill Drost.

When I shared this story with his grandson, who is also a missionary, he told me that after evangelizing South America, Bill Drost took on the challenge of bringing the gospel to Spain. Buried in a small Spanish cemetery, today his legacy lives on as many of the tens of thousands of people that this one Pentecostal life touched travel from all over the world to visit his grave. Even now, decades after his death, the locals respond to these Pentecostal pilgrims, *" Oh, Drost the Pentecost! You want to see his grave!"* In death, Bill Drost's identity is still hidden in Christ. He is forever . . .Drost the Pentecost. Today, the world-wide harvest of souls that spirit-filled Pentecostals are reaping did not come without a price. Are there still believers among us that would cheerfully pack their clothes, their Bibles and a little red stapler?

Chapter Seven
" Search And Rescue"
" Quit praying! Get the people moving!" (Ex.15:14)
- Witnessing -

The fact that Bill Clinton is a master politician escapes no one. Both his political allies and foes acknowledge that he is a consummate compromiser. And Bill Clinton's rare ability to "co-op" his opponents ideas and make them his own continually frustrates his critics. Oftentimes Republicans have had to settle for the bittersweet victory that their ideas are working, but Bill Clinton's political party is reaping the rewards. In a similar way, society-at-large has co-opted many of the messages of the church. Those who say no one preaches against smoking, drinking, drugs, and promiscuous sex anymore haven't been listening to their radios. Society has gotten the message! Though it wraps the idea of *"responsible"* sex in a condom instead of within marriage, secular messages suggesting restraint-or-suffer-the-consequences are filtering through.

Obviously these human vices still abound, but society no longer considers the Christian stand against these types of sins-of-the-flesh an outlandish proposition. Yet having come to the same lifestyle conclusions from vastly different moral positions, to the casual observer it would seem the holiness church and society are harmoniously marching in lockstep on some issues.

In a recent book, *" A Return To Modesty: Discovering The Lost Virtue"*, social critic/author Wendy Shalit promotes the old-fashioned idea of modesty. In a People Magazine interview (April 19,1999), she states, *" Our society has lost sight of the value of feminine modesty, and young women pay a heavy price for that loss - not only in a climate that fosters date rape, stalking, harassment and body-image problems, but in a loss of control over their own lives and fortunes. "Respect for modesty,"* Shalit offers, *"made women powerful."*

24

t seems that the Bible-based warning against becoming a nation that has forgotten how to blush is finally getting through. The classic text, " *Were they ashamed when they had committed abominations? Nay, they were not at all ashamed, neither could they blush:" (Jeremiah 3:12)* has been preached from Christian pulpits for decades. Now it appears that at least a segment of our secular society is remembering the advantages of blushing and how to blush.

n recent years, the U.S. government has taken over many of the ministries that Christ has called the church to. For example, caring for the poor is really the job of the church and family, but we have allowed government to do it. Taking a stand against the excesses of such fleshly vices as drinking, smoking, drugging, adultery and fornication has become another message of Big Brother government, though for reasons other than morality. When disaster strikes the smitten community turns to secular agencies such as the *Red Cross* and to *FEMA*, the domestic crisis arm of the U.S. government. These agencies' acts of human kindness are rewarded by votes and donations from a grateful public.

On a spiritual level, God may be thanked. But the church? The spirit-filled church? Too often the church is considered, as author Peter Cook states it, " *An island of irrelevance in a sea of despair".* We appear to do little that could engender loyalty or gratefulness from the citizens of our communities. We're *too* full-of-the-Holy Ghost and gifts-of-the-Spirit to lower ourselves to give a cup of water in Jesus' name! Instead being turned to as a source of help, we are often thought of as just another tax-free organization standing by wanting our own donation! So heavenly minded . . .

What is my point? There is one area in which the church cannot be replaced by government, society, the devil and all his minions, and that's in the salvation of human souls! That was the main mission of Jesus Christ, and that is the main purpose of His true church today!

" Remember the main thing is to keep the main thing the main thing!"
is the maxim that Rev. T. F. Tenney has made famous throughout the
Pentecostal world. Bro.Jesse Williams preaches a message entitled,
" The Critical Transaction" that reviews all of the high-tech support
systems behind an international airline business. But he makes the
point that all of the systems are worthless if the *"critical"* transaction
is not made at the sales counter. Selling seats on the aircraft is what
keeps the jets flying and the stockholders happy! Comparatively
speaking if the salvation of souls isn't kept the number one priority of
the church, on Rapture Day, millions of souls will be left here on the
ground instead of meeting Jesus in the air!

We can have the best literature, the most proficient Bible-study
materials, high-tech CD-ROM references, capable activity leaders,
youth & young married counselors, camps, conferences, seminars on
prayer, fasting, soul-winning and holiness, as well as lock-ins, mission
marches, choirs and orchestra programs. We can have the most
anointed teachers, speakers and evangelists feeding the flock. But if
no one ever steps away from all of these support systems and
personally reaches for a soul, the world will be eternally lost!

Society can preach lifestyle issues but can never win a soul. Prayer,
fasting and Bible study are essential to Christian growth and
discipleship, but a passion for souls expressed in *actual* witnessing
should always be encouraged. A warrior that builds his strength for
the conflict but never actually fights never wins any victories! A
Christian that continually prays, fasts and studies but never witnesses
or wins souls is an unprofitable servant. You'll never experience
victory without fighting in the battle!

In the Old Testament, God showed impatience with this type of
sedentary service. Have you ever notice how He phrased it?. *" And
the Lord said unto Moses, Wherefore criest thou unto me? Speak
unto the children of Israel, that they go forward!" (Exodus 14:15)*
Did you catch that? God was asking why they were praying and not

moving! On an individual basis, we have to make the *critical* transaction of reaching lost souls the *main* thing! The battle for human souls was won at Calvary! Since then, a search-and-rescue mission has been underway in the fields of the enemy. You are desperately needed in this final soul-saving effort before He comes.

Your prayers aren't enough.

Chapter Eight
" When Revival Knocks "
" She opened not the gate . . ."-Acts 12:14
-Opportunity-

One of the most traumatic experiences that my wife, Marilee, and I experienced in our early parenthood happened when our daughter Gina was just one and a half years old. Residing in Odessa, Texas, we had decided to return to the evangelistic ministry after the Christmas holidays. Planning on basing out of my father's church in Rapid City, South Dakota, we made a quick trip up to South Dakota to allow Gina to stay with them while we finished up our Texas jobs, packed and moved the household up to South Dakota by truck. It would be a long three week separation from our little girl, but our financial situation seemed to dictate that this was our only choice. My parents? They loved the chance to spoil their only grandchild without Marilee's or my interference!

The trauma? At first Gina did cry for us, and we would console her over the telephone. But after a week or so, she seemed to adjust to the situation. The trauma came three weeks later when after emptying our Texas apartment, loading the truck and then making the long tedious thousand-mile journey in a bright yellow *Ryder* truck, we finally pulled into Mom and Dad's country home in South Dakota. We jumped out of the truck and ran into the house to see our daughter. She was being held by my oldest sister, Sherri. When Marilee reached for her, Gina clung to Sherri and screamed in terror. When I attempted to take her, she did exactly the same thing! She didn't recognize us! Our released emotion and excitement at seeing her had frightened her! My wife was heartbroken and with tears streaming down her face, she extended her arms toward Gina and asked *" Gina, don't you remember Mommy? "*

After about an hour, she consented to being held and as we brought in familiar toys, bedding and possessions, a gleeful smile of recognition would cross her infant face. I'll never forget when she finally pointed at me and said, " *Da!*" Needless to say, until she left for college Marilee and I wouldn't think of allowing her any extended visits anywhere! Though she missed us and longed for us, when we actually returned, she had forgotten us and didn't recognize us!

After the death of Jesus and the birth of the Church on the Day of Pentecost, the persecution of believers had been stepped up by Herod Agrippa I in his campaign to ingratiate himself to the Jewish leaders. Being a Jewish convert himself, he arrested one of the three apostles that had made up Jesus' inner circle, James (the son of Zebedee). Upon beheading James, Herod received welcome news of the pleasure James' death had brought the Jewish leaders, so he arrested Peter also.

But by now the observance of the 7 Days of the Feast of Unleavened Bread along with the Passover was underway. Herod decided to wait until after the eight holy days were over before he would put Peter on trial. He chained a soldier to Peter on either side while also posting two guards at the cell's door. A total of four squads of four soldiers working six-hour shifts guarded Peter. Church tradition tells us that Peter was locked up the famed Tower of Antonia located in the northwest area of the Temple; it's obvious that Herod was taking no chance of Peter escaping.

What was the Jerusalem church doing? They immediately gathered at the house of Mary, mother of John Mark, and set up a 24-hour prayer chain! They were praying that God would set Peter free! They knew that James had been decapitated, but since no news of Peter's death had reached them, they were bombarding Heaven with their intercessory prayers.

And Peter? He was willing to die for God, but God needed him to live for Him! An angel awoke him, broke the chains, helped him to dress, and though Peter thought he was seeing a vision, he obeyed and was guided to an intersection away from the jail before the angel disappeared. He immediately headed for Mary's house where tradition places the true location of the Upper Room. No better place could've been found for a prayer meeting, right?

Let the Bible tell the rest of the story. *" And as Peter knocked at the door of the gate, a damsel came to hearken, named Rhoda. And when she knew Peter's voice, she opened not the gate for gladness, but ran in, and told how Peter stood before the gate. And they said unto her, 'Thou art mad.' But she constantly affirmed that it was even so. . .But Peter continued knocking: and when they had opened the door and saw him, they were astonished!"* (Acts 12:13-16) When Rhoda realized it was Peter at the door, she shouted about it to the rest of the church, but she didn't let him in! When they opened the door, they were astonished to see that God had answered their prayer!

Today we often find ourselves in a similar situation. Example? How many times have you prayed, *" Oh, God! Send me the victory!"* And when you immediately become deeply mired in a spiritual battle, you murmured, *" Why didn't God answer my prayer?"* The fact is He did! Most of us just aren't spiritually mature enough to realize that there are no victories without battles! God sent you a battle so you could have a victory!

How many times have you gone to prayer meetings to pray for your city? *" Oh, God, please send us revival!"* And like Rhoda, when God answered your prayer you didn't allow revival to come in. As a church, we shout and prophesy to the choir, *" Thus saith the Lord, revival is at the door, a great revival awaits your efforts, etc. "* But since revival doesn't often bust the door down with deaf mutes talking in tongues, cripples walking, blinded eyes opening, i.e. revival rarely comes in the way you expect it to, you don't even allow revival to come in at all! Sometimes revival presents itself as an opportunity for you to revive others!

The word revival means *" bringing back to life that which is dead"*. In reading the Gospels, it is readily apparent that Jesus is the Christ of the crisis! Whether healing the sick, raising the dead, forgiving the thief on the cross or feeding the multitudes, Jesus always responded to the needs of people that confronted Him. We live in a country where mothers are killing their children, homes are being destroyed by drink, drugs and sexual promiscuity, and yet in the midst of this spiritual crisis, the church is largely singing *" Shouting On The Hills Of Glory!"* and not recognizing the opportunity that is knocking at our doors!

Where can you find revival? In the weeping of an unwed mother. The violent sounds of domestic violence. The pitiful vomiting of an alcoholic. The bulging veins of a drug addict. The hurt and anger of someone rejected because of the color of his skin. The opportunity for revival is here! Those who need revival are all around us. The stench of spiritual death hangs over our cities like an enchanted fog. Those who need revived line our streets and fill the public arena. What is *really* absent is an empowered church made up of Christians like yourself who are willing to become revivers! When spirit-filled revivers revive, *then* our nation will be filled with testimonies of revival!

Our world needs people whom God can use to heal the sick, comfort the broken-hearted, stop the violence, bring salvation to the lost! Jesus declared that *" The harvest truly is plenteous, but the labourers are few: Pray ye therefore the Lord of the harvest, that He will send forth labourers into His harvest."(Matt. 9:37-38)* While interacting with pastors across the nation, I've been told countless times that in most churches 80% of the work is done by 20% of the people. Should we pray for revival? Yes, but you also must be willing to become a reviver when Christ sends the needy to your door!

You should become more familiar with the Great Commission, familiar enough to obey it. You know, *" Go into all the world and preach the gospel to every creature"?* I find it interesting that the majority of Christian ministries require the world to *come to us* instead of having us *go to them.* Ever wonder what God thinks of our apathetic mind-set in the midst of an epidemic of spiritual hunger that is crying out to be fed? Our world is *Desperately Seeking The Supernatural!*

How should a spirit-filled Christian respond to the fact that a novel about the endtime called *Assassins* has been high on the *New York Times* best-seller list? Or a movie called *The Omega Code,* written and produced by a spirit-filled Christian hit the nation's Top 20 at the box office? Just shrug and get prepared for Bible drill? Christians that are seeking a deeper lifestyle in the Lord should do more than hop on their soapboxes and start condemning the church world for offering half-truths to the spiritually hungry. Shouldn't we take a hard look at our own *lack* of effort that just simply lets the world starve to death and go straight to Hell?

Our world's spiritual hunger is evident even to the secular press. Why does it seem that the church-at-large is missing it? In the Dec.3,1999 issue of *Entertainment Weekly,* writers Daniel Fierman and Gillian Flynn revealed," *The new world of Christian pop-culture includes hard rock bands and action movies, serial killer novels and war-based computer games, writers who shroud their sermons in sci-fi and rockers who prefer to wear their crosses as tattoos. With hundreds of millions of dollars (not to mention souls) at stake, purveyors of evangelical entertainment are suddenly exploring terra incognita, while some fans praise them for spreading the Word and others damn them for dancing with the devil!"* He that winneth souls is wise, right? Is this the wisest choice to reach the lost? Is this the way to obey Paul's injunction to become all things to all people to save some?

No, I don't believe you should become a drunk to reach the drunks. Or smoke pot to reach the dopers, or frequent bars, night clubs, strip oints or other entertainment centers to reach the people who are found there. But you should attempt to find some common ground with this generation of mankind to try and win their souls for the Kingdom! Did Jesus intend for us to withdraw into our own sub-culture and ultimately give the world a Christian organization? I think not. If so, the hungry soul would only be saved by *coming* to us. Or did Jesus intend for us to *go* to all the organizations of the world to be available to lost souls and to make our influence felt everywhere? Like Christ, shouldn't we be out where the sinners are?

How can we affect spiritual change in the lives of people we rarely have any contact with? We *are* to change the world! But as a salty seasoning, not as tasteless paprika! We are to change the world by our presence, not by our absence! When revival knocks, i.e. the opportunity to revive hungry souls, answer the door and let Jesus into your life to flow through you to a lost and dying world.

Knock, knock! Revival is here!

Chapter Nine
" Shout It From The Desktops!"
" Be witnesses unto me . . .unto the uttermost part of the earth!" - Acts 1:8
- Internet Witnessing -

" Red, yellow, black and white, they are precious in His sight . . ."
The timeless refrain of the children's church chorus kept running
through my mind. Seated on the platform of the Apostolic Lighthouse
of Pompano Beach, Florida, as the visiting guest speaker, I was
amazed at the diversity of the worshipping congregation that sat
before me. When I had entered the building, a small, slight Pakistani
woman, wearing the shiny, colorful garb of her native country
approached me with a smile. Extending her hand that was laden with
multiple rings and glistening jewels, she gushed, *" Oh, you must be
the evangelist! Have you ever heard of the living God?"*

" Sure, it's none other than Jesus Christ!" I quickly answered.

Smiling broadly, she grasped my hand and spoke, *" I was raised with
many lords and many gods. We took great care to worship all of
them, but I never heard of the living God who died to wash away my
sins until I met our pastor, Bro. Clifford Jones! Brother, I love this
living God, Jesus!"* She proceeded to tell me she had just received the
Holy Ghost in the morning service.

The atmosphere was hot with fervent worship! The blaring of the
organ, the singing of the praise singers, the exuberant shouts of joy
from the cosmopolitan audience, made up of African-Americans,
Cubans, Columbians, El Salvadorans, Indians, Pakistanis, Italians and
Jamaicans, as well as those of European descent, presented a colorful
quilt of waving hands, dancing bodies and happy faces!

After the final notes of the song service had faded away, the powerful
voices arose again in testimony! Individual after individual shared
their stories of spiritual victories, personal challenges, and valleys that

God was bringing them through. Then, a short, slight man stood and shyly awaited the testimony leader to recognize him. *" Brother, what has God done for you?"* the leader inquired with a smile.

With a nervous glance at the audience, the standing man began speaking, *" Well, Brother, you all know how shy I am!"* The audience laughed appreciatively. *" I always get under conviction when the preachers talk about soulwinning. I am so quiet and nervous around strangers that I just can't talk about the Lord though He knows that I love Him."*

His glance dropped to the pew in front of him as he continued, *"So, I've begun witnessing in the religious chatrooms on the Internet. I've been communicating with a young lady up in Oklahoma about baptism in the water and in the Spirit. Tonight while I was showering, my phone rang, and I was unable to answer it in time. When I finally got to the phone, the message light was blinking on my answering machine. When I pushed the button, the message said . . .well, I brought the tape for the sound man to play."* He looked back toward the sound booth in the back of the auditorium.

Immediately a tinny-sounding voice came over the sound system. *" Dave? This is Jenny, up here in Oklahoma. I just wanted to call you and let you know what's happening. I've just packed my clothes; I'm headed to the local Pentecostal Church near me, and tonight I'm going to be baptized!"* Upon hearing that exciting announcement, a great roar of praise came from the approving crowd! Standing to their feet, they raised their hands toward Heaven and continued to give God honor for what He had done!

If you have an honest desire to be used of God in winning souls, He will find a place for you in the harvest! If you're too shy to shout it from the housetops, God has provided you another way to win the lost through the Internet. Shout it from the desktops!

35

Chapter Ten
" God Gave Me A Word!"
" Study to shew thyself approved unto God"- II Tim.2:15
- Bible Study -

I know it didn't start with the Jesus People movement, the Charismatic movement or the Latter-Rain movement nor perhaps any of the many historical renewal movements that have surfaced since the time of Christ. Quite simply, the flame of desire to hear from God began to burn in me in early 1970.

" Do you have a word from God?" a brother would question.

" C'mere brother, God gave me a special word for you!" A lot of that stuff was floating around in the Christian coffee houses, Bible rap groups and campus organizations. When confronted with this kind of offer, usually a feeling of confusion would come upon me.

If God had a message for me, certainly I wanted to know what it was. But why would God tell someone else? Why wouldn't He tell me? Or tell my parents? Or my pastor? In most cases, unless the guy was from the School of Wild-Eyed Reformed Presbyterian Latter-Drained Monks, I would humbly bow my head, and allow them to babble over me. Usually a generic message of self-exaltation and personal prosperity that would come into my life. Never a warning though I might be in sin. Never judgment, though the fear of it would have done me some good. Always I would be a prophet to the nations, unlimited wealth would be at my fingertips and all opposition would fall before me! Great!

Several years later I discerned that these guys offered no guarantee with their *word* from God! The prediction of the prophet must have been fulfilled when as a radio announcer, I would predict the weather at the top and bottom of each hour! You know, *" On K-SKY's skywatch . . .winds out of the south at 24 m.p.h., the barometric*

36

pressure stands at, etc." Unlimited wealth at my fingertips? Probably when I managed a shoe store and had to count out the register each night. Opposition falling before me? Well, that one was true. It happened every Saturday when I would attack the front and back yard with a gas-fired weed wacker!

No one believes in the present-day word of wisdom or word of knowledge more than I do. But, in many circumstances, the word that you're looking for is right below your nose! No, I'm not talking about your upper lip! I'm talking about the Bible, the Word of God, available in bound leather, with onion-skinned pages, edged with gold, with chain-reference, concordance, and 4-color Biblical illustrations! How many of us who are always *"seeking a word"* from God ever read the Word?

With the explosion of Christian literature, Christian radio, Christian seminars, camps, rallies, crusades, music festivals and concerts . . .all talking *about* the Bible, singing *about* the Bible, writing *about* the Bible . . .how many of us ever break through the crowd sitting about that written *Pool of Siloam* and dive into the Word of God and experience the healing of the washing of the water by the Word for ourselves?

Andrae Crouch once sang, *" You'll never know that it's true until it happens to you!"* While camp meeting speakers can thrill you by preaching the Word, and anointed singers can bless you by singing the Word, you need to discover for yourself that the answer to every one of life's problems, the fulfillment of all of life's hopes and dreams is sitting there unopened on your coffee table gathering dust under the latest contemporary Christian magazine!

No Christian would ever declare that the Bible is just another book! But ask yourself, *" Do I treat the Bible as if it were just another book?"* I'm not talking about treating the physical Bible reverently, i.e. not dropping it, or soiling the pages, etc. I'm talking about, Do we give it more time, more reading than other books, periodicals and information sources that demand our attention?

Are you constantly seeking a *"word"* from God and NOT reading His Word? Why do you think God went to the trouble of giving us a written record of His dealings with His people? Can you honestly say, *" Thy Word have I hid in my heart?"* Or could you more honestly say, *" My heart have I hid from thy Word!"* God's Word is full of blessing, healing, power and truth. In the Psalms it is stated that His Word is forever settled in Heaven! HIS Word comes with a guarantee!

Chapter Eleven
" The Cry Of The Soul "
" The Spirit itself maketh intercession for us . . ." - Romans 8:26
- Prayer Language -

I still remember old Sis.Carter leaning over the altar rail encouraging me to speak in tongues. *" Ok, Jimmie, Jr.. . . . say Je-je-je-jesus!"* she commanded. I would valiantly try to obey her well-intentioned instructions. But by concentrating on what my tongue was saying, my human spirit never could quite release it's deep longing for God. While possessing a good vocabulary, personally, I find that often I still am unable to adequately express to God what I feel in my heart. Through speaking in other tongues, allowing *" the Spirit to give utterance . . ."(Acts 2:4)* I've discovered that God has provided me with a bypass of my intellect and vocabulary that gives a direct voice to the deep cry of my soul!

Communication outside of established language structures is an every-day occurrence. Impossible? Ever notice how the family pet *"reads"* a visitor to your home? Within seconds, the dog or cat knows whether or not your guest is partial to pets or not. It's simply a case of communication between species outside of a known language. Or while visiting a foreign country, all of a sudden you hear a horrific cry of pain. Though ignorant of the native language, you immediately understand what is being communicated. How? Because there are some basic life experiences that eclipse the normal boundaries of human expression. Messages of pain, grief, sorrow, anger, betrayal or humiliation can be conveyed in a single sound, a heart-felt groan or a troubled cry that reaches across normal language barriers.

In the 60's, pop psychiatry experimented with a type of treatment known as *primal scream therapy.* An individual who had difficulty in expressing deep feelings in the typical *on-the-couch* method, would be placed in a sound-proof room and encouraged to scream as loudly as he could. By removing the usual obstacle of vocabulary, *primal scream* therapists theorized that the patient could then release the bottled-up fears, insecurities and frustrations with extended screaming. Often, a passionate, powerful demonstration of raw emotion would erupt from repressed patients that enabled them to *"get it off their chests"*.

When God fills us with His Spirit, instead of requiring us to pour our petitions through the narrow funnel of our personal vocabulary, God releases our human spirits by freeing us to speak to Him in other tongues! Then our souls can directly communicate with God! Without the limitation of known language, the deepest, innermost thoughts of *each* individual is freed to rush directly to the ears of a waiting God. And after the initial tongues experience of receiving the Holy Ghost, God continues to keep you *"on-line"* so you can communicate with Him, anytime and anyplace in this heavenly language.

Paul speaks of this great communication gift in his letters, both to the Romans and to the Corinthians. *" Likewise the Spirit also helpeth our infirmities: for we know not what we should pray for as we ought: but the Spirit **itself** maketh intercession for us with groanings which cannot be uttered." (Romans 8:26)* Through speaking in other tongues, our spirits directly express our petitions to God in a way that our intellect cannot. Then to the Corinthians, Paul tells of *" divers kinds of tongues"(I Cor.12:10)*. This versatile release of the human spirit, i.e. speaking in other tongues, gives supernatural voice to everything from receiving the gift of the Holy Ghost to operating in the various gifts of the Spirit.

Through the years, many have used the illustration, *" You don't seek tongues, you seek the Holy Ghost! It's like when you buy a pair of shoes! You don't ask for tongues, you buy the shoes and the tongues come with it!"* A sense of grief steals over me when I am introduced to *chronic seekers* who have unsuccessfully sought for the Holy Ghost for several years. It's true that sometimes there is secret sin that prevents God from inhabiting their human spirit, but often it is a case of too many advisers telling them *how-to-receive* the Holy Ghost! When they pray, their minds are so full of all the external advice they've received through the years, that it becomes impossible to submit to the Spirit. Every time they open their eyes, someone's ear is at their mouths listening, or everyone present is staring at their tongues. It's no wonder that the chronic seeker can't get his mind off of speaking in other tongues.

Shouldn't we encourage seekers to just give themselves to God? To speak from the heart? To open themselves up to God? To release those deep feelings whereby giving their deep spiritual yearnings that well up inside of them to Jesus? Isn't it true that what is inward in a man *will be* manifested outwardly? If you see an egg about to hatch, and you reach over and help the chick crack the egg and leave the shell, there's a good chance that it won't live. Why? Because it was born before it's time. God makes the shell tough so the chick builds a desire to be born. It's muscles grow strong by throwing itself against the inner curvature of the shell. When it is strong enough, the chick cracks the egg by itself and steps out of the shell with a proud chirp!

How many people have been brought to a premature spiritual birth by well-intentioned Christians? They may have spoken in tongues but their human spirit did not receive the full Upper Room experience. The experience of *tarrying* to receive power from on High. Have you ever noticed that over five hundred heard the commandment to go and tarry but only around one hundred-twenty actually stayed in the Upper Room *until* they received the power on the Day of Pentecost? Critics of tarrying protest by saying, " *The Holy Ghost is gift to be received! It's not earned!*" And though that is certainly true, I'd like to point out that *tarrying* is not begging! In fact, *tarrying* is not praying! W.E. Vine's Expository Dictionary of Old & New Testament words defines *tarrying* as " *to abide or wait !*"

What is wrong with encouraging a seeker to wait on God? Jesus commanded his attentive disciples to " *Tarry ye in the city of*

Jerusalem, until ye be endued with power from on high!"(Luke 24:49) Obviously there must be some benefit in tarrying. A building of desire? A separation unto God? A sifting of an individual's true motives? Despite human reasoning to the contrary, the fact remains that Jesus commanded them to *" Go, wait!"*

Let's look at the biblical record. The one hundred-twenty Jews *tarried* until the Day of Pentecost when they received it, along with the spontaneous outpouring upon an additional three thousand. Shift to Philip's efforts with the half-breed Samaritans. Though they repented and were baptized in the name of Jesus, they *tarried* for the Holy Ghost until Peter and John came down to lay hands upon them. The Gentiles? In many ways it was a repeat of the Day of Pentecost. The Gentiles knew nothing other than Peter would reveal the gospel to them. The word reveals that Cornelius himself had been *tarrying* in prayer, and perhaps his whole household, for upon hearing Peter's message they immediately received the Holy Ghost, *" for they heard them speak with tongues and magnify God!"(Acts 10:46)*.

The Bible has no record of either Holy Ghost altar workers or coaches. All of us are called to spread the gospel, to preach the good news that Jesus Christ died to cover the sins of mankind. Without question, exciting sanctuary music and enthusiastic prayer warriors can help create an atmosphere where God can move in the hearts of seekers. But just like the original church, today, we, too, must seek the genuine infilling of the Holy Ghost! That spiritual transformation is given in response to the impassioned cry of a human soul pouring out of penitent lips. No one must settle for the repetitive parroting of an altar worker's well-intentioned coaching. How many souls that have been rushed to receive still grace the pews of the church? Is there anything inherently wrong in tarrying or waiting upon the Lord? After all, whose Spirit is it? And Who freely gives it in answer to the cry of the soul? At Pentecost, didn't God prove that good things come to those that wait? For if a soul is born before its time, it may not continue to live. Isn't it worth the wait?

on? This is a rhetorical question
our nation's periodicals. Where
)s? Instead of inspiring rags-to-
:ration of achievers, my son's
s Rodman who displays his
body sitting atop a Harley-
s autobiography, *As Bad As I
Want To Be!,* available in your city's nearest bookstore. Players with
classic values such as Michael Jordan, Reggie White, and Dennis Byrd
are hard to find.

Growing up a preacher's kid, my heroes were the camp meeting
preachers! Living in Bloomington, Illinois, where my father pastored
and also served as the Illinois District Youth Secretary, each summer
we spent three glorious fun-filled weeks at the district campground
near Murphysboro, Illinois. Brother M.J.Wolfe was our district
superintendent, and I remember that we sang his favorite chorus,
" Reach Out And Touch The Lord As He Passes By!" almost every
service. Why? Bro.Wolfe was in charge, that's why!

I heard several preachers as a kid, but my favorites were Winfred
Black, T.F.Tenney, Nathaniel A.Urshan, and Roland Gardner
(Bro.Wolfe's nephew). I'll never forget Bro.Winfred Black's famous
sermon, *Sixty Minutes Until The Rapture!* He took his audience on a
journey that would conclude with the Lord coming at the end of the
hour. As he described the events that were taking place around the
world, the listeners anxiety about their personal relationships with
God began to crack their stony hearts. After fifty-five minutes of
anointed terror, we kids started running to the altar! At the sixtieth
minute, an unexpected blast from a trumpet ignited a startled scream

from the congregation as they stood as one and stampeded to the front of the building! Hundreds were saved!

Brother T.F.Tenney was the International Youth president in the sixties, and the United Pentecostal Church headquarters wasn't far from the Illinois campground. As a child I admired his one-liners and unique thoughts. He had the ability to speak on everyone's level at the same time. I can still hear my dad hooping and hollering during the services. At the snack bar after service, Dad would run up to me and exclaim, " *Jimmie, Jr., did you hear Bro.Tenney tonight? Boy, that Tenney can preach!"*

We loved Bro.& Sis.Urshan's singing, and we laughed, cried, and were terrified by whatever fascinating story Brother Urshan chose to include in his unique messages. Bro.Roland Gardner was simply a dynamic preacher who kept us kids spell-bound. These four men were the camp meeting heroes of my youth.

Today, my eighteen-year old son cannot get enough of the preaching of Wayne Huntley, Jeff Arnold, Anthony Mangun, and Paul Mooney. If these preachers are within driving distances, I'll hear him on the phone arranging his work schedule so that he can attend these meetings. When he roars off to the events, I know that I'll hear the evenings message on tape for weeks to come. Smiling to myself, I reflect that if we had had cassette tape ministries when I was a kid, I would have played T.F.Tenney's *Jacob's Limp* sermon until the tape broke!

I'm glad for my camp meeting memories. I'm glad I had God-fearing heroes that taught me about Jesus and good, wholesome values. Heroes that did not disappoint me by selling their talents to the highest bidder. I'm thankful that the ministries of Winfred Black, T.F.Tenney, Roland Gardner, N.A.Urshan, J.T.Pugh, James Kilgore, and others had such a powerful influence on me. That campmeeting tradition must continue. Now as parents, we must continue to send

Chapter Thirteen
" The Cult Of Personality "
" Everyone of you saith, I am of Paul, and I am of Apollos" - I Cor.1:12
- Respect -

Talent is a two-sided coin that can feature blessings on one side and curses on the other. Gifts of talent have placed spiritually immature individuals on the cutting edge of the church's voice to the world and eventually allowed them to be destroyed by the worship and admiration of the faithful. Such worship of musical or speaking talent can completely distort the spiritual focus of gifted singers and preachers. Humans commit to talent; God commits to character! The difference between the anointing and the approval of God must be understood.

The truth is God uses whatever we submit unto Him. It's becoming common to see ex-Holiness preachers and singers who *evidence* the anointing in their meetings, publicly reject the basic Bible doctrines and holiness lifestyle that originally birthed their ministries. Further investigation reveals a personal mind-set that affirms *feeling the anointing of God* on their gifts and talents add up to *the approval of God* on their new worldly lifestyle. In reality, nothing could be further from the truth.

In Romans 11:29, the Apostle Paul taught, *" For the gifts and callings are without repentance."* To say that God is not an Indian-giver, may be politically incorrect, but nevertheless it's true. He doesn't give with strings or conditions. Once He endows you with a supernatural gift or talent, it is yours for the using. How and when you use it is up to you. The phrase, *" without repentance"* means that the gifts, callings and talents from God are not subject to recall. He doesn't try to take it back. For example, when taking out a life insurance policy, often an *irrevocable* beneficiary is named. It means that the beneficiary CANNOT be changed. So, too, are the gifts and calling of God. They are irrevocable.

when Bro._____ wheeled in driving his cherry-red Cadillac that he was totally drunk! We helped him to a private area where we began the showering, coffee-drinking, walking around-process of getting him sober enough to preach and pray. I'll never forget the tortured words as he blearily looked at the hundreds of people waiting on his prayer of faith, he would cry out to the heavens, " God, please use me just one more time! God, look at the people who believe in your Word! God, forgive me, please use me just one more time!"

Within minutes the electrifying introduction went forth, *" Here's God's Man of Faith and Power, Reverend _____!!!!"* The crowds would cheer, the prayer of faith was made and hundreds would be healed!!! His ministry exercised the anointed gifts of healing, but obviously God did not approve of his drunken lifestyle. Bro._____'s spiritual gifts had placed him on a pedestal in the hearts of many believers. In fact, in cultic fashion, he founded his own heaven-on-earth city where thousands of the faithful moved to live near him. A drunk! But a drunk who could preach and heal the sick like no other man of his time. Simply, the gifts and callings are without repentance.

Jesus knew that people would be swayed by the gifts and talents of great personalities. In a word of caution, He spoke, *" Not everyone that* **saith** *unto me, Lord, Lord, shall enter into the kingdom of heaven; but he that* **doeth** *the will of my Father which is in heaven!"* *(Matthew 7:21)* Note the stark contrast between saying and doing. God just doesn't want to be sung about and preached about. God wants more than lip service. God wants REAL service from those He has endowed with gifts of singing and preaching.

To further prove the point, Jesus continued. *"Many will say to me in that day, Lord, Lord, have we not prophesied in thy name? And in thy name have cast out devils? And in thy name done many wonderful works?"* And then Jesus delivered the final blow, *"And then will I profess unto them, I NEVER KNEW YOU; depart from me, ye that work iniquity!" (Matthew 7:22-23).* His attentive audience knew that those chilling words *"I never knew you!"* were from a formula often used in excommunication ceremonies by the Jewish rabbis. The commandment *"Depart from me, ye that work iniquity,"* a familiar quotation of King David found in Psalm 6:8.

The fiery apostle Paul preached against the four developing cults of personality in the Corinthian church. In the first three chapters he railed against the schisms of preacher-worshippers that were dividing the body of Christ. *" There are contentions among you. Now this I say, that every one of you saith, I am of Paul; and I of Apollos; and I of Cephas; and I of Christ." (I Corinthians* 1:12). One group claimed Paul as their leader; one followed Apollos who had a more rhetorical, eloquent style of speaking that was very popular with new Greek Christians. One group followed Cephas (Peter) the acclaimed hero of Pentecost (probably conservative Jewish followers), and another group said they followed Christ.

Paul protested being compared to Apollos, like you and I would protest being compared negatively to some of the great orators of our time. In I Corinthians 2: 1-5, Paul made his case, *" And I, brethren, when I came unto you, came not with excellency of speech or of wisdom, declaring unto you the testimony of God.* He was saying that

48

Today we can fall into the same trap of personality worship. We must be careful to build only the Kingdom of God and not various cults of personality! Our salvation must be placed on the received message from God delivered by the speaker or singer! Our worship must be God-directed and not merely a cry of admiration for a dynamic statement or beautiful lyric! For our sakes, and for the sakes of the gifted individuals that minister on the platforms of our gathering places.

The biggest name in Christianity must remain JESUS! Are we ignoring the apostle Paul's warning against building cults of personality? A humorous statement that is more true than funny portends that if a jet plane carrying a certain twenty speakers and a certain ten singers ever crashed, most denominations would have no one left to minister at their conferences! The tendency for leadership to play favorites and use their friends exists in all denominations. True or not, let just the thought of such a situation should prompt us to develop the next generation of leaders and be careful to place our faith in Christ alone!

We are nothing without Christ! Our speaking and singing gifts fall flat without His anointing! Let's allow Paul the final word in this matter,

" Who then is Paul, and who is Apollos, but ministers by whom ye believed, even as the Lord gave to every man? I have planted, Apollos watered; but God gave the increase. So then neither is he that planteth any thing, neither he that watereth; but God that giveth the increase!" (I Corinthians 3:5-7)

process that God uses to release energy

or flammable material! In receiving the Holy Spirit, God's tongues of fire have released a spiritual energy, i.e. power in you that has enabled you to live a holy life before a not-yet-holy world.

First you need to understand how special you are to God. God created all other living creatures by fiat, by decree, but the first human beings were lovingly formed by God's own hands, brought to life by His own breath. The atheist is not really denying the existence of God as much as he is denying the right of people to be different from animals, saying that what they do makes no moral difference! But there IS a difference! Within every man and woman, God has implanted the potential to be human, to see beyond animal instinct and choose goodness over evil.

In his book, *To Life! (Little, Brown And Company, 1993)* Rabbi Harold Kushner writes, " *What makes human beings different from other living creatures? We have eaten of the fruit of the Tree of the Knowledge of Good and Evil! Where other creatures can be obedient or disobedient, only human beings can choose to be good! How can we exercise our humanity in the direction of goodness? By freely choosing to do what God would have us do, instead of following our instincts as all other animals do!"* In areas of basic instincts, it's significant that human beings are the only creatures who engage in sex face-to-face, because only to humans does it matter with whom they are making love! Many of insights that you'll read in this chapter come from *To Life!*, a book that I heartily encourage you to buy!

Rabbi Kushner continues, *" We fast to prove, to ourselves as much as to anyone else, that we are human. All other living creatures are 'programmed' by instinct. You can train a dog not to eat through fear of punishment, but you can never teach a dog voluntarily to go on a diet or to pass up food for ideological reasons. Only humans can do that! A day of abstinence represents another symbol of control over a basic instinct. "* It's interesting to note that chimpanzees can communicate through sign language, dolphins and whales have a system of sounds and squeals, in fact, all animals make noises to communicate, but only humans talk, discuss, pray, apologize, convince, write poetry, novels or symphonies!

In response to the question, *" Is there anything unique about the human being?"* Evolutionist Charles Darwin replied, *" Man is the only creature that blushes!"* We are uniquely made in the image of God, and God wants to see His image reflected in our lives. Our physical self is what we share with the animal kingdom. Our minds and conscience makes up the spiritual dimension that we share with God.

Again, Rabbi Kushner expounds, *" One might say that the Jewish concept of God is largely an idealized version of how an authentic human being, fashioned in God's image would behave! I take the claim that the Jewish people are a **chosen** people to be not a moral or biological statement, but a historical one. It is a historical fact that the Jews, and no one else gave the world the Bible. It is a historical fact that the Jews introduced to the pagan world the idea of a God who demanded righteousness. "*

The fact that the Jews are God's chosen people has always been taught by Christianity. But always the aspect that the Jews were more absolute right or wrong.

As Christians, we are to example Christ to the world! We are the standard-bearers of New Testament holiness. A foundational truth of God's word, Paul informs us, " *Follow peace with all men, and holiness, without which no man shall see the Lord!*" (*Heb. 12:14*) Jesus declared, " *Ye shall be hated of all men for my name's sake! But he that endureth to the end shall be saved!*" (*Matt. 10:22*) It's true that he who Christ has set free is free indeed! But we must use that freedom to choose good over evil!

After the Temple at Jerusalem was destroyed by Titus in 70 A.D., having no place to sacrifice unto the Lord, the Jew's words of worship and praise became the currency of communication to God. Animal sacrifice had reflected the sense that in order for a person to take worship seriously, it had to cost him something. Now having no central house of worship, much of Judaism was practiced in the home which help build a sense of community and strong families. Judaism took the common and ordinary actions of life and made them into an occasion for obeying or disobeying God. Rabbi Kushner continues,
" *The goal is not to teach us how to escape from the profane world to the cleansing presence of God, but to teach us how to bring God into the world, how to take the ordinary and make it holy.*" Out of the

Temple and into the world, so to speak! Or in Christian terms, out of the church house and into the streets!

Today, you, the spirit-filled Christian, battle the same basic human instincts. You must not deny or stifle your instincts of hunger, sex, anger, etc., but you must make a holiness commitment to control them, to rule them rather than to let them rule you. You must learn to sanctify them by dedicating your living of them to God's purpose! The freedom you receive from Christ is the freedom to say, *"No!"* to a fleshly appetite. In a Christian's lifestyle, the whining excuse, *" I'm ONLY human!"* can be turned into a proud affirmation of divine purpose and self-control, *" No, I'm a human made in the image of God with the power to say 'No!' and mean it!"*

In living a holy life before a cynical world, you must not buy into the skeptics that say you're living in bondage, a religious fanatic, a slave to human rules twisted into the shape of a cross! Because while they're ridiculing your abstinence from alcohol, drugs and promiscuous living, you can just kick back and bask in the love of God! What can you say? How about this? *" Isn't it fantastic! Over six billion people on the face of the earth, and the God I serve cares about how I expose my body, what I drink, what I eat, what I ingest into my body! He cares about who I sleep with He cares about what kind of language I use! Isn't it wonderful how finite and careful is His love for me?"*

Your own personal holiness is more than spiritually separating yourself unto God. It is bringing God into your everyday activities and making them holy! In Judaism and now in Christianity, holiness and sanctification should refer to the way individuals relate to each other instead of just the act of withdrawing from a sinful world into a life of greater purity. Jewish theologian Martin Buber once defined theology as talking about God and religion as experiencing God. He went on to say that the difference between them is the difference between reading a menu and having dinner! You must help the world

Chapter Fifteen

"The Challenge Of Compassion"
"Inasmuch as ye have done it unto the least . . ." Matt.25:40
- Compassion -

Out of the swirling drifts of nature's fury arose stories of human tragedy that dwarfed even the headlines filled with reports of frozen freeways, cars held in the grip of ice and cities imprisoned by huge drifts of snow. True, winter was a great inconvenience to millions of Americans, but beneath the storm-laden headlines, frozen by human indifference, lay cold brutal facts of human death. Though the frigid streets and highways contributed to the harvest of death, the ghoulish form of the grim reaper had swung his scythe greedily through the houses of the poor and elderly. As a result of the bitter storm, over one hundred people froze to death in their own homes.

Did they want to die? Of course not! Living on fixed incomes, confronted with the high prices of an inflationary economy, many elderly had been faced with the cruel choice of a heated starvation or a freezing life. They chose to eat in a frigid house with hopes that the raging storm would soon pass. But the winter storm wasn't kind to them. In every sense victims of a cold world, dozens froze to death in their homes.

When I read of an elderly couple that froze to death in an apartment building located right next to the church that would perform their funeral, I wondered in my heart, *" Why would they rather freeze to death than ask the church for help?"* Have we Christians become that unapproachable? Were these senior citizens too embarrassed to call? Their need certainly would have been responded to, right? Maybe they called and were referred to a government agency? Or maybe they didn't believe that Christian people and churches really care anymore? In spite of our high-sounding rhetoric, perhaps this poor deceased couple didn't sense the compassionate spirit of Christ

Galatia instructing them to bear one another's burdens, and in doing so they would *" fulfill the law of Christ!"(Gal.6:2)* Did you catch that? Paul didn't refer to compassion as a *suggestion* of Christ, but a *LAW!*

Why have we allowed the government to steal this ministry from Christians? Laziness? Indifference? Resentment of the needy? Many in the political spectrum feel that the needy would be better served by a government check than the empty promises of an impotent Christianity. I contend that the poor need the compassion and practical help of their friends, family, church *and* community. Everyone wants to help the *truly* needy, but no one wants to give their resources to those that *could* help themselves but *won't*. But it certainly isn't the way of Christ to *assume* that all needy people are deadbeats.

I once wrote an column entitled *" The Politics of Compassion"*. In it I contrasted receiving help from friends and family as opposed to government assistance. Here are a few paragraphs . . ." *When your immediate family, friends or church are helping you through hard times, your conscience makes you get out of bed and search for a job. Your conscience is pricked every time you put your able-bodied hand out for another personal check, food, rent payment or borrowed car keys from a family member. On the other hand, when you roll out of bed at noon to pick up your unemployment check, your help is coming from a faceless, nameless monolithic mass of taxpayers. Hmmmm, sounds a bit cold and impersonal, doesn't it? Society-at-large calls that compassion.*

Years ago, the Peruvian government conducted an experiment with a group of orphaned infants. Two groups of infants received proper food and basic care. But one group was held and cuddled by the nursing staff. The other group was ignored. Was personal human touch important? You bet! The group that just received food became chronic criers and developed a disproportionate amount of disease. The other group that received personal love and attention were found to be much healthier.

My government can feed me, clothe me, and educate me, but my government cannot love me! It cannot give me that spiritual lift that my discouraged self-image needs. That can only come from my church, my family or my friends. To true Christians, government handouts are cold, impersonal, unfeeling and dehumanizing. Nothing can replace the personal love shown by friends that give of themselves to help a friend or needy stranger in the spirit of Christ. It's the difference between an ATM machine and a human teller. Both can take or give your money, but with a human teller you touch another life and get a smile with your deposit slip! Society may desire to shut out Christianity and keep the welfare machine grinding out checks. And face it, they've had to do it because of our lack of concern! Christ wants us Christians to bring compassion back to a more personal, human level."

Along with the spiritual thirst to do the supernatural exploits of Christ such as healing the sick, raising the dead, opening blinded eyes and unstopping deaf ears, we need to have an awareness that Jesus also ministered to the daily practical needs of those He came in contact with. Those living a deeper lifestyle will discover that the more they

these things. But seek ye first ... ...g ...
righteousness; and all these things shall be added unto you." (Matt.
6:31-33). Great advice but tough to follow, right? In the next chapter
you'll discover that when you're ready to respond to the needs of
others, God may even supernaturally direct the needy to you or your
church!

Chapter Sixteen
" Loving The Loveless "
- Sensitivity To The Spirit -

Being the first night of revival services at the *First Pentecostal Church of New Orleans,* pastored by Bro.John Cupit, I was anxious for a sovereign move of the Holy Ghost! I was well into my sermon on faith when the Lord spoke to me, *" Read the 23rd Psalm . . ."* My thought pattern and speech flow became confused as my mind reacted to this request of the Lord. God had used me in the word of knowledge before, but Psalm 23 had absolutely nothing to do with what I was preaching about.

Desperately I searched the faces of the crowd, trying to see a visible sign from God. A black cloud. A shining light. ANYTHING to indicate that the voice speaking inside was God and not my imagination. Being an aisle-preacher, I was standing in the center aisle between the front two pews. All of a sudden it seemed that the Lord was drawing my attention to a young family sitting on the back row.

" Sir . . ." I called out, " Yes, you, your wife and your daughter. The Holy Ghost wants you to come up here with me. God wants me to read you something." The young couple looked at each other, a bit intimidated by my request. Smiling quietly, I encouraged them again, " Come on up! I don't mean to embarrass you, but God has a word for you." When they stood up, I realized that they must be visitors. Walking toward the front of the auditorium in old shorts, sneakers and tattered shirts, I could tell by their tentative steps and lowered gaze that they were very shy and more than a little scared.

Positioning them in front of me, I opened my Bible and demanded " Repeat after me, THE LORD IS MY SHEPHERD . . ." Obediently they echoed the psalm. I continued, " I SHALL NOT WANT . . ." As they repeated the phrase, I noticed small tears begin to trickle down

tightly. " THY ROD AND THY STAFF THEY COMFORT ME!
Openly weeping, the young couple repeated the words of David
through heartbroken sobs. " THOU PREPAREST A TABLE
BEFORE ME IN THE PRESENCE OF MY ENEMIES!!!" That
holy voice that had prompted this supernatural demonstration spoke
in my mind again. *" Son, invite my people to show their love to this
family! "*

Closing my Bible, I stepped away from the young family who were
worshipping God from the depths of their souls. Looking at the
congregation, I said " The Holy Ghost wants you to show your love
to this family. I sense they've experienced rejection and heartbreak.
God has put His mark upon them, and desires you to express your
compassion. Just step out of your pew and surround them with your
love. " The saints of the First Pentecostal Church of New Orleans
needed no further invitation! They poured out of the pews and
proceeded to pray with this young family. Within minutes, both the
father and mother were speaking in other tongues as the Spirit gave
them utterance. God baptized them with the Holy Ghost and fire!

While rejoicing in their baptism, the Spirit of the Lord moved on the
saints to begin stuffing money in the pockets of the father. When the
service was over, the young family's story was shared with the

congregation. Having moved recently from Buffalo, New York, the man had obtained work; however, he would not receive his first paycheck until the upcoming Sunday, just four days away. Having no money, they were living on the streets, digging and salvaging food wherever they could find it. The unsolicited gifts of money placed in their pockets amounted to enough to get them a place to stay, and enough food to last until the father received his paycheck! Hallelujah!

Several months later, I preached a fellowship rally in that same area. I was gratified to find out from First Church members in attendance that the young couple was still attending church and now had their own house to live in. As that young family discovered, His Lordship is timeless! His promise was not just to David; it was even for the homeless of New Orleans. In times of trial and tribulation, never forget that you are not alone! For you, too, can lift your gaze to the Heavens and cry *" The Lord is MY shepherd! And I SHALL NOT WANT! "*

delicious taste that caused my heart to melt? No, it was the ~~~~~~~~~ motive that warmed my heart. My new bride, Marilee, not only wanted to be my wife, but she wanted to please me as well!

After reading the book of Esther, one of only two books in the Bible named after a woman, I've come to the conclusion that that could be one of the reasons Esther was chosen to be King Ahaserus' new queen. Granted she was very beautiful, but in addition she *desired* to be queen. And secondly, I believe that Esther had inside information on how to please the King! Follow closely what the scriptural record reveals. *" He (Hegai) speedily gave her her things for purification, with such things as belonged to her, and **seven maidens**, which were meet to be given her, **out of the king's house.**"(Es.2:9)* After twelve months of purification, each potential queen was presented before the King for his pleasure. The Bible notes that each woman was allowed to take anything she wanted with her that could potentially help her become the King's choice.

I imagine a great cook would request the necessary ingredients for a tasty dish. A dancer might require musicians. A musician might ask for an instrument to play. Perhaps they were each given their choice of fine clothing or jewelry, but the Bible informs *" Now when the turn of Esther, the daughter of Abihail the uncle of Mordecai . . .was come to go in unto the king,* **she required nothing** *but what Hegai the king's chamberlain, the keeper of the women, appointed"(Es.2:15)* Remember Hegai had appointed the seven maidens to her service. Did Esther have a confidence born of knowledge gleaned during her time of purification? Or was her beauty so stunning that she needed no props to enhance it?

Born a Jewess, she was part of the millions of Jews who chose to disobey God and stay in Persia when they were unexpectantly set free by Cyrus. It's sad to note that only 60,000 chose to go with Nehemiah and Zerubbabel to suffer the hardships of re-establishing the nation of Israel. And though God had commanded the Jews not to intermarry with pagans, her cousin Mordecai further disobeyed God by encouraging her to enter the competition to become King Ahaserus' wife. It was definitely a gamble for if she wasn't chosen, she would be forced into the King's harem to live a life of a concubine.

Please be aware that the book of Esther is a secular history of how a people not in God's will were still directed by God. Only by His divine providence did they escape the annihilation planned for them by Haman. Neither God, prayer or any divine title or pronoun are ever mentioned in the book of Esther, nor is it quoted in the New Testament. It still remains a wonderful record of how the providence of God leads people who will not be led. One writer defined providence as the hand of God in the glove of human events. In this case not only the hand of God, but the beauty and wisdom of Esther was about to turn the cultural tide against the enemies of the Jews. When Esther was presented to the King, he was overwhelmed by her and immediately chose her as his new queen.

How did this happen? The fact that Esther entered the kingdom-wide contest revealed her *desire* to be queen. During her time of purification she surrounded herself with seven maidens that had been with the King. I believe she took advantage of their knowledge! I can just see her asking, " *What's Ahaserus like? What's his favorite* deeper lifestyle in Christ, you and I must surround ourselves with people who have been with the King! We can get to know Him by the experiences of God's people recorded in the Bible. We must become conversant with the eight writers of the New Testament: Matthew, Mark, Luke, John, Paul, Peter, James, Jude! As well as the writers, poets, prophets, movers and shakers of the Old Testament!

We must surround ourselves with experienced Christian friends who have weathered many spiritual storms sent their way by Satan! Remember, God is making you over into a new creation! Paul put it this way, " *Therefore if any man be in Christ, he is a new creature; old things are passed away; behold ALL things become new"(II Cor,5:17).* We must immerse ourselves into a lifestyle that pleases the King. Everything from faithful church attendance to getting rid of all worldly influences such as books, magazines, tapes, CD's, videos, etc. that may have a detrimental affect upon our spiritual life! Why would I do all these things? Because I want nothing in my life that will displease the King of kings! I desire to be His Bride and I desire to please Him!

Did you ever wonder if the story of Esther was upon the mind of Solomon when he wrote, " *Wisdom hath builded her house, she hath hewn out her seven pillars"(Proverbs 9:1)?* Did Esther build her case upon what she gleaned from the seven maidens out of the King's house? Curious, I looked up the definition of the word, *hewn.*

" Hewn: shaped or cut with an axe, knife, chisel, etc. stone." Some effort was apparently required on Esther's part. Unlike God's injunction to Moses, *" And if thou will make me an altar of stone: thou shalt not built it of hewn stone: for if thou life up thy tool upon it, thou has polluted it."(Ex.20:25).* God did not want the hands of man to shape Him an altar, He wanted no stone to be hewn or cut out of the rock. He wanted no evidence of man's works or effort upon the altar. It was to be a simple stone made by God, untouched by man.

But Wisdom built her house to rest upon seven pillars she had *hewn* or cut out of rock: And just what is a pillar? Again my dictionary supplies the meaning, *" Pillar: a long, slender vertical structure that supports living on a higher plane or level".* Esther's desire to reign as queen in the house of the King caused her to surround herself with maidens, i.e. pillars whose information would support her or promote her up to that higher level where she wanted to live!

Do you desire to live on a higher level with Christ? What seven pillars of truth can you and I build our spiritual house upon that will enable us to consistently live on a higher plane or level? In Revelation 3:1 we find reference to the seven Spirits of God! *" These things saith he that hath the seven spirits of God, and the seven stars . . ."* A quick glance at the reference to Isaiah 11:2-5 reveals what the seven spirits of God are that will help lift us to life on a higher level!

Pillar 1 / The Spirit of the Lord: To be like Jesus we must have the Spirit of the Lord resting upon us. In Luke 4:18-19, Jesus put it like this. *" The Spirit of the Lord is upon me, because he hath anointed me to preach the gospel to the poor; he hath sent me to heal the broken-hearted, to preach deliverance to the captives, and recovering of sight to the blind, to set at liberty them that are bruised, to preach the acceptable year of the Lord."* Note that this

Pillar 4 / The Spirit of Counsel: Having the type of spirit where we are not too proud to seek out counsel or make ourselves available to others who seek to counsel with us.

Pillar 5 / The Spirit of Might: We must have the spiritual power to carry out the task that Christ sets before us.

Pillar 6 / The Spirit of Knowledge: To live on a higher spiritual level, we must have knowledge of the character and nature of God.

Pillar 7 / The Spirit of Fear: We must live in reverence and obedience, recognizing God's right to our faithfulness and worship.

In Revelation 3, Jesus was speaking to the seven churches of Asia. It makes sense that if he was rebuking or correcting spiritual problems that whatever he held in his hands would provide the proper solution. For example, if I seen you jacking up your car with a tire iron in your hand, I would naturally assume you are changing a flat tire. Or if you headed off to work with a pouch full of nails and a hammer in your work belt, it would be a safe guess that you planned to nail something! Jesus held the seven stars which represented the angels or pastors that were over the churches, as well as the seven spirits of God! For us to live on a higher level, we must have a pastor in our lives as well as the spirit of the Lord resting upon us! Also the spirits of wisdom, understanding, counsel, might, knowledge and fear!

Wisdom requires us to build our house upon the Rock, Christ Jesus! His advice is easy to understand, " *Therefore whosoever heareth these sayings of mine, and doeth them, I will liken him to a wise man, which built his house upon a rock: And the rain descended and the floods came, and the winds blew, and beat upon that house; and it fell not: for it was founded upon a rock."(Matt.7:24-25)* Seeking a deeper lifestyle will lead you to living on a higher level with Him!

8,000 feet below the earth's surface!

It brings to mind an obvious question. *Why IS gold so valuable?* The answer? Mainly because it is so scarce. Gold is a beautiful, soft pliable metal that is easy to work with and can be molded into almost anything. Gold will not tarnish and is resistant to chemicals, while having a resplendent natural glow. God desires his holy church to be a beautiful church that He can work with and shape into His own image. A church that is resistant to the influences of the world and will not compromise and tarnish it's spirituality! A church made up of people that have an inherent spiritual glow! A light that shines into darkness! A city that is set on a hill that cannot be hid!

24 karat gold is *pure* gold. Most often, objects are made of 18 karat gold. Being cheaper, 18 karat gold is diluted with other materials to form a much harder alloy. Subsequently, by diluting the gold, the resulting material is significantly less valuable. Gold becomes hardened when linked with other materials. In the spirit world, God desires us to become *pure* gold tried by the fire! The church that becomes hardened against the will of God also becomes more resistant and less pliable to his divine touch. When mixed with sinful attitudes that dilute spirituality, we become less than God wants us to be.

Another fascinating fact we discovered at Homestake Gold Mine was the fact that it takes 10,000 pounds of rock, mined, smelted and processed to produce just one ounce of pure gold! Incidentally, one ounce of gold is approximately the size of an average chocolate chip! It takes a lot of machine power and manpower to mine just a little bit of gold!

When trials and tribulations, heart aches and suffering enter our lives, we have to realize that we are processing into pure gold! We are becoming pure gold in His sight! Job declared, " *But He knoweth the way that I take! When He hath tried me, I shall come forth as GOLD!*" The Apostle Peter who died a martyr wrote, " *That the trial of your faith being much more precious than of GOLD that perisheth, though it be tried with fire might be found unto praise and honour and glory at the appearing of our Lord Jesus Christ.*"

When Moses and Joshua descended from Mt. Sinai and found the children of Israel dancing before the golden calf, Moses destroyed the calf by burning it in the fire and grinding it to powder, and he threw the golden powder upon the stream of water which flowed out of the side of Mt.Sinai. *Why would he do that?* A little known fact is whenever GOLD is finely ground to almost like baby powder, and it is mixed with water, **it turns the water blood red!**

G.T.Haywood's classic song, " *I See A Crimson Stream Of Blood That Flows From Calvary*" comes to mind as we envision that spectacular blood-red stream that flowed out of the side of Mt.Sinai! Without the shedding of blood there is no remission of sins. Standing before this ancient *type* of Calvary, Moses demanded of the backslidden people " *Who is on the Lord's side?*" Immediately, those who drank of the stream of repentance received forgiveness! Those who didn't were slain by the sword of the Levites! In that one day alone, over 3,000 died in their sins!

One of the primary, non-jewelry uses of gold is in conducting electricity. Much electric current is sent through gold wire and cable! Though fiber optics now abound, *nothing conducts power like gold!*

That is why God desires a church of pure gold. A church not diluted with the spiritual evils of our time. Through His pure gold church, God longs to send healing power, saving power, delivering power to help bind up the wounds of a lost and dying generation. Why the suffering? Why the persecution? Why the trials and tribulations? To echo the patriarch Job, *" That when He hath tried me, I shall come forth as GOLD!"* Why? Because nothing conducts the supernatural power of God like a church made of pure gold! He desires us to be pure gold Christians!

Chapter Nineteen
" Energized By Power "
" You shall receive power after that the Holy Ghost is come upon you!"(Acts 1:8)
- Authority -

In November '94 while driving across the frost-bitten corn fields of northwestern Indiana, I was listening to America's most listened-to radio talk show host, Rush Limbaugh while he chortled with glee at the election day's Republican victory! An unexpected ballot-box victory that had just captured both the House and the Senate for the Republican party! In his opinion legislative gridlock would now be over and the nation was about to see just how a national government should *really* be run!

Just a few scant years later even Rush came to the realization that the Republicans just didn't know how to rule. Occupying the fringes of political power for decades, having finally achieved control, the Republicans promptly squandered it with years of infighting and lack of accomplishment. Though a historical opportunity had been given by the nation's voters, it remained largely unrealized because the Republicans had no expertise in being the party-in-power.

In a spiritual sense, we Christians are often like those lackluster Republicans. We don't know how to exercise the power of the devil that Christ has given to us! We tend to procrastinate using our spiritual authority until maybe sometime in the distant future, like perhaps during the Millennium, which is really illogical because Satan will be bound throughout the entire one thousand year reign of Christ! So why would we wait until then to exercise our authority? In an era of human history in which there will be nothing left here on earth that seeks to harm or destroy.

In a very real sense when someone sarcastically comments, *" You spirit-filled Christians walk around with your heads in the clouds!"* They are actually telling the truth! Our Head *is* in the clouds seated on

power to them. ... ...
with POWER from on high"(Luke 24:49). Luke continues his report of the transfer, *" But ye shall receive POWER after that the Holy Ghost is come upon you . . ."(Acts 1:8).* And the supernatural power surge that hit the Upper Room on the Day of Pentecost confirmed the transfer of Jesus' power to humankind!

Paul wrote the church at Ephesus, *"What is the exceeding greatness of His power to usward who believe, according to the working of His mighty power! Which He wrought in Christ, when He raised him from the dead and set him at his own right hand in the heavenly places. Far **above** all principality, and power, and might, and dominion, and every name that is named, not only in this world but also in that which is to come."(Eph.1:19-21).* Later in the same letter, Paul continued, *" Even when we were dead in sins, (he) hath quickened us **together** with Christ, (by grace are ye saved;) And hath raised us up **together**, and made us sit **together** in heavenly places in Christ Jesus"(Eph.2:5-6).*

Hallelujah! When the Head was raised up and placed in the position of authority at the right hand of power, so was His Body! The Head and the Body were exalted together! The authority conferred upon the resurrected Savior was conferred upon the saved, too! The Head wasn't separated from the Body! Think about it, when someone is decapitated, both the severed head and the remaining body parts die. An individual's head and his body are thought of as being one person, right? It's the classic symbiotic relationship.

The devil seeks to blind the church to the inherent intimacy that we have with Jesus! Not only as His Body do we sit with Him in heavenly authority, but we sit, *" Far above all principality, and power, and might!"* Our spiritual authority is far above any trial, temptation or tribulation Satan may send our way! In fact we are over him, too! We should live a deeper lifestyle that takes authority over sin, sickness and defeat! For God's work is carried out by His spiritual Body on earth; that's you and me! It's a biological fact that the head only controls it's own body, not any other adjacent bodies. In the spirit realm that's why God only directs the church.

Not only does Christ give us **spiritual authority on earth**, He also gives us authority over the devil. *" These signs shall follow them that believe, in my name shall they cast out devils . . .(Mark 16:17).* We are to cast out devils in Jesus name. We have power over the enemy in our own lives and households. I've never seen people simply walk down the street and cast the devil out of everyone they meet. It just doesn't work that way! Individual human will is a decisive factor. If the human host is enjoying the sins being experienced under satanic influence, *no one* can cast the devil out! One evangelist typified it as being like money. You have control over your money, but you don't have control over mine. You have authority over your children, but you don't have authority over mine. You can cast the devil out of your world, your friends and family, but not in mine! Human will *cannot* be cast out!

James, the Lord's half-brother and pastor of the early church in Jerusalem commanded us to *" Summit yourselves therefore to God, Resist the devil and he will flee from YOU!"(James 4:7).* It's worthy to note that the Bible didn't say he would flee from God, it says that he will flee from YOU! It's ineffective when you mix up the order of new accomplishment in their lives.

Too often that happens to Christians. When first saved, we learn to lean on the ministry and other Christians for prayer and strength. Years later, when we should be praying and discipling other Christians, we are still constantly petitioning the church for ourselves. You and I must become strong in the Lord! Learn to take authority in the spirit world yourself! Without question Jesus transferred the power to us at Pentecost.

I live near the city of New Orleans, Louisiana. One of the world-famous tourist attractions is the French Quarter. This historic section of town features Bourbon Street, Jackson Square, the Moonwalk, the Aquarium of the Americas, cute little gourmet restaurants, tasty French beignets with hot chocolate, street musicians, horse carriage rides, corner tap-dancers, street artists who will paint your portrait for a small fee. To say that the French Quarter attracts huge crowds would be a laughable understatement! Especially around the time of the Sugar Bowl or the annual Mardi Gras parade season.

Once while walking along a Canal Street sidewalk that was jammed with out-of-towners, a uniformed policeman motioned me off the sidewalk so a tradesman could roll a loaded dolly into his business.

Though the officer was short and sleight of build, I immediately obeyed him. Why? Because of the authority he represented! Even though I towered over him at a lofty 6'3", my compliance acknowledged that the authority he represented was more powerful than I. That's why a powerful supernatural entity such as Satan flees at our emphatic resistance. The authority we represent not only created him but will one day banish him to the Lake of Fire forever and ever!

Walking in a deeper lifestyle gives you an awareness of the authority that you have. You are seated with Christ *over* all the real and imagined powers of the devil. When you submit yourself to the Lord, the devil will flee from YOU! A popular saying in Pentecostal circles, *" The power behind you is greater than the task before you!"* finds it's scriptural base in the simple statement of John, *" Greater is He that is in you, than he that is in the world!"* When the disciples rushed into the Upper Room, they were seeking power. Understand that seeking power *is* seeking the Kingdom. For the Kingdom of God isn't in word but in power! You are energized with supernatural power that was transferred to the church at Pentecost!

Peering into the darkness, you breathe, *" I love you, Jesus. I love you, Lord. Please let me know your will for me today."* Instantly the spiritual current intensifies as God pours our His love to you. Almost swooning under His benevolent power, you slide off the side of the bed and fall to your knees still crying out, *" Oh, Jesus! I love you! I want to please you and do your will!"*

Your heart pounds as the Lord begins to reveal His will to you. Though unspoken, He plants pictures of people who you haven't seen or thought of in a long time into your mind. Your personal opinion of them surfaces and then fades away as God's will for them is revealed to you. *" God, are you leading me to contact them?"* you whisper into the darkness. The silence builds to a joyful crescendo as torrents of heavenly love confirm His will in answer to your query.

" But, God, they hate me!" you cautiously remind Him. Again the Lord impresses something on your mind that all of you have in common. The word of knowledge has been accompanied by a word of wisdom in how to use the knowledge. God will always prepare you for battle. Taking a quick glance at the clock, you calculate that if you hurry, you can stop by their house on the way to your job. Hurriedly dressing, you gulp down breakfast, hop in your car and head for the object of your prayer's home.

After knocking on the door, the man of the house opens it. When recognizing you, he snarls, " *What are YOU doing here? You know we have no use for you hypocrite Christians!*" Suddenly, the Lord reveals to your mind that the angry greeting is just a facade. Deep in the heart of the angry man, he is glad that someone cares.

Quickly, you reply, " *I heard that Jim has contracted AIDS. I just thought that I would stop and visit with him for awhile.*"

Grabbing your arm, the angry father proceeds to throw you off the porch stoop! " *Get out of here, you phony holy-roller! You're not coming around here praying for us, acting like your better than us!*"

Having discerned his *real* spirit, you quietly respond, " *Mr. Smythe, I've lost a cousin to AIDS last year. I know the hurt and suffering you must be going through. At our house, we are still grieving over the loss of my cousin.*" The sincerity of your plaintive plea stops him cold! Removing his hand from your arm, he gestures for you to enter while dropping resignedly into a waiting armchair. Pointing towards the couch, he unexpectedly starts pouring out his heart.

Listening quietly, the Lord again gives you the courage to pray aloud. " *Mr. Smythe, can we pray for Jim together? Father, in the name of Jesus, I ask your love to fill the heart of this broken man today. I ask you to bind up his wounded spirit! I bind any spirits of confusion, of insecurity or unbelief that may be attacking the Smythe family. Remove all of those spirits of unproductive guilt about their son's condition. Father, in the name of Jesus, we turn it all over to you!*"

With tears running down his face, Mr. Smythe asks you, " *Son, how did you know we've been blaming ourselves? When you prayed that prayer, I felt such a load lift from me! I believe that God is working on our behalf!*"

you quietly speak, " *Jim, the Lord just revealed to us that He will work a miracle in your behalf today! God is going to heal you of AIDS!*"

A bitter sound, a barking laugh erupts from the pathetic, lifeless form, " *Sure, God is going to heal me! Go away! Leave me alone to die!*" Jim mutters.

Bending over the bed, you ask, " *Jim, are you ready to die? Have you asked Jesus to forgive you of your sins? Have you been baptized? Have you been born again?*" Sensing the earnestness of your questions, Jim nods in the affirmative, then explains that he has received the infilling of the Holy Ghost. Apologizing for initial response, he now asks you to pray for him.

" *In the name of Jesus Christ the Son of God,*" you begin, " *Lord, by your stripes, Jim is healed! I command the spirit of disease to leave this body! I take authority over this AIDS condition and cast it into outer darkness! In the name of Jesus, let your healing virtue flow! Jim, Jesus wants you to get out of that bed right now!*"

Struggling slowly, Jim begins to work the miracle in his own life. By faith, he weakly slides off the bed and starts hobbling toward the adjacent restroom. By the time he touches the handle of the restroom door, the healing power of God races through him and Jim begins shouting and dancing for joy! After rejoicing with the entire Smythe family for a few minutes, you then excuse yourself and head for work! The day has just begun and God has already exercised seven of the gifts of the Spirit in your life! As you continue walking in the deeper lifestyle of a spirit-filled Christian, God will do mighty works through you, each and every day. Hmmmmm, just now punched the time clock? Don't you wonder what will happen before lunch?

Sound like a holy-roller fantasy? Sound a bit overdone? I agree that it's more than a bit idealistic, but with Christ it *is* within the realm of possibility! Does God expect *every* Christian to be used like the one in the preceding story? No, because His Body is made up of different members with different functions. But we must allow our fellow Christians the spiritual freedom to be used differently than us! We all have unique functions in His Body, we must recognize and respect that fact!

Jesus declared, *" Ask and ye shall receive, Seek and ye shall find, knock and it shall be opened unto you!"* The spirit of God seeks out individual Christians who want more than to just save themselves and obtain eternal life. God seeks those who will allow Him to heal the wounded spirits and broken lives of mankind through their own spiritually submitted lives. Those that seek a deeper lifestyle will find it and change human history for the better.

Could you be one of those people?

THE END

Deeper lifestyle : insi...
BOOK
ue: 2/24/2010,23:59
Item: 3183304213566

Total items checked out: 4

Telephone Renewal: 421
Website Renewal: www.

FACT, FRAUD, AND FANTASY

The Occult and Pseudosciences

Morris *Herbert* **Goran**

Littlefield, Adams & Company

Published 1980 by
LITTLEFIELD, ADAMS & CO.

© 1979 by A. S. Barnes and Co., Inc.

Library of Congress Cataloging in Publication Data

Goran, Morris Herbert, 1916–
    Fact, fraud, and fantasy.

    Bibiography: p.
    Includes index.
    1. Occult sciences—Controversial literature.
2. Psychical research—Controversial literature.
3. Science—Miscellanea. I. Title.
BF1042.G63   1980   001.9   80-16320
ISBN 0-8226-0356-X

For my students

Contents

Introduction

The problems faced by late-twentieth-century human beings appear to be difficult and often insoluble. Confidence in human reason has consequently been eroded, and the beckoning siren of other ways of knowing have become appealing. Pseudo- and occult science have been presented as tempting replacements for the use of mankind's cerebral cortex and associated organs.

During the days when newspaper, magazine, and radio advertisers attempted to associate themselves with science, pseudoscience was a minor matter and analyses were few. Disenchantment with recent events has brought many people closer to the occult and esoteric and away from science. What are they missing?

One aim of this volume is analyses of the pseudo- and occult sciences so that an intelligent person can view them objectively. Apprehending them in a proper context is both educational and entertaining.

Another objective of this book is to show how some characteristics of science and scientists are also the distinguishing features of pseudo- and occult sciences. The chapter titles as well as some paragraphs in each chapter delineate the particular aspect highlighted. However, the ultimate goal is not to describe similarities but to pinpoint differences. Why similar procedures produce science on one hand and pseudoscience on the other is examined herein.

9

FACT, FRAUD, AND FANTASY

1 Correlations

PHRENOLOGY

Have you ever formed an immediate opinion about a person seen momentarily? Are you enchanted with your seeming ability to gauge character and personality with minimum data? Only when enough wrong impressions are made do you begin to question your supposed special talent.

A rapid, accurate judgment of human personality and capabilities has long been sought. Dress, gait, height, weight, eye color, amount and distribution of hair, complexion, neatness, and cleanliness have a history of use, and one or more are still trusted in some circles today. Who can deny the formation of conclusions when faced by an individual wearing spotted, torn garments and having disheveled hair?

Shape of head, hand lines, and facial features are in the same category of instant correlation, with an added advantage of organization backing. Phrenology and palmistry, for example, are taught and promulgated as the truth. Each began in early times.

In ancient Greece Melampus is reported to have said:

A mole on a man's forehead signifies wealth and happiness; on a woman's forehead, it denotes that she will be powerful, perhaps a ruler. Close to the eyebrow of a man, the mole predicts a happy marriage with a pretty and virtuous woman; and it foretells similar fortune to girls. Moles on the bridge

13

of the nose mean lust and extravagance for both sexes. When appearing on the nostrils, the mole signifies constant travel. Moles upon the lips of men and women betray gluttony and on the chin—they will possess gold and silver! Moles in the ear and on the neck are lucky omens; they predict wealth and fame. When upon the nape of the neck, however, the beauty spot carries an ill omen, that of being beheaded! Moles upon the loins are unfortunate signifying mendacity, and ill luck for the descendants. When appearing on the shoulders, they predict captivity and unhappiness; on the chest, poverty. Moles on the hands announce many children; and under the arm-pits, they bring luck as they promise a wealthy and handsome husband or wife. Ominous are moles when found upon the heart and bosom and belly, as they signify voracity. They are a good omen when seen on the upper leg, announcing wealth; when upon the lower part of the stomach, they presage intemperance for men but the contrary for women.[1]

No record is available of how many mole-people Melampus studied before reaching his conclusions. Probably he made no survey because unless he was adept in securing confidences, men and women did not reveal their hidden skin blemishes.

During Renaissance times in western Europe, an Italian physician and mathematician, Jerome Cardan, extended the correlation of moles and personality to astrological signs. According to him, moles on the bridge of the nose were Libra indicators; on the cheekbone, Scorpio and Sagittarius; on the jaw, Capricornus; on the chin, Pisces. About a century later, Richard Saunders wrote: "That man and woman who hath a mole on the right side of the forehead under the line of Saturn but not touching this line, in the first figure, they shall have another on the right side of the breast; this party may claim good fortune in building, in sowing, planting, and tilling of the earth. And this mole, if it shall shine with a honey or ruby color, he and she shall have good fortune during the whole course of their lives; if black, his condition shall be mutable; if like a lentil, he shall be advanced and the first and chief person in a family. For a woman, it denotes the fortune of inheritance and gifts from the dead. This mole is of the nature of Venus, Mercury, and Mars, and receives its denomination from Lyra, a star of the first magnitude."[2]

Phrenology, correlating various sections of the human head with ability and personality, originated with Franz Joseph Gall, a German who received an M.D. degree at the University of Vienna in 1781. He was a renowned neurologist and is called the godfather of the principle of cortical localization of mental facilities.[3] During his early years, judging people through facial features, physiognomy, was very popular. The theme that character could be read from the contour of the skull, was therefore not very distant.

Gall's pupil, Johann Gasper Spurzheim coined the word phrenology and was chiefly responsible for the beginning of popular acclaim. He toured Great Britain and the United States, speaking to crowded lecture halls and influencing molders of opinion.

For Gall, thirty-seven faculties of the mind, localized in different regions of the brain, were good and evil. For Spurzheim, however, all the faculties were intrinsically good. Moreover, he, unlike Gall, speculated about religion, education, and penology.

Spurzheim influenced George Combe, a lawyer who became the leading exponent in England. For eighteen months, 1838–40, Combe lectured in the United States and was elected to the American Philosophical Society as well as to the National Academy of Sciences. When he lectured in New Haven, Connecticut, most of the faculty of Yale College were in his audience.

During the early nineteenth century, many associations in support of phrenology were formed in the United States. In Washington the Surgeon General of the United States was secretary of the local phrenology society. In Boston there were 144 members, and one-third were medical doctors.[4]

Opponents of phrenology were not muted. Newspapers,

magazines, and individuals argued against it. At Amherst College in 1833, Henry Ward Beecher won his debate against phrenology, and then announced his conversion. He said later that it was the basis of his ministry, and the best preparation for a Christian was "a practical knowledge of the human mind as is given by phrenology."[5]

Acceptance of phrenology gained momentum because eminent men embraced it. In the United States, educator Horace Mann confessed to be "a hundred times more indebted to phrenological than to all the metaphysical works I ever read."[6] In England, Alfred Russel Wallace, co-discoverer with Charles Darwin of the natural selection mechanism for organic evolution, wrote in 1899, "In the coming century phrenology will assuredly attain general acceptance. It will prove itself to be the true science of mind. Its practical uses in education, in self-discipline, in the reformatory treatment of criminals, and in the remedial treatment of the insane, will give it one of the highest places in the hierarchy of the sciences."[7] Charles Darwin was involved in a different way. When he applied in 1831 to Captain Robert Fitzroy of the *Beagle* for the post of ship naturalist, Fitzroy was tempted to reject the twenty-two-year-old Darwin because his nose did not show "sufficient energy and determination." Fitzroy believed in a system of character analysis based on the shape of the face.

Perhaps the appeal of phrenology was simplicity. An avenue to understand human behavior was available without tedious study and abstract conceptions.

However, phrenology in the United States had the advantage of a promotion campaign rivaling the best efforts of those who sold soap, deodorants, mouthwash, and political candidates during the late twentieth century. Beginning in 1835, the Fowler brothers and their sister were publishers, lecture agents, merchandisers, and general entrepreneurs for phrenology. The firm was augmented in 1843 when a young medical student, Samuel Wells, married the sister. The profitability of the venture can be judged by the sales price of a Fowler home, $150,000. Fowler and Wells operated the Phrenological Cabinet, a museum where they also gave character readings. For four dollars, they would also do the same by mail "from a good daguerreotype, the ¾ pose preferred."[8] They had branch offices in Boston and Philadelphia, founded a Phrenological College, sold the Phrenological Almanac, with a circulation of more than 20,000 a year, edited and published the *American Phrenological Journal*, and offered plaster casts, models of the brain and anatomical drawings for a fee to other lecturers.

The phrenologists correlated sections of the head with such human traits as cautiousness, secretiveness, hope, firmness, self-esteem and combativeness. The cranium was divided into more than forty areas called phrenological organs or faculties. The practitioners examined skulls but really described personality traits and the future of the individual.

Religious people who objected to phrenology cited the lack of human freedom as well as the vague, distant position of God within the framework of the subject. The study of scripture would have little if any influence on character; man's divine origin would be suspect.

Scientific opponents could argue that brain dissection did not reveal divisions or compartments, and cranial bones masked any protuberance adversely affecting any exterior examination. A Scottish thinker, William Hamilton (1788–1856), argued that the correlations were contrary to fact; for example, he cited the claim that the size of the cerebellum was an accurate measure of sexual appetite and proceeded to measure more than 1,000 brains of 50 different animal species, and the ratio of cerebellum to total brain size was always greater in females. In all animals the cerebellum reached its maximum size before puberty. The most damaging criticism was that there was no change in a trait even when the particular brain section was injured or destroyed.

Phrenology did not collapse after anatomical studies during the nineteenth century gave support to the critics. In 1876 the pioneer in criminology Cesare Lombroso, as a young Italian army doctor, asserted that he could distinguish between the criminal and normal recruit on the basis of certain gross morphological characteristics. Some of the contentions of the subject were absorbed into accumulated lore and barroom tales so that even men and women today instantly associate forehead protrusions with alertness, or closeness of ears to the skull with intelligence. In 1945 the respectable publishing firm of Blakiston distributed *Fortune Telling for Fun and Popularity* by P. Showers, and beginning on page 324 is a claim for correlation of mole and character: on the right side of the forehead it is a sign of talent and success, whereas one on the left side indicates stubbornness, extravagance, and dissipation. In 1970 Macmillan published Sybil Leek's *Phrenology*. In 1975 a kind of phrenologist employed by a Chicago restaurant was tested by a journalist. He showed pictures of (a) Hitler's lieutenant Joseph Goebbels, (b) gangster Al Capone, (c) the proprietor of a pornography store, (d) a mass murderer, (e) a newspaper columnist, (f) gangster John Dillinger, and (g) another criminal. The analyses, in order, were (a) gentle and sensitive thinker, (b) incapable of any success, (c) a faithful husband, (d) a considerate person, (e) friendly and cultural, (f) charming lover of life, and (g) a quiet, sensitive individual. When shown a photograph of former Chicago mayor Richard Daley, the physiognomist reported that the mayor did not have a good relationship with his brothers—and Daley had no brothers.

The correlation of shapes with character may be ingrained at an early age. Mass media inundate viewers, listeners, and readers with identical conceptions of the beautiful. Parents and peers help the process. Often the printed word, verified or not, can be an important influence.

PYRAMIDOLOGY

The movement correlating pyramid shape with marvelous events was nurtured largely through books. Modern pyramidology begins with an 1859 book by John Taylor, *The Great Pyramid: Why Was It Built? And Who Built It?* Here the Cheops pyramid at Giza in Egypt is described as containing a variety of mathematical revelations such as the value of the biblical measure, the cubit. The speculation was promoted by Professor Charles Piazzi Smyth of the University of Edinburgh; he went to Egypt to investigate. He presented numbers to show how the pyramid indicated, among other facts, the distance of the Earth to the sun, the Earth's mean density, precession period, and the mean temperature of the Earth's surface. Pyramidology was extended by the founder of the religious sect Jehovah's Witnesses, Charles T. Russell of Allegheny, Pennsylvania, who noted that the pyramid revealed the invisible Second Coming of Christ.[9]

Adherents to pyramidology today include actress Gloria Swanson, who sleeps under a pyramid-shaped tent because it "makes every cell in every body tingle," and those who suggest that the shape is useful for the alleviation of arthritis and rheumatism.[10] An organization in Los Angeles claims that the pyramid shape is an incubator of "thought forms."[11] The pyramid shape is also said to maintain razor-blade sharpness, retard food spoilage, increase static electricity, and serve as a hothouse for growing plants. Adherents continue to argue for the thesis that the pyramids are the work of extraterrestrials.

Pyramid study is not an Egyptian monopoly, although about 70 pyramids of significant size are in the country. Scholars continually argue about how they were built and their significance. Tourists are inevitably impressed by their width and height; the base of the Cheops pyramid covers 13 acres, and the structure was originally 450 feet tall.

Pyramidology is commercialized. There is a Cheops Razor Blade Sharpener, a Toth pyramid, as well as pyramid-shaped milk and yogurt cartons.[12]

Traditional scientists have scored the pretensions and falsities of pyramidology. The chairman of the chemistry department at the University of California called it "hogwash"; the head of the physics department at the University of Miami described it as a fantasy; the head of the Oriental Institute at the University of Chicago shows his contempt by refusing to discuss it with newspaper reporters. And like all other occult and pseudo-sciences, traditionally trained scientists are among the defenders of pyramidology. Professor Michael Kosok of the physics department at Fairleigh Dickinson University is studying the effect with two large copper-lined pyramids. Ed Downs, a Houston theoretical physicist, and physicist G. Patrick Flanagan, author of the popular *Pyramid Power*, are devotees.

Pyramidology became even more popular after the Columbia Broadcasting System television special of April 20, 1977. Yet pyramidology does not yet rival the popularity attained by phrenology or another correlation, that of human personality and handwriting. Graphology is widely practiced today and has not suffered the contumely of being characterized as occult. It is not even labeled a pseudoscience, being confused with an allied discipline, handwriting analysis, used in court and other places to establish authenticity. Graphology, however, attempts to match handwriting with character and is in the same league as phrenology.

PALMISTRY

Palmistry or chiromancy is another attempt to relate shapes and human destiny. In this case the lines, crevices, bumps, and lumps on the hand are the alleged key to personality. Like graphology, palmistry suffers less from adverse criticism because of the stature of fingerprinting. Governments and criminologists have great confidence in every person having a unique print. But fingerprint experts do not attempt to read an individual's abilities and future as do the chiromancers.

Palmistry's other name stems from Count Louis Hamon, a nineteenth-century fortune-teller who called himself

"Cheiro." He had scores of patrons and made a fortune even before he supposedly pinpointed the death dates of Queen Victoria, Edward VII, and other notables. Palmists before him had classified hands, making analyses more standardized. Four types accepted today, for example, are called *practical*, with square palms and short fingers; *intuitive*, with long palms and short fingers; *sensitive*, long palms and long fingers; and *intellectual*, square palm and long fingers.

The left hand is supposed to show inherited tendencies, while the right indicates developed qualities; otherwise the alleged correlations are identical.[13] The mound under the index finger is said to represent ambition and social prestige. If the development is closer to the side of the palm, family pride is the chief ambition; when closer to the second finger, scholarly attributes are indicated. Under the little finger is the mound area of Mercury, representing practical, managerial facilities or scientific aptitude. When developed toward the third finger, the mound indicates love and appreciation for beautiful surroundings. If toward the base of the finger, business before pleasure is the rule. When toward the thumb, a spirit willing to fight for a cause is shown; development in the other direction means a good sense of humor, clear quick thinking, liveliness, and talkativeness.

Chiromancy attempts to interpret every part of the hand, not only the palm. The first phalange of the thumb, for example, represents will power, and the second, reasoning ability. If the first phalange is longest, there is more will than logic. If the second phalange is longer than the first, there is native intelligence but not a great amount of will to carry things through.

The lines on the palm and wrist are interpreted, especially if they are clearly traced, without variance of form or color. Light-colored lines purportedly indicate indecision and a weak person who tires easily. The line of life surrounding the thumb shows the vitality and energy that a person can expend. If the line begins close to the forefinger, the individual is supposed to be governed by great ambition and not easily deterred by disappointments or frustrations.

Data needed to establish the veracity of the judgments rendered by the chiromancers is not available. There is no record of any study, statistical or qualitative, seeking to chart the truth of the relationships held with confidence by the palm readers. Names such as Alexander, Aristotle, Pliny, and Caesar can be cited as having an interest in palmistry; Napoleon had his palms read. But investigation into the basic relationships adopted is nonexistent. Reasonable men and women seek verification for correlations as well as a sizable population for the testing.

Lyall Watson in his *Supernature* purports that congenital disorders have been connected with particular palm patterns.[14] Neither this, if true, nor the so-called simian crease of Mongoloids is support of the thesis that the future of an individual can be read from their hands. The Japanese physicians reported by him to have studied 200,000 palm prints and found diagnostic significance in the lines to be able to foretell whether the individual will contract infectious diseases is likewise not an evidence for palmistry. If this claim is substantiated, the palm is shown to be a medical aid rather than a fortune-telling device.

In 1975 Dr. Ira S. Salafsky of the Evanston Hospital, Evanston, Illinois, pediatrics department, made plans to test his theory that palm prints can predict learning disabilities in young children. His preliminary research indicates a correlation between the formation of faint edges on the skin and genetic disorders that portend learning problems.

Phrenology, pyramidology, and palmistry do have medical overtones, not accepted as widely as are their prediction properties. Conventional anatomy and physiology are enough concerned with shapes and lines to squelch any unproved assertions about the value of this or that geometry.

NUMEROLOGY

When numbers were presented to the Western world as significant, they, too, were given medical meanings. The followers of Pythagoras, however, emphasized another direction. Sambursky quotes Philolaus: "Actually, everything that can be known has a number; for it is impossible to grasp anything with the mind or to recognize it without this. The nature of Number and Harmony admits of no Falsehood; for this is unrelated to them."[15]

Other approaches became accredited to the Pythagoreans, and numerology was founded. The number 1 was identified with reason because it alone could produce a consistent whole; 2, with opinion; 4, with justice since it is the first number that is a product of equals; 5, with marriage, being a union of odd and even; 7, with health; 8, with love and friendship. The even numbers were said to be feminine and the odd ones masculine.[16]

Numerology today has a different correlation of the numbers. According to Vera Scott Johnson and Thomas Wommack[17] the number 1 represents aspects of creation and self; 2, aspects of gestation and union; 3, aspects of self-expression; 4, aspects of self-discipline; 5, aspects of re-creation and is the apex for change in the cycle; 6, social consciousness; 7, intellectual and spiritual development; 8, material accomplishment; 9, selflessness and universal awareness; 11, impractical idealism; and 22, practical idealism. The odd numbers tend to be related to thoughts and ideas and are active in nature; the even numbers tend to be related to practical realities and are sometimes passive in nature.

Numerology assigns the numbers 1 through 9 to the letters A through I; J through R are also 1 through 9 with the exception that K is given the number 11; S through Z are 1 through 8 with the exception that V is given the number 22. Thus, the letters in the name Bill are represented by the numbers 2, 9, 3, and 3; adding them yields

17 and adding the two digits yields 8. The letters in the word China are represented by the numbers 3, 8, 9, 5, and 1; adding yields 26 and adding again yields 8. Other rules observed in numerology assign numbers 1 through 9 to the months through September; October is 1; November is 11, a master number (as is 22); and December is 3, the sum of 1 and 2.

In name analysis by numerology, there are three essential numbers. The sum of the vowel numbers is the *motivation* number; the sum of the consonant numbers is the *impression* number; and the sum of all numbers is the *expression* number. Impression number 5, for example, is the prophecy, "You fantasize life as a great epic adventure. You are free and irresponsible, taking all of the sensual pleasures of life as they come and moving on to the next episode the minute you are bored. All of life's sensual delights—sex, food, drink, and stimulants—are yours in great abundance. The world is your home, and you have seen it all."[18]

A person's inclusion table specifies the missing numbers as well as the abundance of numbers in the name, and each has personal significance. A person's birthdate allegedly gives a timetable of achievements and challenges.

A total forecast is made with a numeroscope, a chart including all of the above and more. Although promoters of numerology boast of the simplicity of this occult science, interpreting the numeroscope is infinitely more taxing than composing it. The practitioner must be familiar with or have available a myriad of correlations.

If neither phrenology, pyramidology, palmistry, nor numerology offer satisfying correlations, a host of other relatedness attempts are available. Gibson and Gibson, in their *Complete Illustrated Book of the Psychic Sciences*, list 97.[19] In their 1973 book, *The Complete Illustrated Book of Divination and Prophecy* (Doubleday), they have 105. Among them are *austromancy*, referring to divination by a study of the winds; *ceraunoscopy*, drawing omens from the study of thunder and lightning; *cromniomancy*, finding significance from onion sprouts; *ichthyomancy*, involving fish as factors in divination; and *tephramancy*, interpreting from ashes.

In some circles the omens are used as a form of entertainment. Rachleff reports that in Austria on New Year's Eve, spoonfuls of hot wax are dropped into ice water, and the formations are interpreted for what the year ahead will bring.[20]

Some erroneous correlations can be traced to ancient and medieval writers. Hippocrates said that the woman bearing a male child is well colored and has a larger right breast. When the Black Death plagued Europe, responsibility was assigned to the mutilated poor or the Jews. A forerunner of modern science during the Middle Ages, Michael Scot passed along several entertaining ones. He wrote: "the right testicle generates males and the left females, not only in human beings but in all animals; that a baby born in a waning moon will have a white skin and yellow or white hair; that hen and goose eggs are larger in a waxing moon; that hens lay better in a waxing moon and southwind, worse in water; that the more a hen is trampled on by the cock, the better she lays and rejoices to find many eggs together in the nest."[21]

Equally good fun can be had with Pliny the Elder's list of fifteen materials alleged to make a pregnant woman abort. Experimental tests were not popular during his day so that his correlations are old wives' tales and products of his imagination. He claimed that fumes from an "asses house" or warts or lichens from the leg of a horse powdered and drunk in water produced abortions.[22]

Individuals who make their own correlations indoctrinate themselves with similar attempts to find connections. One may say that good luck will appear if fifteen Chevrolets with green vinyl tops are seen during an hour, or excellent health will be theirs should an individual with a ruddy complexion and at least six feet tall pass them on the street. The rationale behind the efforts may be the conceit that they have the special ability to discover the relationship, or saturation with it to the extent that a self-fulfilling prophecy is available.

If and when individuals confess to a belief in what appears to be a strange correlation, they may take refuge in the contention that scientists practice the same tendency. The celebrated men and women of science seek out patterns in nature, such as "pressure and temperature of an enclosed gas at constant volume are directly proportional." The ecologists preach the principle of interrelatedness with their statement that everything is connected to everything else.

The correlations devised by scientists may be in words, equations, or diagrams. The mathematical formulas connecting variables are favored by the physical scientists, and the diagrams or graphs are found in all sciences. At the beginning of the century, astronomy had one independently prepared by Hertzsprung and Russell. The R-H diagram relating color and luminosity of stars at first appeared to be an academic novelty. Now it has become the basis for investigation of stellar development.

Correlations honored in science have an important characteristic not found in pseudoscience. *The scientific relationships yield fruitful results, and those capable of being quantified have a high, positive correlation.*

Pseudoscience connects sunspots with a large variety of factors. Among the better known are wars, stock-market prices, growth of hair, and economic depressions. Data to support these and other correlations is not available, and, consequently, the scientist rejects them. On the other hand, the connection between sunspots and precipitation or sunspots and radio reception has been established. Scientists study these to wrest a pattern enabling quantitative prediction.

Some of the correlations once accepted in scientific circles have been shown to be erroneous and are dropped. Pseudoscientists tend to cling tenaciously to their favorites, and their percent of rejection of ideas is probably much smaller.

In meteorology, the British during the late nineteenth century believed barometric measurements to be a clear indicator of weather. Barometers on British warships were marked similar to some household ones today. Each barometric number is associated with kind of weather from fair to foul. Meteorological investigation revealed several other factors besides atmospheric pressure developing weather. Professionals today must take into account such items as wind speed and direction, height and type of clouds, visibility, fronts, air masses, and dew point. The simple correlation between barometric pressure and weather characteristics is therefore closer to pseudoscience.

Scientists are faced with many correlations needing research to establish or reject the contention. Unfortunately, the public may take them up when first announced and may be loathe to relinquish them. In 1975 *Newsweek* reported a preliminary study showing a link between creased ear lobes and a tendency toward heart ailments. Despite the disclaimer by one Mayo Clinic physician that a person who finds that his lobes are creased should not worry, the scene was set for amateur, dogmatic diagnosticians.[23]

Physicians and others have also maintained the thesis that an elevated level of cholesterol in the blood indicates a greater-than-average risk of suffering heart disease. The cholesterol theme has been widely accepted, yet the Coronary Drug Project seeking definitive evidence that lowering blood cholesterol concentrations can prevent heart attacks, gave negative results.[24]

Scientific research finds many correlations demanding closer investigation. In medicine, a connection is suspected between diabetes and virus. In meteorology, in North America at least, there is extreme precipitation for the month near the middle of the first and third weeks after new moon. A Canadian investigator of parapsychology believes that psychics received a severe electric shock before the age of ten. During the summer of 1975 a Canadian psychologist reported to the *New Scientist* a positive correlation between difficult births and subsequent left-handedness, suggesting the latter trait is a symptom of brain damage occurring during birth. In 1976 a professor at the University of West Virginia, in a paper delivered at the annual meeting of the Acoustical Society of America, claimed a general idea of an individual's appearance can be obtained from the sound of the recorded voice.

None of the correlations investigated or accepted in science are random, based upon chance, notwithstanding the first law of ecology that everything is connected to everything else. The dictum is not a rationale for an attempt to relate diverse items; it is a principle to underscore the interconnectedness of significant factors. Thus, nitrate fertilizer seeps into the ground and eventually seeks out ground water, which may be adversely affected; the added chemical for deficient soil was not until recently thought to be deleterious to water. The first law of ecology does not make connections of anything with everything in the manner of games of chance.

I CHING

Pseudoscientific correlations based on chance include I Ching (Book of Changes) and Uranai. In his foreword to the 1949 version of *I Ching*, Carl Jung, the psychologist with a proclivity toward the occult, wrote: "The Western mind sifts, weighs, selects, classifies, and isolates while the Oriental picture of the moment encompasses everything down to the minutest nonsensical detail, because all of the ingredients make up the observed moment."

The *I Ching* addict throws forty-nine yarrow stalks or three coins to find out the beneficial day for travel, marriage, business transactions, home building, and other aspects of daily living. In Japan the comparable information and guidance is obtained from *Uranai* charts. The extent to which it is followed is indicated by the decidely lower birthrate in Japan in 1966, a year according to *Uranai* when female babies were destined to be spinsters. In 1967 the Japanese birth rate was above normal.

Devotees of *I Ching* appear to be increasing in occidental countries, perhaps as a matter of entertainment along with fortune cookies, tarot cards, and tea-leaf readings. If the motive be a kind of devotion to chance correlations, then the Western world may also be witness in due time to such exhibitions as a band of chimpanzees before type-writers; by chance alone, they can type out the great works of mankind.

The Book of Changes or *I Ching* contains sixty-four hexagrams that may be used at random. Traditional dev-otees use the yarrow sticks, and others toss three coins six times in order to find the hexagram to interpret. Each gives short poems wherein the answer lies hidden. The hexagrams have such names as "Revolution," "The Joyous," "Oppression," "Standstill," "Peace," and "Difficulty at the Beginning." The judgment accompanying the latter is

> Difficulty at the beginning works supreme success,
> Furthering through perseverance.
> Nothing should be undertaken.
> It furthers one to appoint helpers.

The poem called "Image" is:

> Clouds and thunder
> The image of difficulty at the beginning.
> Thus the superior man
> Brings order out of confusion.

The interpretations are aided in some *I Ching* books by opinions of both Chinese philosophers and Western trans-lators. No one is deprived because of an inability to read between the lines. No one is prevented from obtaining any type of answer. Perhaps this may be the reason for testi-monials by users, Psychologist Jung, for example, saw verification of his idea called synchronicity, or noncausal coincidences.

TAROT CARDS

Tarot cards, credited to the ancient Egyptians, like *I Ching*, make correlations at random. The popular fatalistic expression "It's in the cards" would appear to give Tarot cards an edge in Western communities, but the ordinary player's as well as the pinochle deck have perhaps been a barrier. The modern Tarot deck has twenty-two cards in its major arcana and fifty-five or fifty-six in the minor arcana. The latter is composed of four suits named swords, staves, cups, and pentacles. The major group is simply symbolic pictures such as the moon dripping blood or a woman leading a lion. Patterns are arranged from both arcana for *general* answers to *general* questions.

NOTES TO CHAPTER 1

1. Kurt Seligmann, *The Mirror of Magic* (New York: Pantheon, 1948), p. 374.
2. Ibid., p. 380.
3. Owsei Temkin, "Gall and the Phrenological Movement," *Bulletin of the History of Medicine* 21 (May–June 1947):275.
4. John D. Davies, *Phrenology, Fad and Science* (New Haven, Conn.: Yale University Press, 1955), p. 25.
5. Ibid., p. 163.
6. Ibid.
7. Ibid., p. ix; see also David de Guistino, *Conquest of Mind, Phrenology and Victorian Social Thought* (London: Croom Helm, 1975).
8. Davies, *Phrenology, Fad and Science,* p. 47.
9. Martin Gardner, *In the Name of Science* (New York: G. P. Putnam, 1952), p. 181; see also "Mathematical Games," *Scientific American* 230 (June 1974):116.
10. Max Toth and Greg Nielsen, *Pyramid Power* (New York: Freeway Press, 1974), p. 164.
11. Ibid., p. 160.
12. Alan and Sally Landsburg, *In Search of Ancient Mysteries* (New York: Bantam, 1974), pp. 100–101.
13. Owen S. Rachleff, *The Occult Conceit* (Chicago: Cowles-Regnery, 1971), p. 54.
14. Lyall Watson, *Supernature* (New York: Doubleday, 1973), p. 191.

15. Samuel Sambursky, *The Physical World of the Greeks* (New York: Macmillan, 1956), p. 40.
16. Morris Kline, *Mathematics in Western Culture* (New York: Oxford University Press, 1953), pp. 76–78.
17. Vera Scott Johnson and Thomas Wommack, *The Secrets of Numbers* (New York: Berkley, 1974), p. 13.
18. Ibid., p. 53.
19. Walter B. and Litzka R. Gibson, *The Complete Illustrated Book of the Psychic Sciences* (New York: Pocket Books, 1968).
20. Rachleff, *The Occult Conceit*, p. 66.
21. Lynn Thorndike, *Michael Scot* (London: Nelson, 1965), p. 51.
22. Letter from Howard McCully, *Science* 165 (July 18, 1969):236–37.
23. *Newsweek*, January 20, 1975, p. 67.
24. Jean L. Marx, "Coronary Project: Negative Results," *Science* 187 (February 14, 1975):526.

2 Periodicity

A correlation bandied about but needing substantiation is that interest in the occult and pseudoscience rises with economic depression. At least one support of the contention is the experience with astrology at the start of a major worldwide debacle. In 1930 the *London Sunday Express* printed a horoscope of newly born Princess Margaret. Reader response was so overwhelming that an astrology column soon became a regular feature of daily newspapers in the Western world.[1]

Astrology has origins in early civilizations, with the first known horoscope being cast in the fifth century B.C.[2] The attempts were crude because astronomical tables were incomplete, but by the Renaissance modern astrological practice began to take form.

Today the United States has about 10,000 professional astrologers and many more amateurs.[3] The number of astrology magazines is several times the number of all kinds of astronomy journals. Moreover, astrologers are more widely known and better paid than are astronomers. Sydney Omarr in Hollywood not only caters to screen personalities, but his column is syndicated in more than 200 newspapers. Carroll Righter has even a larger following, his work being printed in more than 300 newspapers. When writer Shana Alexander accepted the *Los Angeles Times* Woman of the Year award from one of the paper's columnists, she said, "You are my *second* favorite columnist on the *Times.* My first is Carroll Righter who tells me every morning that something nice is going to happen."[4]

The proponents of astrology do not view it as occult, nor as pseudoscience. Their position is that astrology is a worthwhile science helping many people. In the November 1968 issue of *Trans-Action,* two psychologists from Northwestern University, Lee Sechrest and James H. Bryan, reported how astrologers can be effective marriage counselors. They claimed "A person can give good advice even if the theory upon which he supposedly bases his advice is absurd. After all, he might simply ignore his theory altogether."[5]

Astrology is based upon a correlation, similar to those delineated in chapter 1 but different from them in being a periodic relationship. Nature abounds in periodicities, and the concept may be one way to have an encompassing integration. It has even been suggested that a major reason for the lack of significant progress in early Chinese science was the belief that cycles were omnipresent, and nonperiodic causal phenomena were veritably ignored.

Periodic phenomena in astronomy include earth rotation, revolution, and precession; tides, phases of the moon, eclipses; star binary systems as well as variability in brightness. Physics has regularly recurring items in uniform and uniformly accelerated motion; the cycle of refrigeration and the cycle of internal combustion engines; the distribution of sound as well as that of electromagnetic radiation. Some biologists contend that a clock mechanism is in every cell, but obvious periodicities involving life are in eating and watering patterns and the menstrual cycle in human females. Chemistry has one of the few periodicities that does not function with respect to time; the periodic table of chemical elements also has several different cycles rather than one. Social scientists, too, deal with periodic phenomena such as wars and economic stagnation.

As noted in the first chapter, attempts have been made to correlate sunspot activity with many other events. The famous English-German amateur astronomer William Herschel told the Royal Society of London in 1801 of a relationship he had detected between sunspot number and the price of wheat between 1650–1800; he said that when sunspots were few, wheat was scarce and prices high.[6] In late 1974 scientists at the Appleton Laboratory in England had a similar conclusion dealing with all foodstuffs. Their thesis was that the low level of world agriculture productivity could be associated with the decline in sunspot activity. However, they went beyond Herschel and accepted the effect of the sunspot cycle on rainfall and hence the growth of plants.[7]

Scientific workers are not often those who cite not-fully-tested and perhaps-erroneous solar periodic correlations. Yet Dr. A. K. Podshibyakin in the U.S.S.R. is credited with the idea that automobile accidents increase in the days after a solar flare eruption.[8] In 1974 two physical scientists in the United States presented analyses of correlations between astronomical and geophysical phenomena and concluded: "A remarkable chain of evidence . . . points to 1982 as the year in which the Los Angeles region of the San Andreas fault will be subjected to the most massive earthquake known in the populated regions of the Earth in this century."[9] Their bold prediction was based on the alignment of the planets to maximize their tidal pull on the sun as well as a maximum for sunspot activity. The alignment occurs every 179 years, but no catastrophe on earth is recorded for 1803 or 1724, and so forth.

Lyall Watson, a Ph.D. in biology and a purveyor of pseudoscience, describes the Czech psychiatrist who used lunar rhythms for an allegedly successful birth-control procedure. When the moon is in a so-called male zone, a male child is produced, and a girl results if the zone is said to be female at the time of conception. According to Watson, "when tested by a committee of gynecologists, who gave him only the time of intercourse, he was able to tell the sex of the child with 98 percent accuracy."[10]

According to Swiss-born George S. Thommen of Clearwater, Florida, introducer of *biorhythm analysis*, a person's physical, emotional, and intellectual ups and downs are cyclic. He cites a 23-day physical, 28-day emotional and 33-day intellectual rhythm. The first half of each cycle indicates strength, while the change of rhythm gives so-called critical days when people are most unstable; the second half of each cycle is a period of weakness or re-charging.

Two psychologists reported in the March 13, 1975 issue of *Science* that the chances of a college woman volunteering for a behavior study could depend on the stage of her menstrual cycle. Richard L. Doty of the University of Pennsylvania and Colin Silverthorne of the University of San Francisco contend that women are probably ovulating when volunteering. They are likely to be more elated and active, responding to peer-group pressure.

In the April 1975 issue of *Psychology Today*, Peretz Lavine and Daniel F. Kropke of the University of California, San Diego, show evidence for a 90-minute cycle in man. Rapid Eye Movements, or REM sleep, occurs in cycles of 90 to 100 minutes, as do periods of mental alertness and the appetite for sexual activity.

Biorhythm charting has been used in industry. The Ohmi Company in Japan used them for 500 bus drivers and claims that accidents were fewer because the men were alerted to their critical days. Mel Lyell, safety engineer for the Virginia Department of Highways, claims that 5,000 firms use the system for accident prevention. Other testimonials, such as from a psychologist who says that he can predict the days when mental patients in a hospital will become violent or Thommen's reported pinpointing of Clark Gable's death from a heart attack in 1960, have spurred sales of biorhythm charts.

Thommen's book, *Is This Your Day?* (Crown Publishers), gives formulas to help compute cycles. His book sold more than 100,000 copies through 1975. Biorhythm Computers, 298 Fifth Avenue, New York, N.Y. 10001, offers charts for six months for $5.00. Edmund Scientific Company, Barrington, N.J. 08007, markets Thommen's do-it-yourself Cyclgraf for $4.50 or a Dialgraf calculator for $10.00. Competitors include M. R. Zaeske, P.O. Box 105, Deerfield, Illinois, with one year of charting for $7.00, and Time Pattern Research Institute, 21 Henderson Drive, West Caldwell, N.J. 07006, with one year of charting including day-to-day interpretations for $19.95. The latter sold 100,000 biorhythm printouts at $10.00 to $20.00 apiece in three years. A kit to chart the cycles is available from Psi Rhythms, Inc., 2832 South Bixie Avenue, Dayton, Ohio 45409, for $4.95. A Japanese company, Casio, Inc., manufactures an electronic calculator, the biolator, automatically charting the rhythms, and it is sold in the United States for $29.95.

Celebrated researchers in biological rhythms decry the popularity. They cite how the Workmen's Compensation Board of British Columbia studied 13,285 time-loss accidents during the first four months of 1971 and concluded: "The results indicate that accidents are no more likely to occur during 'critical periods' than at any other time." Dr. Franz Halberg, professor at the University of Minnesota School of Medicine and president of the International Society for the Study of Biorhythms claims: "The rhythms we know of are actually wobbly. They vary quite a bit, though they vary predictably."[11] Andrew Ahlgren, an associate of the Minnesota-Twin Cities Chronobiology Laboratory calls biorhythm "a hideous marriage between the quackery of numerology and perfectly sound technology." He said, "thousand of articles in reputable medical and biological journals establish that rhythms in any one person are variable, rhythms are different for different people. . . ." Gay Gaer Luce in *Biological Rhythms in Human and Animal Physiology* (New York: Dover, 1971, p. 8) traces the beginning of biorhythms as a pseudoscience to a friend of Sigmund Freud, and remarks how the originator's "blatantly unsophisticated understanding of simple mathematics is evident in his formula, which is transparent junk." Professor Frank Brown of Northwestern University, a leader in biological clock studies, calls biorhythmic theory "wholly artificial" and "in the area of clairvoyance and astrology." Professor A. James Fix of the University of Nebraska College of Medicine analyzed biorhythms in the first issue (Fall/Winter 1977) of the *Zetetic*, a quarterly published by the Committee for the Scientific Investigation of Claims of the Paranormal. He cited the untested assumptions: that each person has exactly the same cycles, totally inflexible and invariable regardless of age, sex, or life events; and that each person always begins at his or her birthdate with an "up" pattern. He studied seventy randomly selected major league baseball players during the 1975 season. Their batting pattern did not show any significant tendency toward greater effectiveness on any certain type of day. He concluded: "In this case there was no evidence that the biocurve theory is helpful in providing personally useful predictions for individual athletic performance." In the January 1978 *Archives of General Psychiatry*, Professor John W. Shaffer of Johns Hopkins University School of Medicine published an analysis of 205 carefully investigated highway crashes. He found no evidence for a link between so-called critical days and highway crashes.

Other cyclic phenomena may not be appreciated in scientific circles, even some bearing apparent credentials. West and Toonder cite several.[12] They claim that a rat in a darkened cage was twice as active when the moon was over the horizon than when it was beneath it, but they fail to report how many rats were tested and how many times the phenomena occurred. They cite Dr. Leonard J. Ravits of Duke University and his plot of human electrical potential, with decided changes coinciding with phases of the moon and the seasons; again, numbers and frequency of test are not given. They note that a physicist-astrologer made a statistical analysis of 134 major earthquakes, and the positions of the planets at the time were "non-random" as were a multitude of other factors of no significance. They even find a cyclic phenomenon in the rate of precipitation of bismuth oxychloride in water. Between 1951 and 1958 Professor Giorgio Piccardi found that the rates followed a pattern throughout any year, with a minimum in March. (Chemists have long known that temperature affects chemical reactions.) They have a large number of 9.6-year cycles such as the population of coyotes, fish, lynx, marten, mink, muskrat, rabbit, and "wildlife in general" in Canada and United States. They cite 18.2-year cycles in marriages in St. Louis, real estate activity, and pig-iron production.

The Foundation for the Study of Cycles was put together in the 1950s by Edward R. Dewey. One offshoot active today is the Society for the Investigation of Recurring Events, Box 477, Linden, N.J. 07036.

Another similar-sounding study is called cyclomatics, promulgated by Cyclomatic Engineering, P.O. Box 382, Glenview, Illinois 60025. It is based on the work of a former head of the psychology department at the University of Kansas, Dr. Raymond Wheeler, who delineated climate periods of 100 years encompassing warm-wet, warm-dry, cold-wet, and cold-dry segments. The followers contend that societies everywhere become seriously ill at least once every 100 years and desperately sick every 500 years.

West and Toonder offer a rationale for the abundance of cyclic phenomena in the subject called *cymatics*, the study of wave forms and their interaction with matter. In this discipline, the solar system is considered to be vibrating, producing a multitude of interacting harmonics. Moreover, "cymatics is essentially the study of this elusive third force which so steadfastly remains immune to our reason; it is the 'idea' between the sculptor and the block of wood; the 'desire' that mediates between man and woman, the Holy Ghost of Christian Trinity."[13]

Eastern religions also recognize the cyclical character of many items and perhaps the entire universe. The Hindu view expressed in *The Mahabharata* involves the continuing rebirth of the individual.

Numerology, too, is based on a kind of reincarnation. Johnson and Wommack report:

The science of Numerology assumes that the mind or the central core of intelligence of man is infinite but ever changing. The eternal plane on which all life exists and evolves is called the cosmic plane. A lifetime or life on a physical plane is just one cycle or incarnation through which each man's infinite intelligence passes in its continual search for perfection and balance with the universe. . . . What we are is the total of what has happened to us and, more importantly, of how we have reacted to it. Each physical reincarnation adds new experiences. We have been through many before and have more to come.[14]

Astrology is a correlation between the character and destiny of an individual and the periodic positions of the sun, moon, and planets. The cyclic nature of these places indicates either the "rebirth" of a person—or else the production of human carbon copies has been abundant.

The time of birth is significant in astrology. The constellation holding the sun at the moment is the sun sign of the individual. Those who inquire whether you are a Virgo, Aquarius, or Gemini are asking for this information.

The twelve signs of the zodiac or sun signs are contained in a strip of sky about 18 degrees wide where sun, moon, and planets appear to travel. At any one time of night, six of the constellations are visible, and with imagination the figures such as the lion and scales can be sketched between the stars outlining the group. The twelve zodiacal constellations are given in this rhyme:

> The Ram, the Bull, the Heavenly Twins
> And next to the Crab the Lion stands
> The Virgin and the Scales;
> The Scorpion, Archer, and Sea-Goat.
> The Man that bears the Watering-pot,
> The Fish with shining tails.

This is a description of Aries, Taurus, Gemini, Cancer, Leo,

Virgo, Libra, Scorpio, Sagittarius, Capricornus, Aquarius, and Pisces.

For a complete horoscope, the accurate time and exact place of birth is necessary. The first is not expressed in the usual way; it is converted into sidereal or star time. The procedure is the change of local time into Greenwich Mean Time, that used for the vicinity of London, England, and the final translation, via astronomical tables called the Ephemeris, into sidereal time. The last essential step is to consider the longitude of the birthplace and find the sidereal time there.

The latitude of the birth place and the sidereal time of birth gives the astrologer a certain degree of the zodiac rising over the eastern horizon called the rising sign or ascendant. During any twenty-four-hour period, there are 360 possible ascendants.

Besides the sun sign and rising sign the astrologer calculates the medium coeli, m.c., or midheaven. It is the highest point the sun will reach on the day of birth.

Various schools of astrology have arisen on the basis of the drawing of lines to indicate the divisions called *houses*. MacNeice states that an unfriendly critic of astrology, Robert Eisler in his *The Royal Art of Astrology* maintains that the ancients had eight houses, halving each quarter of the sky.[15] Generally, there are twelve segments, and the process of achieving them is complex. Shumaker reports that a modern handbook describes briefly eight methods.[16] MacNeice claims "very few astrologers understand the various mathematical theories of house division, since an expert knowledge of spherical astronomy is required."[17] The reason for the problem is that both latitude and longitude must be considered in deciphering a horoscope, unless everybody at a given time on the same longitude is assigned the same horoscope. In any event, the methods of division result in an unequal number of degrees for the twelve strips.

Position is important in astrology and planets, basically influencing character, affecting space an accepted number of degrees. For example, Jupiter projects its "sphere of virtue" 4½ degrees in every direction. Whether sun and planet be in conjunction (0⁰), opposition (180⁰), in trine (120⁰), in quartile (90⁰), in sextile (60⁰), and so on apart has much significance. Rules of interpretation, such as Saturn and Mars in conjunction is bad while Jupiter and the sun in conjunction is good, are applied. Astrologers have a plethora of rules of unknown origin, and their degree of acceptance varies; the generalization may even become widely accepted by the public. For example, Shakespeare had Othello observe that Desdemona's hand was hot and moist, an association with Venus and lechery.

Horoscopes today give the planets and zodiacal signs qualities and characteristics influencing human beings. Aries is supposed to affect the head, Taurus the neck, Gemini the arms, and Cancer the breast. Each planet has a gender as well as a day and night house, or zodiacal constellation where it "rules"; planets, sun, and moon also "rule" one of the seven ages of man, such as Venus over adolescence and Mars for late maturity.

Astrologers who seek the fundamental basis of their work recognize it to be correlations of human factors with periodicities in the skies. Marc Edmund Jones says: "The continual recurrence of phenomena in the heavens, the rhythmic reality of the ages in the firmament, are a prophecy of man in his immortal reality."[18] Astrologers do not rationalize about the rules used for casting horoscopes, save some general statement such as Jones's: "that the individual is the cosmos in miniature, while the greater universe is the total man in his real being—has been traced from the earliest Greeks. . . . on down into the modern period."[19]

Modern astrologers try to garner support from the work of Michel Gauquelin, a graduate of the Sorbonne in statistics who rejects the claim that his research is evidence for astrology. In 1950 Gauquelin was impressed by the statement of a French astrologer that Mars "aspected" the ascendants in the horoscopes of 134 politicians; Venus did the same for 190 artists; Mercury for 209 actors and writers; and Mars and Saturn for 576 professors of medicine. Gauquelin made a new group of 508 physicians and found a similar result. Next he studied other professions, and the position of specified planets at the moment of birth appeared to be unique. His investigations were published in France in 1955, but he continued obtaining new data in Western Europe verifying the thesis. Mars was found 666 times in 3,305 scientist births; 634 in 3,142 military leader charts; 327 for 1,485 athletes. He maintained "We reject from the onset occult explanations, according to which the planet, at its rising 'casts a spell' more or less immaterial or symbolic upon the newly-born, a spell which will follow at his feet the duration of his life, and will decide his destiny. Such aphorisms are of no interest, for in science one cannot propose hypotheses except that they be firmly material, limited and precise."[20]

The definition of work done by each profession must be clearly stated if Gauquelin's research is to have any meaning. A scientist can spend most of his time writing and a military leader can do mainly politicking. Since he chose eminent men in each field, administrative functions probably occupy a large percentage of their working hours. Moreover a teacher may call himself a scientist, and an athlete, say Muhammad Ali, could have most of his yearly activity in politics and religion.

John McGervey, associate professor of physics at Case-Western Reserve University, tabulated the astrological signs of 16,634 listed in *American Men of Science* and 6,475 in *Who's Who in American Politics*. He found a statistically "flat" pattern tending to contradict the statistical "bulge" found by Michel and Francoise Gauquelin suggesting that sports champions are more likely to be born with Mars in the rising or culminating sky sectors.

Astrology defenders also cite the work of psychologist Vernon Clark. He collected horoscopes for ten people—a herpetologist, a musician, a bookkeeper, a veterinarian, an art teacher, an art critic, a puppeteer, a librarian, a prostitute, and a pediatrician; half were men. The horoscopes were given to twenty astrologers as well as twenty social workers and psychiatrists. They were to match the horoscopes with the professions; the astrologers scored well while the others made selections equivalent to chance. Clark also provided his test group with ten pairs of birth data, with one of each pair having cerebral palsy. The astrologers were able to choose the afflicted of the pair with greater success.

Clark admitted that his test did not "prove" astrology; he simply claimed a failure to disprove it. Perhaps Clark's arrangement showed how much more shrewd astrologers are with people or descriptions of them.

The comment of the English journal *New Scientist* in a comparable situation may also be apropos. Their competitor *Nature* reported that more science journalists are born under Pisces than any other sign. *New Scientist* complained that only the London staff of the journal was used and continued:

> Instant research in the *New Scientist* office last week showed that the hypothesis is false: neither the editorial, nor total office staff of the *New Scientist* show the overwhelming Piscean bias indicated in the *Nature* paper. This does not mean that the *Nature* results are of no value. That they may indicate that the *Nature* staff is an aberration in the field of science journalism will possibly come as no surprise to others in that field. Of more consequence to scientists planning to submit papers to *Nature* are the effects which may result from a Pisces-oriented staff. According to authoritative astrologer Christopher McIntosh: "The Piscean has the Jupiterean intellect, but is negative in personality, reacting to situations and people rather than imposing himself on them. He has the Neptunian qualities of sensitivity and nervousness and tends to live in a world of dreams and imagination". (*The Astrologers and Their Creed* [Hutchinson, 1969]).[21]

The reaction of scientists to astrology is seldom as witty. More often, they deny its truth in flat terms. Astronomer

Fritz Zwicky said, "We astronomers know that birth at some date when the sun passes through this or that constellation of the zodiac in no way predetermines the course of life. . . ."[22] Harold Spencer Jones emphasized: "Such claims are absolute rubbish. No astronomer could possibly say anything else. But they pander to the desires of many people to peer into the future. They foster the primitive instinct to cling to the belief that our lives are directed to some extent by supernatural forces."[23] Astronomer George O. Abell's popular college textbook *Exploration of the Universe* had no mention of astrology in the first two editions. The third edition contains an entire chapter on the topic and has the comment, "It is hard to imagine that the directions of these planets in the sky at the moment of one's birth could have anything to do with one's personality or future" and "the astrological claims seem so farfetched as to be ludicrous."[24] Astronomer Bart J. Bok listed the zodiacal sign of every name in *American Men of Science* and there was not one predominant constellation. He drafted the statement, issued in September 1975, published in *The Humanist*, and signed by 186 scientists including 18 Nobel prize winners, challenging "the pretentious claims of astrological charlatans." They announced: "We are especially disturbed by the continued uncritical dissemination of astrological charts, forecasts, and horoscopes by the media and by otherwise reputable newspapers, magazines and book publishers. This can only contribute to the growth of irrationalism and obscurantism. We believe the time has come to challenge directly, and forcefully. . . ." Most scientists publicly and privately applauded. One who did not is editor of the journal for high school and junior college students, *Chemistry*. His editorial in the December 1975 issue reported: "Our scientists mistake the function of modern astrology. Some very brilliant students and scholars read the astrologers' columns. Their reading in no way detracts from their allegiance to excellence and accuracy in scholarship. For many it is a parlor game, a conversation piece, a way of showing one is not all brain or at least is aware that the brain doesn't yet know everything. And Capricorns do seem to behave like Capricorns. It's uncanny." A physician, too, like many of those of much earlier times, may also be an astrology advocate today. A reader wrote T. R. Van Dellen, M.D., conductor of the "How To Keep Well" column in the *Chicago Tribune,* March 20, 1976, that his pediatrician was consulting the stars for help in his practice. Physicians seeking to emulate can read Dr. William J. Tucker's *Astromedical Diagnosis,* sold by a purveyor of food fad and occult books, Health Reasearch, Box 70, Makelumne Hill, California, 95245. Also available is C. Norman Shealy, M.D., *Occult Medicine Can Save Your Life* (New York: Dial, 1975).

The testimonial of science writer John J. O'Neill of the old *New York Herald Tribune* is also atypical of someone in science or peripheral to it. His endorsement was: "Astrology is one of the most important fields for scientific research today, and one of the most neglected. . . . No stigma of any kind should be associated with it in the mind of any scientist or layman."[25] West and Toonder's list of arguments against astrology—they also supply answers—is more characteristic of what scientists have to say.[26]

West and Toonder deny that the heliocentric theory and the discovery of new planets has invalidated astrology; they state their confidence in action at a distance of the sun, moon, planets, and stars. Their response to the contention that precession of the equinoxes is not considered is—"collective experience testifies to the validity of the standard Tropical zodiac." A more telling adverse criticism, that lives are genetically determined with sperm and ova union at fertilization is handled through an experiment with rats. Those inbred for over one hundred generations so that genes would be identical were still quite varied. West and Toonder offer no substantial counterpoint to the presentation of varying horoscopes for identical twins as well as time twins, babies born the same minute in the same place. In the case of induced births, they confess, "like the question of twins, this one is so complex and so unpromising that most astrologers prefer to admit their incompetence in the matter." Their answer to the question of how to account for mass tragedies such as the slaughter of Jews by Hitler is to "contend that the individual's destiny is subsumed in the greater laws governing his city, state, nation or race." The final objection they raise, that the zodiac, houses, aspects, and the like are purely arbitrary and man-made, admittedly a "master objection," is turned aside on the basis of aesthetics: astrology is a beautiful theory.

West and Toonder do not raise all the possible adverse criticism. For example, horoscopes for plants and animals are not considered, and the pragmatic test for predictions is avoided. Astrologers have made many erroneous forecasts, but their percentage of misses compared to say, meteorologists, has not been tabulated.

A grand flood was supposed to occur after the lineup of planets in Pisces in 1524, but the deluge failed to materialize. Indian astrologers predicted doom in 1962 because seven planets would be in Aquarius. Perhaps the twenty-one-day prayer session by 250 priests in Delhi stayed the catastrophe. Robert Eisler in *The Royal Art of Astrology* compiled the forecasts of English astrologers during World War II and found very poor agreement with actual events. Astrologers said that Jacqueline Kennedy would not marry again and the Vietnam war would end much sooner than it did.

Some allegedly accurate predictions may be what draws a few to astrology. In 1651 English astronomer William Lilly is supposed to have warned that a great fire would sweep over London in 1666. This is what he actually wrote:

When this absis, therefore, of Mars shall appear in Virgo, who shall expect less than a strange catastrophe of human affairs in the commonwealth, monarchy, and Kingdom of England? There will then either in or about these times, or near that year, or within ten years more or less of that time, appear in this kingdom so strange a revolution of fate, so grand a catastrophe and great mutation under this monarchy and government, as never yet appeared; of which as the times now stand, I have no liberty or encouragement to deliver my opinion—only it will be ominous to London, unto her merchants at sea, to her traffique on land, to her poor, to all sorts of people inhabiting her or her liberties, by reason of sundry fires and a consuming plague.[27]

Those were the days without organized fire departments and almost any blaze could cause extensive damage.

Reasoned analysis hopefully sways opinion, particularly if the criticism comes from someone with the same outlook. Astrologers, however, have not been influenced by the statement in 1952 of their friend Carl J. Jung (whose daughter Gret Baumann-Jung became a well-known Swiss astrologer): "If astrologers had concentrated more on statistics to justify scientifically the accuracy of their forecasts, they would have found out long ago that their pronouncements rest on unstable foundations."[28] Similarly, antiastrologers have not generally sought to investigate, and the quotation of Grant Lewi, former editor of *Horoscope* and a member of the English department at Dartmouth College is apropos: "Astrology is 'believed in' by a lot of people who know practically nothing about it, and it is 'disbelieved in' by even more who know *absolutely* nothing about it."[29]

NOTES TO CHAPTER 2

1. John Anthony West and Jan Gerhard Toonder, *The Case for Astrology* (Baltimore, Md.: Penguin Books, 1973), p. 113.
2. Jack Lindsay, *Origins of Astrology* (New York: Barnes & Noble, 1971), p. 49.
3. John Godwin, *Occult America* (New York: Doubleday, 1972), p. 3.
4. C. Robert Jennings, "Swinging on the Stars," in *Beyond Reason, Playboy's Book of Psychic Phenomena* (Chicago: Playboy Press, 1973), p. 16.
5. In Roy A. Gallant, *Astrology, Sense or Nonsense* (Garden City, N.Y.: Doubleday, 1974), p. 153.
6. David Williams, "Scientific Findings Which Vindicate Astrology," in

Martin Ebon, ed., *The Psychic Scene* (New York: Signet Books, 1974), p. 68.

7. *Nature* 252 (November 1, 1974):2–3.

8. West and Toonder, *The Case for Astrology*, p. 191.

9. John R. Gribbin and Stephen H. Plagemann, *The Jupiter Effect* (New York: Walker, 1974).

10. Lyall Watson, *Supernature* (New York: Doubleday, 1973), p. 69.

11. *Chicago Tribune*, January 4, 1975.

12. West and Toonder, *The Case for Astrology*, pp. 179 ff.

13. Ibid., p. 200.

14. Vera Scott Johnson and Thomas Wommack, *The Secrets of Numbers* (New York: Berkley, 1974), pp. 4–5.

15. Louis MacNeice, *Astrology* (New York: Doubleday, 1964), p. 247.

16. Wayne Shumaker, *The Occult Sciences in the Renaissance* (Berkeley, Calif.: University of California Press, 1972), p. 2.

17. MacNeice, *Astrology*, p. 243.

18. Marc Edmund Jones, *Astrology, How and Why It Works* (Baltimore, Md.: Penguin, 1971), p. 15.

19. Ibid., p. 16.

20. In West and Toonder, *The Case for Astrology*, p. 172; and Michel Gauquelin, *The Scientific Basis of Astrology* (New York: Stein and Day, 1969).

21. *New Scientist* 64 (December 19, 1974):880. This article first appeared in *New Scientist London*, the weekly review of Science and Technology.

22. Fritz Zwicky, *Discovery, Invention Research Through the Morphological Approach* (New York: Macmillan, 1969), p. 13.

23. In West and Toonder, *The Case for Astrology*, pp. 123–24.

24. George O. Abell, *Exploration of the Universe*, 3d ed. (New York: Holt, Rinehart & Winston, 1975).

25. Jennings, "Swinging on the Stars," p. 19.

26. West and Toonder, *The Case for Astrology*, pp. 137–51.

27. In Daniel Cohen, *The Magic Art of Foreseeing the Future* (New York: Dodd Mead, 1973), p. 47.

28. Gallant, *Astrology, Sense or Nonsense*, p. 12.

29. Jennings, "Swinging on the Stars," p. 14.

3 Analogy

ALCHEMY

Galileo, when first using the telescope, saw sunspots, features of the moon, phases of Venus, and the first four moons of Jupiter. He and those who supported the heliocentric view proposed by Copernicus could use the natural satellites of Jupiter in their argument. The moons of Jupiter, they said, went about the planet in the same way as the planets revolve about the sun. It was reasoning by analogy, a weak procedure used often by scientists then and now. A presentation via analogy may be educational but is very seldom persuasive.

Johannes Kepler, Galileo's contemporary and yeoman supporter of the heliocentric doctrine, was a student of theology before he became a teacher of mathematics. Perhaps it was because of his own background or in line with the spirit of the times that Kepler used the analogy that the sun was the Father, the planets were the Son, and the relationship between them the Holy Ghost. There is no record of how many were convinced by the comparison.

Analogy is widespread in science through the employment of models. These are not literal pictures of reality but comparisons revealing insights. The liquid-drop model of the atomic nucleus and the billiard-ball model of a gas are convenient fictions.

Pseudoscience, too, is laden with analogy. Sheila

Ostrander and Lynn Schroeder in their *Handbook of Psychic Discoveries* (New York: Berkley, 1974, pp. 25–26) describe how plants, too, wither and die if the "mother" plant is destroyed.

The pseudoscience of alchemy is based upon reasoning by analogy. Both the goals and content of the discipline are laced with erroneous comparisons.

The ancients knew seven metals—copper, gold, iron, lead, mercury, silver, and tin. The seven were associated with the seven heavenly objects displaying eastward drift among the stars, the sun, the moon, and planets visible to the naked eye. The sun was gold, moon silver, Mars iron, Mercury quicksilver, Jupiter tin, Venus copper, and Saturn lead. The days of the week were similarly used: Sunday is for the sun, Monday for the moon, Tuesday (in French, *mardi*) for Mars, Wednesday (in French, *mercredi*) for Mercury, Thursday (in French, *jeudi*) for Jupiter, Friday (in French, *vendredi*) for Venus, and Saturday is for Saturn.

Alchemy was not the only discipline of early man using analogy extensively. A standard medical work in the China of Han times, *Canon of Medicine*, made comparisons of man to the state and universe. Because the heaven is round and the earth is square, the human head is round and human feet are square; because there are four seasons and twelve months in a year, man has four limbs and twelve joints.[1]

In Islam, analogy was widely adopted. Mason claims:

> The "Brethren of Purity" were opposed to the deductive, geometrical kind of reasoning which the orthodox Muslim scholars had inherited from the Greeks. They exalted mystery above reason, and they held that mysteries could be explored empirically. The conception that man is a microcosm of the whole world, which throughout history has found favour with the alchemists and religious mystics, was taken up by the "Brethren of Purity" and made the basis of their world system. They were indeed the first to work out in detail the consequences of the idea that man is a microcosm or an

epitome of the whole universe, finding analogies and correspondences between all aspects of the anatomy and physiology of man and the structure and workings of the world which were then known.[2]

The ancients who accepted the Stoic and Platonic philosophies found analogy pleasing. The Stoics believed that everything was alive, growing, and developed from seed according to plan. The idea of the growth of metals became so widespread that mines were occasionally closed so that the supply of metal could be renewed. Plato promoted the thought that form as well as characteristics could be transferred; alchemists would therefore have no difficulty in thinking that metals were living things gradually developing toward gold. This idea could be prompted by transferring the form or soul of gold to the metals.

Among the terms used were *body, soul,* and *spirit.* The first was the outward manifestation, the second was the inward individual volatile material, and spirit was a universal in all men. A seventeenth-century European alchemist wrote, "The essences of metals are hidden in their outward bodies, as the kernel is hidden in the nut. Every earthly body, whether animal, vegetable or mineral, is the habitation and terrestrial abode of that celestial spirit, or influence, which is its principle of life or growth. The secret of Alchemy is the destruction of the body, which enables the Artist to get at, and utilize for his own purposes, the living soul."[3]

During the early Renaissance, thinkers in alchemy and allied fields maintained the theme of comparison between man the microcosm and the universe the macrocosm. Paracelsus wrote: "He that knoweth the origin of thunder, wind, and storms, knoweth where colic and torsions come from," and Jan Baptist von Helmont a little later said: "Sublunary things do express themselves on analogy or proportion of things above."[4]

The words of the alchemist can best show the omnipresence of analogy. A 1974 English translation of the revelations of Morenius, ancient adept and Hermit of Jerusalem to Khalid Ibn Yazid Ibn Mu'Awijya, king of the Arabs, is very revealing. At one point Morenius said:

> For the conduct of this operation, you must have pairing, production of offspring, pregnancy, birth, and rearing. For union is followed by conception, which initiates pregnancy, whereupon birth follows. Now the performance of this composition is likened to the generation of man, whom the great Creator most high made not after the manner in which a house is constructed nor as anything else which is built by the hand of man. For a house is built by setting one object upon another, but a man is not made of objects. His substance, rather, before he is formed, improves through successive changes until the living being is made, which then continues from day to day and from month to month, so that the Creator most high at last finishes this his great handiwork at the appointed time of maturity. So also did the Creator first make the seed of the four elements, and set for them a certain time in which they should be formed, after which they might be finished as he would suffer and ordain it. And this operation is but the secret of secrets of great God most high, which he reveals to his prophets, whose souls he has gathered to himself in paradise.[5]

When alchemy was popular, openness and communication between its practitioners was nonexistent. The tradition was secrecy, and consequently the confessions of Morenius were not extracted easily.

Many of the alchemists referred with great respect to Hermes Trismegistos, allegedly a founder of the discipline who lived about 2,000 B.C. He was said to have inscribed the secrets of alchemy on an emerald that he presented to Sarah, wife of Abraham. There are authorities on Hermes who identify him as a myth or as the Egyptian god Toth and the emerald as being given to Miriam, the sister of Moses. A poem "The Emerald Tablet" is supposedly his, and it begins with a rationale for the microcosm-macrocosm comparison inherent in alchemy:

It is truth; truth without lies; certain truth
That that which is above is like that which is below.
And that which is below is like that which is above
To accomplish the miracles of one thing.[6]

The reason for the secrecy can be found in alchemical writings. One who lived in the fourth century wrote: "The [true alchemists] only express themselves in symbols, metaphors, and similes, so that they can only be understood by saints, sages, and souls endowed with understanding. For this reason they have observed in their works a certain way and a certain rule, of such a kind that the wise man may understand and, perhaps after some stumbling, attain to everything that is secretly described therein." Geber, also famous now, declared: "One must not explain this art in obscure words only; on the other hand, one must not explain it so clearly that all may understand it. I therefore teach it in such a way that nothing will remain hidden to the wise man, even though it may strike mediocre minds as quite obscure; the foolish and the ignorant, for their part, will understand none of it at all."[7]

The reason for secrecy, if true, is analogous to how they viewed materials. Gold and silver were sacred and noble compared to others. True alchemists differed in the same way from ordinary mortals and so deserved a particular and special form of communication.

The operating procedures of the alchemists were also laden with analogy. The base metals could only be transmuted into silver and gold by first being reduced to their *materia prima*. Burckhardt reports: "If the base metals are regarded as being analogous to one-sided and imperfectly 'coagulated' states of the soul, then the *materia prima*, to which they must be reduced, is none other than their underlying 'fundamental substance,' that is to say, the soul in its original state, as yet unconditioned by impressions and passions, and 'uncongealed' into any definite form."[8]

In their work with mercury and sulfur they found much to compare to human beings: "When sulphurous dryness joins one-sidedly with mercurial coldness, so that coagulation and contraction come together (without the action thereon of the expansive heat of Sulphur or the dissolving humidity of Quicksilver), a complete *rigor* of soul and body ensues. In terms of life, this is the torpor of old age, and on the ethical level, avarice."[9]

Shumaker emphasizes the point that "alchemical manipulations were based, . . . on the assumption that the behavior of matter imitated, or could be made to imitate, that of plants, animals, men, and of God Himself in His work of creation and redemption. . . . Even in the most primitive fashion, the alchemist did not analyze but analogized."[10]

An alchemist cited by Redgrave compares the philosopher's stone to "the Stone which the builders rejected, Christ Jesus," commenting: "I have briefly and simply set forth to you the perfect analogy which exists between our earthly and chemical and the true and heavenly Stone, Jesus Christ, whereby we may attain unto certain beatitude and perfection, not only in earthly but also in eternal life."[11]

Redgrove describes the work of another alchemist presented in a series of pictures depicting alchemical processes. First is the palace of the king, representing gold, surrounded by his son, mercury, and five servants, the metals silver, copper, tin, iron, and lead. The son kills his father; and the blood of his parent stains mercury's robe, indicating that an amalgam of mercury and gold is prepared. In the next sequence a grave is being dug, meaning a furnace is made ready. Both father and son fall into the grave, and the son is prevented from escaping; the intent is to show that the amalgam is placed in a sealed vessel. Ultimately, the father king is resurrected, and the son and five servants are also kings.[12]

Lynn Thorndike in his multivolume *A History of Magic and Experimental Science* (New York: Columbia University Press, 1923–58) quotes from *Secrets of Nature*, attributed to Arnold of Villanova (1235–1311), which compares the manufacture of the philosopher's stone to Christ's crucifixion and resurrection. Since the world was lost through a

woman, the recovery must be through a woman, and therefore the alchemist directs: "Take the pure mother and put
her in bed with the sons according to your intention and
there let her do strictest penance until she is well cleansed
from all sin." She will then give birth to a son who will
preach to all, "Signs have appeared in sun and moon." He
must be "taken and beaten well and scourged lest by reason
of pride he perish." Then you must "put him in bed to
enjoy himself" and afterwards "take him pure and extin-
guish in cold water." After you have repeated this process,
"hand him over to the Jews to be crucified. And while he is
crucified, sun and moon will be seen, and then the veil of
the temple will be rent and there will be a great earthquake.
So then the fire is to be increased and then he will give
up the ghost."

It would seem unlikely that the goal of changing base
metals into gold is viable today. The explosion of scientific
activity, particularly modern chemistry, would appear to
preclude the probability. In 1667 John F. Helvetius published at The Hague an account of a transmutation. In the
next generation, Isaac Newton did alchemical experiments.
During the early 1920s, Nobel prize winner in chemistry
Fritz Haber was ecstatic when observing an alleged conversion of metal into gold. "Gentlemen, we were here," he
told bystanders. Within a few days, more critical analyses
showed that the experimenter's gold-rimmed spectacles
had contributed the gold, and Haber bitterly withdrew his
seeming approval.

In theory, gold can be made from other materials; the
transmutation of chemical elements is a modern accomplishment. Yet no one is seriously interested in changing
base metals into gold because the cost of the change is
manyfold times the value of the gold obtained. Pauwels
and Bergier in their pseudoscientific tract *The Morning
of the Magicians* argue that alchemists, albeit a small number, are operating in France, England, Germany, Italy,
Morocco, Czechoslovakia, and the United States. They
even cite a professor at West Point Military Academy,

erroneously identified as a United States senator, who con-
jectures that the elixir of life had to do with heavy hydrogen, that a secret society of immortals knowing the secret
could still exist.[13]

The elixir of life has had numerous candidates since the
demise of alchemy—magic potions from vaccines to vita-
mins. Sulfa drugs, antibiotics, alcohol-laden proprietary
medicinals, fresh mineral water, and goat milk have been
touted. Oldsters may claim much for a variety of juices,
and unscrupulous promoters have pushed mysterious liq-
uids.

During the middle of the twentieth century, an outstanding American physiologist, Andrew Ivy, became a
protagonist for a cancer cure called *krebiozen,* allegedly
prepared from horse serum. The aftermath of the affair was
the dismissal of George Stoddard from the presidency of
the University of Illinois, ostensibly for "general administrative ineptness" but really for blocking Ivy's krebiozen
research. Stoddard said in 1953: "It is my considered opinion that except possibly as a common, harmless, inexpensive
ingredient, krebiozen does not exist." In 1955 Ivy sued him
for libel and sought $300,000 in damages. In 1966 Ivy
dropped the suit, and in 1968 the University of Illinois
awarded Stoddard an honorary degree. The discoverer of
the drug, Dr. Steven Durovic, is classified as a fugitive
from justice after leaving the United States following indict-
ment on income tax evasion of $900,000, based on 1960–62
sales of krebiozen. His brother Marko, an attorney, is also
accused of income tax evasion. The Durovics, Ivy, and
another physician were adjudged innocent of fraud and
violation of federal drug regulations.[14]

Alchemy, if it does exist today, is a minimal activity,
but the basic rationale, analogy, is widespread and often
brings confusion rather than edification. The metaphor and
simile of the poet is an excusable employment, but the
use of analogy in scientific argument is harmful. For example, John J. O'Neill, science editor of the old *New York
Herald Tribune,* once wrote: "The hypothesis of the astrol-

ogers that different [terrestrial] effects will be produced by different configurations of the heavenly bodies is entirely consistent with modern developments in the field of chemistry, in which the properties of substances are stated in terms of the architectural configurations of the atoms within the molecule, and with the theories of the atom physicists state that the properties of the atom are associated with the orbital architecture of the electrons."[15]

The argument starts with the assumption that the heavenly bodies have an effect on human beings, the very thesis denied by critics of astrology. Moreover, the analogy, like all of them, falls asunder upon examination. The molecule and its parts are very much closer in space and more causally connected than are the astronomical universe and objects on earth.

Analogy is a principal argument of those who urge the adoption of the scientific method or the scientific spirit in all human affairs. The contention is that the supposed successes of the laboratory can be obtained in other areas. In 1961 the U. S. Office of Education circulated a pamphlet entitled "Science As A Way of Life." In 1966 the National Education Association published a larger booklet, "Education and the Spirit of Science." Philosophers, too, have argued for more science. John Dewey said that the future of mankind depends upon the widening spread and deepening hold of the procedures of science. Max Otto's small book, *Science and the Moral Life* (New York: Mentor, 1949), was a post-World War II success. Scientists have also pushed the theme. Jacob Bronowski published an eloquent appeal in *Science and Human Values* (New York: Harper, 1959); in England, biologist C. H. Waddington paid respects to *The Scientific Attitude* (Hammondworth, England: Penguin, 1948).

Analogy is employed by popular historians who compare the Roman Empire's decline to current U.S. events. Some educators claim that analogy circumvents boredom and enhances learning. As developed by the Synectics Education System of Cambridge, Massachusetts, analogy is supposed to help the art of thinking. Konrad Lorenz's Nobel Prize address was entitled "Analogy As A Source of Knowledge." He described the usual morphological homologies and analogies as well as what he saw as cultural-behavioral ones.

Analogy may be a valid pedagogical tool, providing instruction not otherwise available. Once used, however, it must be tempered with critical analyses in order to avoid serious errors. The theory of organic evolution, for example, can be used as a prototype for other developments, but the doctrine cannot be indiscriminately applied. The concept of the solar system can be employed to introduce the structure of the atom or vice versa, but introduction is the only function. Likewise, the atmosphere of the planets may be compared to the earth's, providing differences are highlighted.

Analogy is only a keyhole in the door of knowledge. Opening the door reveals the truth. Peering through the hole yields a distorted picture.

NOTES TO CHAPTER 3

1. Stephen F. Mason, *A History of the Sciences* (New York: Collier Books, 1962), p. 78.
2. Ibid., pp. 97–98.
3. H. Stanley Redgrove, *Alchemy: Ancient and Modern,* 2d rev. ed. (1922; reprint ed., New York: Barnes & Noble, 1973), p. 32.
4. Mason, *A History of the Sciences,* pp. 233–34.
5. Lee Stavenhagen, ed., *A Testament of Alchemy* (Hanover, N.H.: University Press of New England, 1974), p. 29. Reprinted from *A Testament of Alchemy* by Morienus, Lee Stavenhagen, ed., by permission of the University Press of New England © 1974 by Trustees of Brandeis University.
6. C. A. Burland, *The Arts of the Alchemists* (New York: Macmillan, 1968), p. 2.
7. Titus Burckhardt, *Alchemy* (Baltimore, Md.: Penguin Books, 1971), pp. 28–30.
8. Ibid., p. 97.

9. Ibid., p. 127.

10. Wayne Shumaker, *The Occult Sciences in the Renaissance* (Berkeley, Calif.: University of California Press, 1972), p. 161.

11. Redgrove, *Alchemy: Ancient and Modern,* p. 13.

12. Ibid., p. 33.

13. Louis Pauwels and Jacques Bergier, *The Morning of the Magicians* (New York: Avon Books, 1968), p. 135.

14. Justin Fishbein, "Krebiozen Foe Lost Job, Not His Honor," *Chicago Tribune,* June 23, 1974.

15. C. Robert Jennings, "Swinging on the Stars," in *Beyond Reason, Playboy's Book of Psychic Phenomena* (Chicago: Playboy Press, 1973), p. 19.

4 Revolutionists

The unknown inventors of the wheel, agriculture, and fire control, among other achievements attributable to early man, were truly revolutionists. Human life-styles were considerably altered after each accomplishment. Revolutionists became more identifiable with the birth of modern science, and their characteristics were hardly in the popular vein of protesters, agitators, orators, and organizers. Nicholas Copernicus, who reintroduced the idea of a sun-centered solar system and made it more scientific, was still a student when in his late twenties and a church administrator when later working. He was a reluctant promoter of the heliocentric thesis, publishing the concept in the year of his death. Johannes Kepler was an introverted mystic who revolutionized the Copernican view by assigning ellipses to planetary orbits. Revolutionist in mechanics, optics, and mathematics, Isaac Newton was more interested in theology and viewed himself with the cryptic comment that he stood on the shoulders of giants. Later revolutionists such as Charles Darwin, Max Planck, and Albert Einstein were quiet, unassuming fellows.

Some revolutionary concepts in science can be associated with nonrevolutionary personalities, but outstanding work can also be cited for the bombastic and outspoken demanding due recognition. Paracelsus, also known as Philippus von Hohenheim, lived during the first half of the sixteenth century and performed miraculous medical work. The English poet and priest John Donne, when comparing the work of Paracelsus and Copernicus, believed that the former more deserved the title of innovator. Paracelsus would denounce physicians and claim "every little hair on my neck knows more than you and all your scribes, and my shoe-buckles are more learned. . . ."[1] The exceptional Tycho Brahe, first Western professional astronomer, chose between the geocentric and heliocentric systems by devising his own, the Tychonic, forgotten as soon as he died. Galileo in both his unrecognized youth and established old age demanded citation of his prior art when others published similar work. He and Brahe had outgoing personalities, were cognizant of their standing as leaders in science, and probably would have been pleased to have their peers point to them as great innovators.

The explosion of scientific activity in the twentieth century has multiplied the number of both types of revolutionists, the modest and humble as well as the egocentric and pushy. There has also appeared, in both categories, those who seem to be scientists, and their work is advanced as revolutionary.

DONNELLY

During the last half of the nineteenth century, Ignatius Donnelly of Minnesota was a self-educated, accomplished lawyer. One of his novels sold more than a million copies. At the age of twenty-eight he was the lieutenant governor of his state, and at the end of his career he was a candidate for vice-president of the United States. In 1882 his *Atlantis: The Antediluvian World* was published by Harper and Brothers.

Donnelly revived the gossip first circulated by Plato that an advanced civilization had existed on a now-sunken island, presumably in the Atlantic Ocean. Donnelly maintained that the kings and queens of this superior culture became the gods and goddesses of the ancient religions. The residents of Atlantis had advanced scientific knowledge, just as had been reported via Egyptian priests through intermediaries to Plato.

Atlantis proved to be very popular. The prime minister of England, William Gladstone, was so impressed that he approached his government about sending a ship to try to detect the sunken continent.[2]

Atlantis received support from the public but only sporadic analyses from the scientific community. Geologists contended that continents had not sunk and generally expected their pronouncements to terminate discussion. Instead the Atlantis cult flourished.

In 1974 some scholars at the University of California, Berkeley, responded to it and other similar mythologies presented as science in their symposium "Lost Worlds and Golden Ages." David Larkin, assistant professor of Egyptology at Berkeley, showed discrepancies in chronology and references in Donnelly's book.

The counterpart to Atlantis in the Pacific Ocean is known as Lemuria or Mu, a fiction developed principally by the occult religion of theosophy. Lemuria was first proposed by a biologist in order to account for the geographical distribution of the lemur. The continent was taken over by the founders and promulgators of theosophy who weaved fantastic tales about the island. According to theosophy founder Madame Blavatsky, the residents of Lemuria were apelike giants, and a remnant offshoot of them migrated to Atlantis to form its society. Other advocates of theosophy have developed equally imaginative stories about Mu and Atlantis. Annie Besant, for example, has Atlanteans about twenty-seven feet tall with bodies so hard that "one of our knives would not cut their flesh."[3] Rudolf Steiner cited Lemurians who lifted immense weights through will power and who could not reason but communicated via telepathy.[4] A more current occult religion using Atlantis as a base is Eckankar, claiming three million members, with 50,000 in the United States.

Another cult established in the nineteenth century was the gospel of the hollow earth. A retired infantry officer,

John Cleves Symmes, lectured throughout the United States about the openings at the North and South Poles leading to five concentric spheres, each supporting life; indeed, one contained a utopian society. A follower who embellished the doctrine was Cyrus Reed Teed, alias Koresh. He founded the settlement of Estero in Florida, and in the 1890s it had several thousand true believers. Koresh might have been more properly named Horos because, according to him, he was so called by a beautiful woman who came to inform him of his mission to enlighten the world about the hollow earth. Theo and Annie Horos were involved in the impersonation of members of the magical Order of Golden Dawn at the turn of the century in London. During the court case, Annie Horos said that she was a founder of a movement known as Koreshan Unity.

HÖRBIGER

The revolutionist Hans Hörbiger became more involved with politics than religion. The Nazis adopted his theme and demanded belief not only by good Nazis but also innocent bystanders. Hörbiger wrote science publicist Willy Ley, "either you believe in me and learn, or you must be treated as an enemy."[5]

Hörbiger was a Viennese mining engineer who published a huge book in 1913, *Glazial Kosmogonie*. Those readers persuaded to his views and others formed the WEL cult, for Welt-Eis-Lehre. In England, after Hörbiger's death, his disciple Hans Schindler Bellamy wrote *Moons, Myth and Man* in support of the theme. The believers accepted several successive moons for the earth, with each coming closer and eventually crashing into our planet. Great civilizations were supposed to have arisen during these intervals when the Earth was moonless. Ice was omnipresent in their universe, with the Milky Way being gigantic sections of ice. When told that photographic evidence showed the

Milky Way to be composed of billions of stars, Hörbiger declared that the pictures were evidently fraudulent.

FORT

Contemporary to Hörbiger, Charles Fort was an American pseudoscientist who proclaimed that the opposition peddled not fraud, but fiction. In one of his books he wrote, "I am . . . obviously offering everything in this book as fiction," but he then added the proviso that it was fiction in the same way as Newton's *Principia*, Darwin's *Origin of Species*, mathematical theorems, and every printed history of the United States.[6]

Fort was a reporter but spent the last twenty-six years of his life collecting and publishing descriptions of odd occurrences in nature such as a fall of fish and frogs from the sky. Friendly literary men organized a society in his honor and later established a magazine promoting the tradition of taunting modern science. Fort's collection was from newspapers at a time when journalism was less professional. Oddities could have been fabrications, printed to boost circulation. Early in the nineteenth century a reporter for the *New York Sun* had a series about life on the moon, based purportedly on the observations of John Herschel in a South African observatory. Before the latter's denying letters reached New York, the newspaper's circulation had tripled. Fort's verified odd occurrences had some evaluations by scientists during his time. However, he rejected all the explanations.

VELIKOVSKY

The response of scientists and scientific organizations to Donnelly, Fort, and Hörbiger was muted compared to the reaction to Immanuel Velikovsky at the middle of the twentieth century. Perhaps the reaction was stronger because science was also more established; or Velikovsky had the most scientific training of the group.

Educated as a physician in Russia, Velikovsky had emigrated to Palestine to practice. In 1939 he came to the United States to continue his work in depth psychology. He also became interested in establishing the reality of the flight of the Israelites from Egypt.

Velikovsky searched for references to a worldwide catastrophe at the time of the Exodus. He found an account in a papyrus from Egypt preserved in Holland's University of Leiden; it also contained a description of a similar event in the literature of ancient Mexico. On the basis of more extensive ancient writings, he postulated an astronomical scenario to acount for the cataclysmic event. He claimed that at about 1,500 B.C., Venus separated from Jupiter in the form of a comet, swept close to the Earth twice, collided with Mars, and finally settled in an orbit. The near misses of Venus colliding with the Earth would have made the tidal force parting the Red Sea enough for the Israelites to cross it.

Velikovsky's *Worlds in Collision* was published in 1950 with much advance publicity, generating an equal amount of anger from scientists. Dean B. McLaughlin, professor of astronomy at the University of Michigan, wrote to the president of the Macmillan Company, May 20, 1950: "In my quarter century of experience as a research astronomer and teacher of astronomy, I thought I had seen just about every form of 'crackpotology' but the publication of *Worlds in Collision* by a nationally famous and erstwhile publishing house is indeed 'something new under the sun.'"[7] McLaughlin acknowledged that he had not read the book claiming that you don't need to "eat a whole egg to know that it is rotten."

Before the book had been released, a February 1950 issue of *Science News Letter* published denunciations by five authorities: archaeologist, orientalist, anthropologist, geologist, and astronomer. The latter was Harlow Shapley, then director of the Harvard College Observatory. Velikovsky had asked Shapley for help in verifying his hypothesis, and the latter had refused, asserting: "The sensational claims of Dr. Immanuel Velikovsky . . . were pretty obviously based on incompetent data. . . . If Dr. Velikovsky is right, the rest of us are crazy."[8]

Leaders in the scientific community pressured the Macmillan company to drop *Worlds in Collision,* and it was reissued by another publisher. The effect of the maneuver was to spur sales and make Velikovsky a martyr. His defenders began to grow in numbers and included science-trained men and women.

By 1970 a journal, *Pensée,* with editorial headquarters at Oregon's Lewis and Clark College, appeared with a principal mission, presenting Velikovsky's theme fairly. Several of the predictions he had made, or "advance claims" as he preferred to call them, proved true. He had said that there are radio signals emanating from Jupiter, a hot surface on Venus, and a magnetic region around the earth.

The February 1974 American Association for the Advancement of Science meeting had a seven-hour symposium on Velikovsky's theories, and Velikovsky, seventy-nine years old, participated. The first confrontation was with Peter J. Huber, a Swiss statistician and amateur in Assyriology. He maintained that Velikovsky had used "obsolete and erroneous translations" and sometimes made "a complete muddle of texts, insights, periods and places."[9]

Another attack was mounted by Carl Sagan, Cornell University astronomer. He read a fifty-seven-page paper and at one point remarked, "Where Velikovsky is original he is very likely wrong; where he is right, the idea has been preempted by other workers."[10] Among the points Sagan stressed were the ejection of a mass the size of Venus from Jupiter would take as much energy as the sun emits in one year; no interaction with Venus or Mars could slow the earth's rotation or start it accelerating; that Mars receives more heat from the sun than it emits, opposite to the Velikovsky claim; and comets are not known to settle in circular orbits in so short a time.

Velikovsky not only defended himself but also had some help from Professor Irving Michelson of the Illinois Institute of Technology. The scientific journals reporting the event judged that Velikovsky came out second best. But the *New Scientist* appropriately wrote, "His theories suffered a serious setback. . . . but this seems unlikely to deter his supporters."[11]

VON DÄNIKEN

The pseudoscience revolutionists popular during the 1970s have a similar coterie of convinced followers. The main contention, that in prehistory astronauts from other worlds visited the earth and instructed the low-grade human beings, was first broached by Charles Fort. His hypothesis was that people on earth were property and the owners visited occasionally. Soon after World War II a spate of other writers adopted the idea; in particular, French authors were active in propagating the theme. Among the most active were Robert Charroux, Jean Sendy, and Jacques Bergier. The latter's *The Morning of the Magicians*, written with Louis Pauwels, had a sale of more than half a million copies. Early in the 1970s the concept took hold with the publication of books by Erich von Däniken, a Swiss. Whatever the causes—economic and political despair, disillusion with conventional science, television and film presentation, simplicity of expression—von Däniken's books hit the cosmic jackpot with a worldwide circulation of more than forty million copies. Von Däniken became a celebrity to be displayed on television and interviewed by the press.

Veritably all the supporters of the ancient astronaut theme make a monkey out of early man. As von Däniken writes in *Chariots of the Gods?*: "Let us not forget that we too were semisavages 8,000 years ago."[12] As a consequence, the writers are overawed by the achievements of ancient civilizations and rush to ascribe them to intelligences from outer space; they easily account for the pyramids, monuments on Easter Island, and stone edifices in South America. To support their position, they attack conventional archaeology and cite a line here or an artifact there as proof positive of early visitations. Typical of the caustic aspersions on archaeologists is Jacques Bergier's comment, "An archaeologist, even one of the present day, looking at a drawing of the LEM vehicle poised on the moon would conclude unhesitatingly that it was an insect."[13] Typical of the artifact displayed as evidence is a "bullet hole" in the skull of a prehistoric bison. Because it is neat and round and could not have been produced by a spear, Peter Kolosimo reports that only one explanation is possible —explorers from space long ago came to the earth with guns and bullets.[14] However, another book in the same realm of fantasy proclaims that the hole was caused by a type of marine shellfish.[15]

The flimsy "evidence" accumulated to support the ancient astronaut idea is more aggravated by the lies that have been used for the same purpose. Archaeologists purport that von Däniken lies. Psychiatric reports on the man when in trouble earlier in life describe him as a compulsive liar.[16] More serious charges are that the ancient astronaut writers misquote, misinterpret, and make no distinction when citing as authoritative the work of certified nuts or established scholars.

The public had available a large number of books in paperback and hard cover dealing seriously with the ancient astronaut theme. These were abetted by radio, television, and motion picture coverage. Oddly, book publishers did not see fit to issue books critical of the idea. One poorly developed paperback volume was available; another was a small collection of articles first appearing in Australia. The author of the first, a clergyman, proceeded next to write a book about his belief in UFOs. The situation in the category of unidentified flying object books is similar: a very large assortment offering the extraterrestrial hypothesis, another space-time continuum or mystery, and very few books explaining away the so-called unidentified.

Donnelly, Hörbiger, Fort, and Velikovsky have never been accused of lying, but they, along with the writers about ancient astronauts, engaged in sloppy critical thinking. When employing deductive patterns they indiscriminately apply their untested generalizations. With inductive modes of thought they make some common mistakes such as jumping to conclusions and not having a good sampling.

When early-twentieth-century American astronomer Percival Lowell thought he saw straight lines on Mars, he jumped to the conclusion that only intelligent beings could build them and thus advanced the theory that life was on the planet. But the lines were not there. Indeed, the checkerboard pattern seen from above the earth characteristic of agricultural and urban pursuits was not photographed by the Mariner 9 survey of Mars. Likewise, inappropriate evidence for the shape of the earth is given in the disappearance of a ship on the horizon, hull first and mast last. The correct inductive development for this evidence is the manner of disappearance at randomly chosen places is the same.

The pioneers of modern science, Galileo and Kepler, as well as all the early believers in the heliocentric theory, could also be accused of improper inductive thinking. They firmly believed in the conception even though a key piece of evidence, stellar parallax, was not detected until 1832. Newton explained away the failure to see the annual shift in position of near stars against the background of more distant stars as due to the huge distances involved, and he had them several hundred times less than measured today.

The writers with the ancient astronaut theme do compare themselves to the pioneers, but not on the above grounds. The pseudoscientists place themselves in the category of misunderstood geniuses whose time will come.

Flindt and Binder illustrate the faulty induction of the writers when describing the uniqueness of man; they assume, therefore, that *homo sapiens* came to the earth from outer space. They cite man's nakedness, copious tears, flexible hand and fingertips, low healing rate of skin, lack of tooth gaps, facial muscle mobility, speaking, slow swallowing, full-color vision, sexuality, long childhood, and schizophrenia prevalence as distinguishing marks without antecedents among related mammals, particularly anthropoids.[17] Last century, Alfred Russel Wallace, with similar evidence, was also unable to decipher the descent of man. However, he simply concluded that organic evolution does not apply to *homo sapiens*.

Established scientists also may jump to conclusions, and their speculations can be truly revolutionary. Thus, Soviet astrophysicist N.S. Kardashev has claimed three general types of civilizations exist. First are those advanced communities on earth; next are societies capable of using the total energy output of the parent star in their solar system; finally, there are civilizations with access to the entire energy of their galaxy.[18] Kardashev without evidence places human beings on earth in the lowest category of intelligent life in the universe, an idea as revolutionary now as the Copernican doctrine was during the Renaissance.

Revolutionists have an imagination par excellence, a necessity in all creative work. If the imaginative effort results in an idea that can be tested or explains away a vexing problem, the community of science welcomes the work. When it appears reasonable in the light of accepted knowledge but must wait for verification, the revolutionary idea becomes less certain. James Clerk-Maxwell's electromagnetic theory had to wait twenty years for Heinrich Hertz's experimental test. How long before the following equation for the number of civilizations in a galaxy is verified?

$$N = R_x f_p n_e f_e f_i f_o L$$

where—

R_x = mean rate of star formation over galactic history

f_p = fraction of stars with planetary systems

n_e = number of planets per planetary system with conditions ecologically suitable for the origin and evolution of life

f_e =fraction of suitable planets on which life originates and evolves to more complex forms

f_i =fraction of life-bearing planets with intelligence possessed of manipulative capabilities

f_o =fraction of planets with intelligence that develops a technological phase during which there is the capability for and interest in interstellar communication

L =the mean lifetime of a technological civilization.[19]

NOTES TO CHAPTER 4

1. Allen G. Debus, *The English Paracelsians* (New York: Franklin Watts, 1966), p. 14.
2. Martin Gardner, *In the Name of Science* (New York, G. P. Putnam, 1952), p. 166; see also Ignatius Donnelly, *Atlantis: The Antediluvian World* (London: Sidgwick and Jackson, 1950).
3. Gardner, *In the Name of Science*, p. 168.
4. Ibid.
5. Ibid., p. 37.
6. Ibid., p. 49.
7. George Grinnell, "Trying to Find the Truth about the Controversial Theories of Velikovsky," *Science Forum* 7 (April 1974):4.
8. George Kolodiy, "Velikovsky—Paradigm in Collision," *Bulletin of Atomic Scientists* 31 (February 1975):36–38.
9. Robert Gillette, "Velikovsky: AAAS Forum for a Mild Collision," *Science* 183 (March 15, 1974):1061.
10. Ibid.
11. Graham Chedd, "Velikovsky in Chaos," *New Scientist* 61 (March 7, 1974):624.
12. Erich von Däniken, *Chariots of the Gods?* (New York: Bantam, 1971), p. 9.
13. Jacques Bergier, *Extraterrestrial Visitations from Ancient Times to the Present* (Chicago: Regnery, 1973), p. 45.
14. Peter Kolosimo, *Not of This World* (New York: Bantam, 1973), p. 9.
15. Jack Stoneley and A. T. Lawton, *Is Anyone Out There?* (New York: Warner, 1974), p. 221.
16. *Playboy*, August 21, 1974, p. 51.
17. Max Flindt and Otto O. Binder, *Mankind—Child of the Stars* (New York: Fawcett, 1974).
18. Carl Sagan, "An Introduction to the Problem of Interstellar Communication," in *Interstellar Communication: Scientific Perspectives*, ed. Cyril Ponnamperuma and A. G. Cameron (Boston: Houghton Mifflin, 1974), pp. 19–20.
19. Ibid., p. 12.

5 Gadgets

Science and technology are characterized by the construction and use of tools, whether by early people with a flint scraper or by *homo sapiens* today with electronic computers. At the start of man's development, tools were necessary for hunting and building. When agricultural pursuits began to dominate, the invention of necessary devices became more frequent. The scientific and industrial revolutions quickened the pace of tool introduction, and by the middle of the twentieth century, mechanical and electrical aids were abundant.

As an example of the pioneer physical scientists in Western society, Galileo had such tools as the telescope and the hydrostatic balance; he used the inclined plane and the pendulum and was the godfather of the mercury barometer. A research physical scientist now may be involved with a nuclear reactor, a particle accelerator, a scanning electron microscope, a gas laser, a recording oscillograph, a spectrophotometer, an electrophoresis cell, a ph recorder, an infra-red spectroscope, a tachometer, a digital gaussmeter, and a chromatography apparatus, among others. Specialists and laymen alike are overwhelmed with the number, size, complexity, cost, and use of instruments and tools.

A science such as astronomy was in a primitive state before the advent of the telescope and other instruments. Early people did know the stars and constellations as well as movements of the sun, moon, and planets much better than does the average urban resident today. Diurnal motion, eastward drift, and retrograde activity of the planets are often a mystery to modern literate men and women but were very much appreciated by the illiterates of bygone days. Those who were in Britain about 4,000 years ago and built Stonehenge, apparently to note the summer and winter solstices and the cycle of eclipses, were astute observers. But theory in astronomy was relatively impoverished until instrumental analyses flourished. First the geocentric conception was abandoned; then the nature of stars was delineated with the help of the spectroscope; and now radio telescopes have been uncovering quasars and pulsars. The present idea of the macrocosm gets major support from using the tools of astronomy.

The success of the sciences and technology, with a cornucopia of gadgets, may have engendered a reaction to have confidence in all operations with tools. Devices of all sorts appear to add another dimension—greater propensity toward belief. Unfortunately, many pseudosciences exploit this faith in gadgets.

Perpetual motion devices, an impossibility according to the second law of thermodynamics, frequently surface and may even be supported by individuals with imposing credentials. In 1812 one entrepreneur in the United States charged admission to observe an operating perpetual motion device. A commission of eminent engineers finally came to examine the complex machine; one of the commissioners brought his nine-year-old son and the boy detected a flaw. He heard the noise of a turning crank although none was visible. Others tore away a wooden partition to expose an elderly man driving the apparatus. In 1898 another promoter was able to convince investors that he had a perpetual motion device; this one had a clockwork mechanism hidden in the base of the machine.

DOWSERS

Much more common than perpetual motion devotees are the water dowsers. With a simple tool they allegedly find underground sources of water. Testimonials about their ability are available from scientists and nonscientists alike. The American novelist Kenneth Roberts was an avid advocate, and the early-twentieth-century English physicist J. J. Thomson was impressed. He reported: "There is no doubt of the reality of the dowsing effect. In fact, in many agricultural districts the dowser is the man they call in when they want to find the right place to dig a well, and he very often succeeds."[1] Lyall Watson contends: "Every major water and pipeline company in the United States has a dowser on its payroll. The Canadian Ministry of Agriculture employs a permanent dowser. UNESCO has engaged a Dutch dowser and geologist to pursue official investigations for them. Engineers from the U.S. First and Third Marine divisions in Vietnam have been trained to use dowsing rods to locate booby traps and sunken mortar shells. The Czechoslovakian Army has a permanent corps of dowsers in a special unit."[2]

In his small book, *The Beginner's Handbook of Dowsing*, Joseph Baum cites an impressive array of testimonials. In 1931 the government of British Columbia employed a dowser; the Bristol-Myers Company, Canadian Industries, and RCA are among organizations successfully using one. His most astounding tale, however, is the report of the art connoisseur Bernard Berenson: "A number of photographs of paintings by the Old Masters were spread out on a table, face down. The dowser, with the guidance of a wand or pendulum, preceeded to make neat little piles of all the photographs, face down. The piles were then turned face up and each pile consisted of all the paintings done by the same artist. Berenson remarked that he studied art for years before he could do that, and then only if all the pictures were face up!"[3]

Baum's speculations explaining dowsing include vestige of an animal instinct still in some human beings, radiations sensitivity, an electromagnetic phenomenon, and extrasensory perception.

Physical scientists have written books attempting to explain why a forked twig held in competent hands can indicate the presence of ground water supplies. Maby and Franklin's *The Physics of the Divining Rod* (London: G. Bell, 1939) found an answer in the assumption of a cosmic radiation yielding electromagnetic waves about ten meters long.[4] *Psychical Physics* by Dr. Solcol W. Tromp, professor of geology at Fouad I University, Cairo, published in 1949, also evoked electromagnetism. According to Tromp, fields surrounding the underground materials affect similar fields in the brain of the dowser.[5] Physicist Y. Rocard at the University of Paris followed practitioners with a magnetometer and claimed they were responding to tiny changes in the earth's magnetic field strength.

The pragmatic test of accomplishment has been heralded by advocate and opponent alike. Seldom, however, has a rigorous test been made to compare the success of the dowser and the geologist. Vogt and Hyman describe such an event in 1949.[6]

During the August 1949 dry season in Maine, twenty-seven diviners—twenty-two men, four women, and an adolescent girl—went through their motions on a selected field. The plot was chosen so that cues on the surface, such as wells, were absent. Each dowser chose the best spot for sinking a well and at the same time stated the estimated depth and the amount of water to be found. The established experts were a geologist and a water engineer, and they likewise gave approximate depth and rate of water flow at sixteen previously chosen places. Test wells were dug at the dowser's spots as well as at the sixteen of the experts. The latter did better in guessing depth necessary, whereas the twig holders were altogether wrong about depth and amount of water at their chosen stations.

Milbourne Christopher in *ESP, Seers and Psychics* (New York: Thomas Y. Crowell, 1970, pp. 140–41) describes a test in 1964 supervised by James A. Coleman, professor of physics at American International College, Springfield, Massachusetts. He offered $100.00 to any dowser who could succeed seven out of ten times. There were no winners, and the professor concluded "dowsing is nothing but self-delusion."

The dowsers maintain that some human beings have the ability to hold a forked piece of wood or a rod over ground to detect the water below the surface. The talent is explained in a variety of ways, with one even encompassing water-witching from a map. Vogt and Hyman, however, opt for unconscious muscular action as the *modus operandi*. As a supporting argument, they cite Clever Hans, a horse of early twentieth-century Germany who could do arithmetical problems and other feats because human questioners gave him detectable, unconscious, muscular movement clues; the pendulum gyrating clockwise or counterclockwise because unwittingly the operator twists the string; Ouija board and other devices dependent on unnoticed human activity.[7] During the nineteenth century, French chemist Michel Chevreul demonstrated virtually the same answer. He worked with an iron ring suspended at the end of a string and swinging as a pendulum over mercury.

How does the twig-holder know, on a conscious or unconscious level, when the bending should occur? In most cases, any time will be sufficient because ground water is present almost everywhere, albeit at varying depths. If the dowser fails, rationalizations such as fatigue, poor atmospheric conditions, and wrong type of shoe leather can be easily invoked.

Since dowsers are often passionate about the value of their device and talent, innocent bystanders may be drawn into controversy about the tool and its success. In many other highly promoted gadgets, an identical flap occurs. A recent one in France had overtones to many segments of society.

Antoine Piore was born in Italy and was an electrical engineer and radar officer in the Italian navy. He settled in Bordeaux after World War II and began working on the use of electromagnetic radiation for killing bacteria. He was without university training, but as a former member of the French underground resistance movement he had access to much electrical apparatus from U.S. military stockpiles. He also had the support of the newly elected Mayor of Bordeaux, Jacques Chaban-Delmas, another resistance fighter. Piore devised a room full of equipment ending in a nozzle that emitted something electrical.

During the early 1960s several members of the University of Bordeaux medical faculty as well as the secretary of the French Academy of Science proclaimed that Piore's machine could cure cancer in rats. The secretary, Robert Courrier, was attacked by another academician who asked why prestige was being given to an apparatus "shrouded in mystery." Piore would not allow examination of his machine.

One of England's cancer research centers sent some cancerous rats for treatment to Piore. They received a group of healthy animals—but not the ones previously dispatched.

The French government sent a committee of scientists to investigate, and one reported, "Anytime we wanted to copy parts of the machine to see which of its components were producing particular effects, Piore said we were not doing it right. When we sent technicians to measure what was coming out of the machine, it turned out that on those particular days the machine was not working properly. We suggested that Piore certify that the machine was working properly and that then we would carry out experiments under our supervision, but it was always impossible to get him to agree to what we considered to be essential conditions. And always there was Chaban-Delmas in the background to protect Piore."[8]

Nonetheless, the Department of Immunology and Parasitology at the University of Bordeaux was able to show, under the scrutiny of a blue-ribbon committee, that Piore's device was effective in treating mice infected with trypanosomes. As a result there was no difficulty in assigning $700,000 for the construction, under Piore's direction, of a more powerful machine. The director of the agency awarding. the money said, "I'll be personally astonished if something comes out of this. Besides, we'll be able to salvage all but about $200,000 of the equipment if it doesn't work out."[9]

MEDICAL BOXES

In England, at about the same time that Piore was beginning to rise to eminence in France, an engineer named George de la Warr constructed a black box allegedly suitable for the diagnoses of human ailments. The device had containers for blood or hair and eight so-called control knobs—but the box was empty. Operators of the instrument turned each of the knobs to obtain a characteristic click, and the number where the dial stopped was noted; digits 07752 meant a bacterial condition while 80810 was for a parasite.

De la Warr's next concoction, a treatment box, brought litigation. Although he was acquitted, the British court in 1960 found him "an exponent and practitioner in the pseudoscience of radionics and that . . . he fraudulently represented that there were associated substances, distinctive waves, vibrations or radiations capable of affecting a device of the defendant called a Delawarr diagnostic instrument."[10]

Physicians have marketed diagnostic and treatment boxes. Among the most widely used early in this century were the invention of Albert Abrams in California. He had a "dynamizer," an "oscilloclast," and a "reflexophone." The latter allowed diagnosis at a distance.[11] Gardner also describes[12] Dr. Elisha Perkins and his son Benjamin, one of the earliest medical quacks in America, profiting handsomely from the patented metallic tractor, a gadget consisting of two three-inch rods. The senior Perkins had promoted the theory that the metals draw diseases out of the body, and many notables had approved.

Dr. Wilhelm Reich was one of the few who suffered because of his black box. In 1954 the Food and Drug Administration banned its sale. In 1956, after a trial was held in Portland, Maine, he was fined $10,000 and given a two-year jail sentence. He was sent to the Lewisburg, Pennsylvania, prison where he died.

After receiving his medical degree from the University of Vienna at the age of twenty-five, Reich became a disciple of Sigmund Freud. He was one of several who split with the master and started his own school of psychoanalysis. His theme was that sexual health was a necessity for personal .as well as societal well-being. Reich invented the concept of orgone energy, the basis of sexual energy; orgone is in the human sexual apparatus during intercourse and in the entire body at orgasm.

The Orgone Accumulator was a three-foot square with wood on the outside and metal on the inside. Wood or other organic materials were said to absorb orgone from the sun and atmosphere. Miniature boxes called *shooters* were applied to an area of pain. Orgone blankets, composed of alternate layers of steel and sheep wool, were also used.[13]

David Hammond in *The Search for Psychic Power* (New York: Bantam, 1975) describes some amazing gadgets in East Europe. One monitors fluctuations in "biological fields." Others "accelerate seed growth," "depollute small quantities of water," and "magnetize any type of material."

KIRLIAN PHOTOGRAPHY

The most popular gadget of the early 1970s was first found in 1939. S. D. and V. Kirlian in the U.S.S.R. showed that an object photographed in direct contact with the film and with an electrical discharge sent through the rear of the photographic plate has a halo around the image. The color, intensity, and geometrical configuration of this "aura" has been correlated with many characteristics. *Psychic Magazine* has called Kirlian photography "a new era in scientific reasearch," but mystic Annie Besant, an important figure in establishing theosophy, wrote in her *Man and His Bodies* (1900) a good description of the "aura." At the 1975 American Physical Society meeting in Denver, two physicists at the University of Northern Colorado showed that the radiation produced during Kirlian photography with inanimate objects could be explained with natural forces only; there was no need to refer to unknown phenomena or factors. Dr. William Tiller of Stanford University, a sympathizer with those interested in the unusual, claims that Kirlian photography is not an effective physiological state monitoring device. At the Second Western Hemisphere Conference on Kirlian Photography, Acupuncture, and the Human Aura, New York, February, 1973, Richard Miller, a physicist at the University of Washington, showed that the human "aura" may be, in part, gaseous emission from the body. In 1974, a group of electrical engineers at Duke University proposed that the phenemenon rather than due to the object being photographed could be caused by electrical breakdown of gases in the environment. The October 15, 1976 issue of *Science* contains a report indicating the variation in the images of a living subject can be accounted for by the presence or absence of moisture.

The believers in the value of Kirlian photography view it as an indicator of bioplasma rather than corona discharge. They point to seeing the pattern for a whole leaf when one-third is torn away and only two-thirds is photographed via the process.

As pointed out in a prior chapter, argument via analogy is, weak. Nonetheless, Kirlian photography may be compared for pertinent insights. When an object is immersed in a fluid, the "absent" fluid buoys up the object. Again, the canals of Mars and a moon for Venus have been "seen". And during the beginning of the twentieth century, a virtual library of material was developed in France about non-existent N-rays.

Gadgets will probably continue to excite laymen and professional alike, especially when offered as panaceas. At the end of 1973, when automobile drivers were inconvenienced by long lines at services stations, several inventors came forward with devices purported to save gasoline. As energy became a popular topic, gadgets to conserve it were featured by mass madia. One southern California man demonstrated the production of hydrogen from tap water and, amid claims of perpetual motion and counterclaims of impossibility, nonetheless secured corporate sponsors.

Among other popular gadgets of the late 1970s was a voice stress analyzer for determining whether or not a speaker was lying. Dr. David Raskin, a psychophysiologist at the University of Utah and a student of voice stress analyzers, said: "There's no way in the world I can see how they can support the accuracy of such an instrument." Likewise, magnets have their accepted uses, but in Britain several thousand rheumatism sufferers bought a Japanese-made magnetic necklace. Specialists at London's Medical Research Council warned that the devices should be treated with the same suspicion as copper bracelets.

NOTES TO CHAPTER 5

1. D. H. Rawcliffe, *Illusions and Delusions of the Supernatural and Occult* (New York: Dover, 1959), p. 338.
2. Lyall Watson, *Supernature* (New York: Doubleday, 1973), p. 112.
3. Joseph Baum, *The Beginner's Handbook of Dowsing* (New York: Crown Publishers, 1975), p. 29.
4. Rawcliffe, *Illusions and Delusions,* p. 356.
5. Martin Gardner, *In the Name of Science* (New York: G. P. Putnam, 1952), pp. 103–4.
6. Evon Z. Vogt and Ray Hyman, *Water Witching U.S.A.* (Chicago: University of Chicago Press, 1959), pp. 72–73.
7. Ibid., pp. 92–120.
8. Daniel S. Greenberg, "The French Connection," *Saturday Review,* May 1973, p. 43.
9. Ibid., p. 44.
10. Christopher Evans, *Cults of Unreason* (New York: Farrar, Straus and Giroux, 1973), p. 43.
11. Ibid., p. 183.
12. Gardner, *In the Name of Science,* p. 204.
13. Evans, *Cults of Unreason,* pp. 207 ff.; and ibid., pp. 250 ff.

6 Imponderables

SCIENTOLOGY

The administrators, salespersons, sports coaches, supervisors, and teachers able to affect men, women, and children in a desired fashion are very seldom guided by a complex theory. When asked for the secret of their success they will respond with a time-worn phrase, a popular slogan, or practical wisdom from handbooks of how to get along with people. The worker is told how important his accomplishment is for the enterprise; the purchaser of an appliance is made to feel good through subtle compliments; the football player is inspired by the elocution in the locker room; and the student is given a gold star and a smile. Practical psychology appears to work and is not based upon an advanced, sophisticated idea.

At the beginning of the twentieth century, depth psychology was developed and gave an alternative basis for dealing with people. Studying hysteria, Sigmund Freud came upon the procedure of free association. The patient spoke at random without restraints, and the analysis of the contents came to be called psychoanalysis. Freud expanded his concept to encompass the interpretation of dreams as well as everyday behavior. He invented terms such as *id, libido,* and *superego,* and redefined others such as the *Oedipus complex* to help explain his fundamental theme that repression, chiefly sexual, was responsible for human aberrations. Anatomical seats for the concepts were not identified, and thus they became imponderables, similar to those in physical science. (Freud's first venture into prominence involved a magic potion. When he was a young physician he came upon cocaine and heralded it as a kind of cure-all.[1] There was no imponderable; the miraculous was accomplished, he claimed, with a tangible substance.)

Ether was a popular science imponderable of the late nineteenth and early twentieth centuries. Even now, some physicists hold the idea in abeyance, awaiting evidence or an opportune time for readmittance as the fluid pervading space. Biology, during Freud's early career, had an imponderable in the *élan vital*, favored by the vitalists who interpreted life processes as being beyond physics and chemistry.

When modern chemistry began to develop, phlogiston was an imponderable used to explain burning; phlogiston was supposed to have been released in the process. The discoverer of oxygen, Joseph Priestley, called the gas *dephlogisticated air*; at about the same time, liberal and intellectual Thomas Jefferson believed in the phlogiston idea. When Priestley pondered about electricity he wrote: "Here the imagination may have full play, in conceiving of the manner in which an invisible agent produces an almost infinite variety of visible effects. As the agent is invisible, every philosopher is at liberty to make it whatever he pleases."[2]

Caloric was another imponderable that reigned in science during the eighteenth century. According to the concept, heat was a fluid called *caloric*: it flowed from high to low temperature regions; it was weightless and self-repellant.

Freud's formative years saw the birth of Maxwell's demon, an imponderable invented to screen molecular speeds and violate the second law of thermodynamics. Perhaps a different kind of demon was responsible for the N-rays, popular in France and finally forsaken as a mistake.

At the start of the century, N-rays caused a flurry of excitement in French circles, but scientists in other countries also had their never-to-be-verified imponderables.

During the middle of the nineteenth century, Baron Karl von Reichenbach in Germany publicized *od*, after the ancient German god Odin. According to Reichenbach, od was omnipresent in both positive and negative forms. Some people were sensitive to the force and could see, for example, a nonluminous stream from the fingertips. In Russia in the 1920s, Dr. Alexander Gurvich called attention to mitogenetic radiation, and he believed that all living cells produce an invisible radiation. In the United States, in the 1950s, Wilhelm Reich proposed that living cells are made up of bions, pulsating units of orgone energy.

Physics today has a wide array of imponderables. Those who desire a fundamental unit of all matter have the *quark*; the theorists who seek an item with a speed beyond that of light have the *tachyon;* the *monopole* is the sought-for single, isolated magnetic pole.

Since analogy only illuminates, the citation of imponderables in both physics and psychoanalysis does not give the latter the status of science. Whether psychoanalysis is a science has been extensively debated with antagonists citing lack of experimentation, open data, laboratory, quantitative investigations, and even a body of verifiable theory. Nonetheless, depth psychology in one form or another has permeated the fabric of twentieth-century society. Its terms and argot are freely used in literature, television, theater, and motion pictures. Psychoanalysis and its peripheral schools have become thoroughly vulgarized.

Freud would not accept the diverging schools during his time, and perhaps he would be aghast at what might be called a splinter group developed since his death in 1939. The originator, LaFayette Ronald Hubbard, cites no prior art and views himself as a first-order creator rather than a disciple or modifier.

Hubbard was born in Tilden, Nebraska, in 1911, took courses at George Washington University, did some exploring, and served as a lieutenant in the United States Navy during World War II. He made a reputation as a science fiction writer; his Dianetics was first announced in

Astounding Science Fiction. The editor, John W. Campbell, wrote in the April 1950 issue: "Next month's issue will, I believe, cause one full-scale explosion across the country. We are carrying a sixteen-thousand word article entitled "Dianetics . . . An Introduction to A New Science" by L. Ron Hubbard. It will, I believe, be the first publication of the material. It is, I assure you, in full and absolute sincerity, one of the most important articles ever published."[3] During the summer of 1950, Hermitage House published *Dianetics: The Modern Science of Mental Healing*. The book was dedicated to popular philosophy writer Will Durant; an appendix on "The Scientific Method" was by Campbell, who identified himself as a nuclear physicist. Hubbard, too, claimed to be a nuclear physicist in his book *All About Radiation*; the book described a concoction alleged to lower susceptibility to radiation damage called *dianazene*. The dianetics book sold a million and one-half copies.[4]

Hubbard devised a new terminology in *Dianetics*. His "reactive mind" was the customary unconscious one; "engrams" were mental blocks filed away in the "reactive bank." The process of getting "clear" of the psychic blocks was called "auditing," and the sessions could turn the individual into a "release," one free of mental aberrations and illness. The procedure of free association and the ubiquitous couch of the psychoanalyst were used.

Dianetics quickly acquired converts, including wealthy ones and some with impeccable credentials. An oil millionaire, Don Purcell, built a Dianetic Research Center at Wichita, Kansas. Those who publicly supported dianetics included actress Gloria Swanson, jazz pianist Dave Brubeck, science-fiction writer A. E. Van Vogt, physician Dr. Joseph Winter, and political scientist Frederick L. Schuman. The latter wrote to *The New York Times* that "history has become a race between Dianetics and catastrophe."[5]

Hubbard continued to expand his conception in *History of Man*, published in 1951. It sold almost as well as *Dianetics*. He postulated the existence of Thetans—omnipotent, indestructible beings who at first played games creating different kinds of universes. They became ensnared several million years ago and have been wandering in human bodies.

The medical, psychology, and psychiatry communities vigorously attacked dianetics. Hubbard and his group counterattacked by changing the name to scientology and claiming to be a religion. The Founding Church of Scientology was incorporated in Washington, D.C., during the summer of 1955. Scientologists became ministers of religion with access to hospitals, and other privileges.[6]

The Church of Scientology has no free services. Instruction can cost as much as $10,000. A so-called free membership for six months leads to the apprentice course and a sequence of instruction following is available and called the *special course, recognized scientologist, trained scientologist, certified auditor, professional auditor, advanced auditor, validated auditor,* and *senior scientologist.* Presumably the pinnacle of learning is becoming a "clear," and by 1968, about 1,000 scientologists were adjudged to be in the category.

Before 1967 the church did sanction family disruption. Some scientology students were required to sever family ties in order to continue study of the religion.

Its discipline is comparable to that of a political organization. The code of the church states that anyone deviating from the church's teachings could be justifiably "tricked, sued, or lied to, or destroyed." An observer living next door to the Founding Church of Scientology in Washington reported "I have seen two instances of screaming people being dragged back into the 'safety' of the Hubbard Guidance Center."[7] Two former scientologists confessed fear for losing their lives, because of the movement's vindictiveness, on an American Broadcasting Company television program, September 2, 1976. They cited a *policy 45,* meaning death via a .45 caliber revolver for followers who strayed.

Hubbard's chief tilt with the law in the United States

arose with the device called an "E-meter," a measurer of electrical impulses in the skin and similar to the lie-detecting polygraph. The Food and Drug Administration had taken 100 E-meters in a raid and then charged that fraudulent curative powers had been ascribed to the device. A Federal judge ruled that Scientology was a religion, and the E-meters were returned with the proviso that therapeutic capabilities not be assigned.

Hubbard was not so well treated in Australia. There the Anderson Commission reported in 1965 after hearing many witnesses. The conclusion was clear and strong:

Scientology is evil; its techniques evil; its practice a serious threat to the community, medically, morally and socially; and its adherents sadly deluded and often mentally ill. Its founder is LaFayette Ronald Hubbard, an American . . . who falsely claims academic and other distinctions and whose sanity is to be gravely doubted.

If there should be detected in this report a note of un-relieved denunciation of Scientology it is because the evidence has shown its theories to be fantastic and impossible, its principles perverted and ill-founded and its techniques de-based and harmful. . . .

Its founder, with the merest smattering of knowledge in various sciences, has built upon the scintilla of his learning a crazy and dangerous edifice. . . .

The HASI claims to be "the world's largest mental health organization." What it really is, however, is the world's largest organization of unqualified persons engaged in the practice of dangerous techniques which masquerade as mental therapy.[8]

Authorities in Great Britain similarly indicted Scientology and refused Hubbard reentry into England. Consequently he cruises in a boat that the organization calls the "Sea Org."

The Australians "gravely doubted" Hubbard's sanity. For example, he wrote President Kennedy that in 1938 the Soviet government had offered him the laboratories of Ivan Pavlov, the research physiologist credited with the discovery of the conditioned reflex. A few months later he described his two visits to Heaven. After his second visit he wrote: "The place is shabby, the vegetation is gone. The pillars are scruffy. The saints have vanished. So have the angels. A sign on one (the left as you enter) says *This is Heaven.* The right has the sign *Hell.*"[9]

Despite attacks, Scientology continues. The organization claims more than three million adherents, with 22 major churches and 100 missions. The international headquarters in Los Angeles has a "celebrity center" for such scientologists as actress Karen Black, the Incredible String Band, and former San Francisco football player John Brodie. During the fall of 1974, 1,500 faithful gathered in Los Angeles for what was called the first National Conference on Public Action and Social Reform.[10] Rabbi Hyman Solomon of Los Angeles responded to *Newsweek's* report of the convention with "I myself have benefited from Scientology's technology."[11]

Defenders of Scientology can also be found outside the faithful. A former United Press International and Reuters correspondent, Omar Garrison, published a defense of Scientology as a religion, claiming that the church has been unfairly treated by both the Food and Drug Administration and the Internal Revenue Service. The government refuses to give it "tax-exempt" status as a religion.[12]

The attitude of scientists can be gauged by their reaction to Hubbard's attempt to organize "Allied Scientists of the World." The men and women of the laboratory were invited to join, and although thousands were solicited less than a handful showed any interest.

Despite the experience in Australia and England, the attitude of legislators in the United States now appears to be more tolerant. At the Scientologist's First National Conference on Public Action and Social Reform representatives of the California legislature gave a special commendation to Narconon, the movement's drug-abuse program. It was instituted by William Benitez, an American who had been a drug addict for almost two decades.

Splinter groups have formed, although salvation and the

path to it are similar in the sects. The Church of the Final Judgment is hardly different from the Church of Scientology.

Perhaps when Hubbard dies, scientology will disappear. At least Wilhelm Reich's orgone, mentioned in the prior chapter, is an imponderable that virtually went with Reich. Other pseudoscientific imponderables did not have the benefit of a strong-personality sponsoring and had short lifetimes. At the May 1950 conference on "Radionics and Radiesthesia" in London, Dr. Aubrey Westlake talked about another version of Reichenbach's od, *odyle,* a remarkable intangible that "quickly penetrates and courses through everything."[13] Odyle never gained supporters, nor did *telluric radiation*, mentioned at the same meeting by Professor H. Lavaron of the University of Rennes.

Perhaps some occult beliefs and pseudosciences appear to attract because their premises and activities seem to be within the grasp of the average person. Nonetheless, practitioners often caution about the diligence and work required. The words of Major J. F. F. Blyth-Praeger are typical:

Radiesthesia is not magic and no amount of enthusiasm and pendulum waggling replaces common sense and as precise a knowledge of one's subject as can be acquired. While the starry-eyed amateur may locate water beneath the dining-room table (they might even be right!) or the site of Camelot just off the end of Wigan Pier without doing anyone much harm, they can be a menace on the medical side. To become a reliable pendulist takes quite as much sweat and discipline as to become a good painter, acrobat, or what you will. Even then, the pendulum is no more than a tool for answering a question: and one must know enough to choose that question correctly and to put it correctly. It would be a disservice to the public and to radiesthesia itself to suggest either that it was easy, that it freed one from intellectual responsibility, or was the complete answer to everything. But to an expert in anything the pendulum can be similar to an x-ray or microscope for giving him accurate information which his five senses alone could not provide.[14]

NOTES TO CHAPTER 6

1. Review of *Cocaine Papers by S. Freud,* ed. Robert Byck, M.D. (New York: Stonehill, 1975), *Newsweek,* March 17, 1975, p. 95.

2. Robert Darnton, *Mesmerism and the End of the Enlightenment in France* (Cambridge, Mass.: Harvard University Press, 1968), p. 16.

3. Christopher Evans, *Cults of Unreason* (New York: Farrar, Straus and Giroux, 1973), p. 32.

4. John Godwin, *Occult America* (New York: Doubleday, 1972), pp. 76–99.

5. Evans, *Cults of Unreason,* p. 59.

6. Ibid., pp. 77–78.

7. *Newsweek,* October 28, 1974, p. 10.

8. Evans, *Cults of Unreason,* p. 83.

9. Ibid., p. 28.

10. *Newsweek,* September 23, 1974, p. 84.

11. *Newsweek,* October 28, 1974, p. 10.

12. Omar Garrison, *The Hidden Story of Scientology* (New York: Citadel Press, 1974).

13. Evans, *Cults of Unreason,* pp. 191–92.

14. Major J. F. F. Blyth-Praeger, "Medical Dowsing with Rules and Discs," in *Practical Dowsing,* ed. A. H. Bell (London: G. Bell, 1965), p. 178.

...wer than any private ceremony can. That's why ritual is ...important to religions and to people. The massing together ...people dedicated to a common philosophy gives confidence ...the power of magic. Man has a basic need for emotion- ...izing through dogma, ceremony, ritual, fantasy, and enchant- ...ent. Modern psychology and intellectual awareness have ...ken man away from religion, but the process has robbed ...m of the wonder and fantasy which religion provided. ...atanism, based on modern psychology and intellectual aware- ...ss nevertheless uses dogma and ceremony to retain wonder ...d fantasy. There is nothing wrong with that if based on ...eas that are cooperative with Nature.[5]

...bout one hundred years ago, witchcraft was examined ...ewhat scientifically by Edmund Gurney, a leader in ...British Society for Psychic Research, in his *Phantasms* ...*the Living*. He wrote: "On a careful search through ...ut 260 books on the subject and a large number of ...temporary records of trial . . . there is a total absence ...respectable evidence, and an almost total absence of ...first hand evidence at all, for those phenomena of ...ic and witchcraft which cannot be accounted for as ...results of diseased imagination, hysteria, hypnotism and ...asionally perhaps, of telepathy."[6] In the April 2, 1976, ...e of *Science*, a graduate student in psychology at the ...iversity of California, Santa Barbara, presented evidence ...t witchcraft at Salem, Massachusetts, was due to ergot ...soning. A parasitic fungus, ergot grows on a large num- ...of cereal grains. Two Canadian scientists examined ...hypothesis, and in the December 24, 1976, issue of the ...e journal reported that records of the events did not ...port the idea.

...ed by popular literature and motion pictures, witch- ...t today is less of a threat to organized religion but is ...arely in opposition to science, despite a contrary asser- ...n by a British sociologist. In his 1974 presidential ad- ...ss to the sociology section of the British Association for ...Advancement of Science, Professor Max Marwick asked, ...Science A Form of Witchcraft?" His reply was affirma- ...because "both hold theories of causation, both derive

7 Contro...

Modern science and technology is alleged to have giv... human beings control over nature. Actually a dispassionate scrutiny of accomplishments in that direction should result in the addition of a qualifying phrase, a small degree of control in limited areas. Even specious observation reveals hurricanes, volcanoes, earthquakes, and weather proceeding without the influence of *homo sapiens*. Nonetheless, the controls realized, such as the domestication of plants and animals and the use of fire, have been great. Recently, men and women have had some success in the area of public health. In Italy in 1945 there were 411,600 cases of malaria; in 1951, thanks to the use of the chemicals DDT and benzene hexachloride against the *anopheles* genus of mos- quitoes, Italy had 392 cases. The occurrence of simple goiter in one district of Switzerland fell from 88 to 13 percent of the population within three years after the addition of iodine compounds to table salt. In Newfound- land, after margarine was fortified with vitamin A and all flour enriched with iron, calcium, and vitamin B, the mortality rate for infants dropped from 102 to 61 per 1,000.

Measures to protect public health have not always had the benefit of scientific knowledge. Magic and witchcraft have a longer history of use and still tempt the unwary seeking control over natural forces, particularly human beings.

Magic and witchcraft in the Western world were first

are, as competition for
mans legislated against

umed supreme power as
:alled upon by his close
s Maecenas, the cultured
nd Vergil, to cleanse his
necromaunts with whom
once a new edict was
official inquisition con-
vitch-manuals, grimocres,
discovered and publicly
burned. In the reign of Tiberias, the successor of Augustus, a decree of the Senate exiled all Traffickers in base occult arts.[1]

Charles Mackay in his classic *Extraordinary Popular Delusions and the Madness of Crowds* (Boston: L. C. Page, 1932; Wells, Vt.: Fraser Publishing Co., 1969). reported that Charlemagne several times banned witches, while Queen Elizabeth of England in a 1562 statute proclaimed witchcraft as a crime of the highest magnitude.

WITCHCRAFT

A historian of witchcraft, Margaret Murray, presented it as a distinct religion that coexisted with Christianity during the Middle Ages. The notion seems substantiated by the bull of 1488 of Innocent VIII describing the evils of witchcraft and the appointment of inquisitors in every country. However, Norman Cohen in his *Europe's Inner Demons* (New York: Basic Books, 1975) challenges the theory and describes witchcraft as a fantasy exploited by the Church in order to punish heresy. Early twentieth-century devotees of magic in England's Hermetic Order of the Golden Dawn, as well as Germany's Order of the Temple of the Orient, saw witchcraft as a debased Christianity. In any event,

witchcraft promoted some false correlations t
affected many European and American lives.

With the Reformation, charges against wit
came more accentuated. An observer of the sc(
land wrote: "Scotland played an unenviable
great witch panic that swept like an epidemic (
during the sixteenth and seventeenth centurie
find the witch trials of Scotland conducted
severity than elsewhere, and with a more {
savage fanaticism of faith."[2]

That Christianity saw witchcraft as evil cor
attested by the means used to detect the gu
pected witch was asked to recite prayers, a
were in any way faulty, a sure sign for conden
at hand.[3]

Witches were assigned supernatural prope
them a great deal more control of nature tha
or scientists. In one trial in Salem, Massachus
end of the seventeenth century, several wit
claimed an accused lifted a heavy gun by simp
a finger into the barrel. At another similar t
court was assured that a cow that had been o
of dying suddenly recovered at the moment of
arrest. Summers reports personal knowledge o
England where farmers who had offended so
were repaid with diseased crops, although
yields were rich and plentiful.[4]

Witchcraft today may be presented in the d
religion. The West Coast favorite, Anton LaVe)
trayed the devil impregnating Rosemary with (
motion picture *Rosemary's Baby*, so organizec
worship. He is the author of a best-selling S<
and calls himself the emissary of Satan on earth
less he views the function of witchcraft as cont

Each of us has power to change events by o
organized ritual magic is better for all of us
provides more of a reinforcement of faith and in

specific explanatory hypotheses from these theories, and both carefully apply recognized tests to these hypotheses."[7] The professor chose to emphasize superficial resemblances of people groping for understanding and ignore the vast chasm between confidence in human reason and faith in supernatural, experimental verification and rationalization, disinterested investigation and personal involvement, the use of talismans, charms, and rituals versus scientific procedures. An examination of current witchcraft practices reveals how it, like science, seeks control of natural forces but through vastly different means and diametrically opposed basic assumptions.

Witchcraft in Africa appears to be of a different character than the Western variety. At the annual conference of the Association of Social Anthropologists of the Commonwealth, King's College, Cambridge, April 1968, the scholars presented witchcraft in Africa as a homeostatic control system; one wherein witchcraft was a weapon and a defense mechanism.

Nonetheless, Professor Marwick's conception of science would have natural forces be susceptible to investigation by divination. He cites one tribal African witch doctor who used a speaking gourd as well as conversation with the professor to determine that a paternal uncle had "sent" owls to plague the professor. Seances and the calling up of demons, devils, vampires, and assorted monsters are ludicrous activities for a scientist.

Newspaper stories reveal the way in which control is sought through witchcraft. American teenagers have been caught nailing hamsters to the cross and in one case, a baby boy was so mutilated. In California, a teacher was murdered and her heart and lungs were used in a sacrificial ritual. A Christian evangelist has vividly described how his Puerto Rican parents practiced witchcraft: "One man asked him to put a curse on his enemy. Papa killed a black chicken, sprinkled the blood over the enemy's picture, and then drove a knife through the face. We heard that the man who had been hexed became violently ill."[8]

It would appear that witchcraft has neither rhyme nor

reason, but by whatever name—*brujeria* in Mexico, *obeah* in South America, or *voodoo* in the Caribbean—the pattern of activity may have some kind of rationale. For some of the deeds of his mother and father in Puerto Rico, Nicky Cruz explains: "Mama was able to enter into such complete empathy with an afflicted person that she bore the person's sickness or trouble in her own mind and body. When this transfer had been made, Mama opened her mind to the spirits, who told her the real cause of the affliction. Then, often without words, Papa communicated with Mama to learn the cause and remove it. But all this ordinarily happened while Mama was in a state of deep trance, and afterward she usually had no memory of what had happened."[9]

Those witches who recite the Lord's Prayer backwards show their contempt for prayer; the revelers in the nude claim that psychic power is diminished by clothing. Undoubtedly some of the first are disgruntled with orthodox religion, and some of the second are simply seeking sexual experiences.

Witchcraft, along with magic, is a system of control. In this respect Colin Wilson in his *The Occult* (New York: Random House, 1971, p. 38) quotes the first sentence of E. M. Butler's *Ritual Magic*: "The fundamental aim of all magic is to impose the human will on nature, on man and the supersensual world in order to master them."

MAGIC

Magic, like witchcraft, can be found in biblical times. One scholar, Morton Smith, professor of ancient history at Columbia University, has charged that Jesus was adept at magic. Smith cites the ability of Jesus to control followers and show healing powers, as well as the claims of Clement of Alexandria, an early Church leader, in a document discovered in 1958 in a Greek Orthodox monastery. Others view the rituals and ceremonials of all religion as a form of magic. Christianity has its flying monk in St. Joseph of Copertino of the seventeenth century. He was able to control his flights, performing before royalty and the pope.

Famous magicians "exposed" during their lifetimes include Count Alexander Cagliostro, an eighteenth-century artist. He died in prison. Before being convicted of fraud, swindling, and heresy, however, he claimed to be several thousand years old, a friend of Cleopatra and the Queen of Sheba. During the twentieth century, Aleister Crowley in England used his knowledge of magic to promote the occult. Others do *exposés*.

During the early twentieth century, magician Harry Houdini did his work as a professional entertainer. He reported that his exhibitions involved careful, diligent, physical and mental training and not any special higher powers. He delighted in exposing those who made such claims. Currently, the Amazing Randi and Milbourne Christopher, among others, are following the same pattern. The latter said in 1975: "I do the impossible, but I do it solely for entertainment. I don't like to see people taken by those who use a magician's tricks and claim psychic powers."[10]

Contemporary magical feats are similar to Houdini's escape from a locked trunk on the bottom of a body of water. In 1956 a forty-eight-year-old yogi was buried alive for several hours at the All-India Institute of Mental Health, Bangalore, India. He emerged without any visible signs of illness; instruments attached to him had shown little physiological activity during the ordeal. At about the same time writer John A. Keel paid to learn how to do the trick and according to him was buried for one-half an hour; his tutor remained underground for twice the time.[11] A Dutch-born American citizen, Jack Schwarz, has been called "one of the greatest talents in the country and probably the world in the realm of voluntary bodily controls." He can hold the burning end of cigarettes to his hand, withstand a rusty spike driven through his palm and stretch out on a bed of nails.[12] Schwarz insists that what he does is a possibility for all human beings.

His comment may be an indicator of modesty rather than realism. Many men and women have tried to be hypnotists, for example, and their efforts have not always been successful.

MESMERISM AND HYPNOTISM

Hypnotism as a means of controlling human beings has origins in the accomplishments of a Viennese physician, Franz Anton Mesmer. At first he had what was called a magnetic clinic in association with a Jesuit professor of astronomy. Then he found that magnets were not necessary for the cure of disease. Seeking a wider audience and acclaim, Mesmer moved to Paris in 1778.

Mesmer believed that a very fine fluid was in and around all objects. The universal agent accounted for gravitational attraction and veritably all energy; it flowed in healthy men, women, and children, and an obstacle to its movement was the cause of illness. His medical treatment consisted of massaging the body's magnetic poles to try to overcome the obstacles.

Mesmer's dramatic treament won converts among the afflicted and some wealthy men but was ignored and condemned by the learned. One medical doctor who tried to support him was read out of the faculty of the University of Paris. The famous chemist C. L. Berthollet charged that the treatments were based upon imagination.[13] Benjamin Franklin was on one French commission that in 1784 rejected mesmerism.

Hypnosis grew out of mesmerism when it was found that some patients were in a strange sleep and able to act out commands. Mesmeric somnambulism may have been an accidental discovery. A pair of French brothers, followers of Mesmer, found the effect with a peasant boy on their estate; the master himself had great success with another peasant named Victor Race who was able to make expert medical diagnoses when under a hypnotic spell.

During the next couple of generations after Mesmer, a significant hypnosis phenomenon was occasionally reported. French physicians Claude Richet and Pierre Janet, working with a young girl named Leonie, found clairvoyance with the hypnotic spell. During one experiment she "experienced clairvoyant perception while in a hypnotic trance . . . (she) shocked Dr. Richet by informing him that his Paris laboratory, many miles away, was on fire . . . the laboratory burned to the ground at the very time Richet and Janet were trying to calm their subject."[14]

Perhaps self-hypnosis was responsible for a similar sort of clairvoyance exhibited by the outstanding Swedish scientist-philosopher-theologian Emanuel Swedenborg in 1759. He was at a dinner party with several others when he announced his vision of a fire in Stockholm, three hundred miles away. He gave details of where the fire had started and of the houses already in ashes. Two days later, arriving messengers allegedly confirmed Swedenborg's vision.[15]

Perhaps mass hypnosis may be the explanation for a good percentage of social, political, and economic activity. Not complex theory but simply control through hypnotic trance could account not only for the success of a Hitler but also for some of the manipulations by American political figures.

The Indian rope trick wherein a horde of spectators are convinced that they see falling parts of human anatomy is explicable on the basis of mass hypnosis. Some interpret the event as a magic trick that can be duplicated, an illusion or mass hallucination. Several versions of the Indian rope trick are available. The one described by Andrija Puharich[16] involves a crowd entertained by an Indian fakir and a boy assistant. The former throws up a coil of rope and the latter climbs it. Parts of his body then fall to the ground to be collected by the fakir who next ascends the rope. Then both boy and fakir come down smiling. The witnesses agree about the details yet a motion picture shows only a fakir throwing up a rope that falls to the ground and he and his assistant are motionless.

PSYCHIC HEALING

So-called psychic healing and psychic surgery may also have a grounding in hypnosis. At least one American stage personality who has earned a living as a "mind reader" terms psychic healing to be a fraud. (The Amazing Kreskin believes that hypnotic trance does not exist. He says that anything done to a hypnotized person can be done without hypnosis, through suggestion. In 1910 Emil Coue, a French pharmacist, said that suggestion and imagination produce hypnosis. Coue promoted self-mastery through auto-suggestion. He said: "I am not a miracle man. I do not heal people. I teach them to cure themselves"[17]).

The American Medical Association, at least one federal grand jury, and lawyers from the Federal Trade Commission have called psychic surgery a cruel and mercenary hoax. In Seattle in 1974 the FTC attorneys obtained a preliminary injunction against some West Coast travel agencies banning the pomotion of tours to visit the psychic surgeons of the Philippine Islands. Testimony given in Seattle showed that the blood and supposed human tumors displayed in advertising films were from animals and that the so-called incisions without knives were magic tricks. Administrative law Judge Daniel Hanscom declared psychic surgery to be "pure and unmitigated fakery."

D. J. West in his *Psychical Research Today* (London: Gerald Duckworth, 1954) reported negatively on the alleged medical miracles at Lourdes, France. He wondered why elderly spinsters claimed benefits more than any other group. Another Englishman, Dr. Louis Rose, studied many cases of purported faith healing and remarked in his *Faith Healing* (Middlesex, England: Penguin, 1971): "What else I might have discovered, I had not come within hailing distance of a single example of the type of 'miracle cure' which I was seeking."

In London during the 1970s, a twenty-one-year-old Irishman, Finbarr Nolan, did his psychic healing at the Northumberland Grand Hotel en masse. He saw hundreds in one day and simply ran his fingers over the afflicted areas of the patient. Instead of charging for his services, each customer was given an envelope for voluntary contributions. Disinterested observers claimed that he became a millionaire.

In Chicago in 1975, faith healer Kathryn Kuhlman at the International Amphitheatre had standing-room-only crowds. Admission was free for her "miracle service." About one-quarter of the main floor audience was taken up with wheelchair followers. Many went with her across the country hoping for the service that will strike them. At every meeting people threw down their crutches, took off braces, or bent where bending was hitherto impossible, and "praise the Lords" were plentiful.

The famous American surgeon William A. Nolen investigated psychic healers and psychic surgery. In his book,[18] he exposes Kathryn Kuhlman, Norbu Chen, an ex-marine posing as a Tibetan monk, and psychic surgeon Tony Agpoa, one of the richest men in the Philippines. Nolen claimed: "With neurotic diseases, if you persuade a person he is going to get better, he often will. Many diseases heal themselves. A great many more appear in cycles." He investigated twenty-three of Miss Kuhlman's so-called cures and reported: "I listened carefully to everything they told me and followed up every lead that even remotely might have led to a confirmation of a miracle. I reached an inescapable conclusion: None of the patients had in fact been miraculously cured of anything, either by Kathryn Kuhlman or the Holy Spirit."[19]

Positive testimonials from public and other personalities are available in the Appendix of Marti Sladek's privately published *Two Weeks with the Psychic Surgeons* (Chicago, 1976), several well-known figures in the occult giving their support, as does Australian tennis star John Newcombe. Dr. Richard O'Wellen, assistant professor of medicine at Johns Hopkins University, says his daughter was "miraculously cured" by Kathryn Kuhlman of a congenitally dislocated hip. "I can't explain it and I can't understand it.

But it has to be God," he claims.[20] Yul Brynner, the entertainer, gives plaudits to Norbu Chen. So do Dr. James
Bruce, an Alabama surgeon, and Dr. E. Stanton Maxey of
Stuart, Florida. Moreover, the faith healers have been
given an intellectual rationalization by psychologist Lawrence LeShan, among others. He says "We are learning
that the psychic attitude of physicians and nurses can
affect the physical rehabilitation of a patient in their care.
And physicians themselves are discovering how to tap
their own unused psychic resources as a whole person who
is involved in the healing process."[21] Dr. Harold Weiss,
head of the department of social medicine at the Montefiore
Medical Center, New York City, took training with LeShan
and became convinced that the latter had discovered what
was missing in modern medicine: love. Sister Justa Smith,
director of the Human Dimensions Institute Laboratory,
Rosary Hill College, Buffalo, New York, showed that a
Hungarian healer affected a solution of the enzyme trypsin
in the same way as a strong magnetic field.[22] In another
experiment by Dr. Robert N. Miller, a chemical engineer,
rye grass was allegedly given extra growth through the
efforts of faith healers sixty miles away.[23]

Exposes of the Nolen type appear to have minimal influence among those not helped by traditional medical
practice. Perhaps the latter tend to ignore psychic needs
and techniques, long used by the adroit. The Prince of
Orange at the siege of Breda in 1625 cured his soldiers
dying of scurvy by giving them a simple medicine with
the proviso that it was a rare and strong material secured
at great cost and possible danger from the East.

SPIRITUALISM

Psychic healing, hypnotism, mesmerism, magic, and
witchcraft as means of human control were never as
popular as spiritualism. More scientists, too, appear to have
been involved.

One of the earliest references to spiritualism in the Western world is in the brotherhood of the Pythagoreans in ancient Greece. They are credited with achievements in mathematics, but occult activities are also theirs. They had great confidence in numerology and reincarnation. One apocryphal story would have Pythagoras intercede in behalf of a howling dog because he recognized the wail of a departed friend.

Christianity and other religions promoted the prime concepts of spiritualism and reincarnation by citing the promise of new lives in heaven. The literati also gave more credence to spiritual existences through their creation of cherubs, sprites, seraphim, and other imaginative beings.

A investigator of mesmerism reports that those interested in the phenomenon finally turned to spiritualism. Darnton also cites the conversion of staunch materialists. Pierre S. Du Pont de Nemours came to believe that "a chain of invisible spirits stretches between us and God; the spirits communicate with our sixth sense by means of an invisible fluid." Robert Owen, the utopian socialist, announced his belief in the immortality of the soul "by the conversations he has had with members of his family, who have been dead for years."[24] Swedenborg was also involved with spiritualistic occurrences. However, student of the occult Colin Wilson in his *The Occult* (New York: Random House, 1971, pp. 276ff.) points out that the evidence for Swedenborg's accomplishments in the realm are confused and conflicting.

During the nineteenth century expert scientist Michael Faraday exposed spiritualism through experimental procedures and may have convinced some, although the popularity of the idea after his time indicates he had no influence. Spiritualists during Faraday's time engaged in table-turning by pressing their fingertips to the table and supposedly concentrating on the effort. Faraday showed that tables moved because they were pushed and in sportsmanlike fashion said: "The parties with whom I have worked were very honorable. It is with me a clear point that [they] do not intend, and do not believe that they move [the table] by ordinary mechanical power."[25]

Charles Darwin's eloquent advocate, scientist, and educator Thomas Henry Huxley also had a similar experience with spiritualism. In 1874 Darwin asked him to attend and report on a séance, and after Huxley's investigation Darwin wrote, "and now to my mind an enormous amount of evidence would be requisite to make me believe in anything beyond mere trickery." Huxley never again dealt with spiritualism, explaining, "I gave it up for the same reason I abstain from chess—It's too amusing to be fair work, and too hard work to be amusing."[26]

A third outstanding English scientist who was unimpressed with spiritualism was physicist Sir J. J. Thomson. He sat at a sizable number of séances and claimed that "at all but two of those I attended nothing whatever happened, and in the two where something did there were very strong reasons for suspecting fraud."[27]

Several important European scientists were more than interested in spiritualism, and some became avid protagonists. Marie Curie and her husband observed the fad. They and physicist Jean Perrin were present at one exposé of a spiritualist with an international reputation, Eusapia Paladino. Pierre Curie, in one of the earliest letters he wrote to his wife, remarked: "I must confess that these spiritualism phenomena intrigue me a great deal. I think that there are things in these questions which touch closely on physics."[28] Biologist Alfred Russel Wallace and physicists Sir Oliver Lodge, Johann K. F. Zöllner, Sir William Barrett, and Sir William Crookes were much more convinced.

Sir William Crookes declared before the British Association for the Advancement of Science meeting in 1898: "Upon one other interest I have not touched—to me the weightiest and farthest-reaching of all. No incident in my scientific career is more widely known than the part I took many years ago in certain psychic researches. Thirty years have passed since I published an account of experiments tending to show that outside our scientific knowledge there exists a Force exercised by intelligence differing from ordinary intelligence common to mortals. I have nothing to retract. I adhere to my already published statements. Indeed, I might add much thereto."[29] Almost a century later, a senior lecturer in physics at Newman College, Birmingham, attempted to give a rationale to the spiritualism activities of Crookes. The claim was that all his scientific work concerned undiscovered forces and was beyond common sense.[30]

Early in his career in 1861, Crookes discovered the chemical element thallium, but soon he shifted the focus of his activities to realms ushering in modern physics. He was close to the three laboratory events that changed the course of physical science research: the isolation of the electron, the discovery of X rays, and the discovery of radioactivity. However, others, not Crookes, were on top of the list for honors in the work. It has been suggested that the death of a close brother instigated his research into the occult.

The belief in spiritualism of another nineteenth-century British scientist, Alfred Russel Wallace, cannot be rationalized away. He was involved with spiritualism from about 1870 until his death in 1913.

With little formal education, Wallace had arrived at the same mechanism for organic evolution Charles Darwin had found: natural selection. Their ensuing cooperation rather than conflict in presenting the theme is one of the classic stories of science.

Wallace and Darwin differed about the descent of man, with the former believing that natural selection was insufficient to explain man's origin. He then eased into an occult or spiritual agency to account for the fact. A contemporary historian of science believes that "Wallace's spiritualist beliefs were the origin of his doubts about the ability of natural selection to account for all of man."[31] Yet when he had his first spiritualist experience he was "so thorough and confirmed a materialist that [he] could not at that time find a place in [his] mind for the conception of spiritual existence, or for any other agencies in the universe than matter and force."[32]

At an early age Wallace was interested in phrenology and mesmerism; spiritualism was in this sense an additional avocation. All three had an origin and spurt of popularity during the nineteenth century.

Modern spiritualism can be traced to the Fox family of Hydesville, New York. In 1848 the two young girls in the family began an episode that brought them fame and some fortune. On October 24, 1888, the *New York World* published a letter from Margaret Fox Kane confessing a hoax and fraud. She wrote:

> We were very mischievous children and we wanted to terrify our mother, who was a very good woman and very easily frightened. At night when we went to bed, we used to tie an apple on a string and move the string up and down, causing the apple to bump on the floor, or we would drop the apple on the floor, making a strange noise every time it would rebound. . . . My sister Katie was the first one to discover that by swishing her fingers she could produce a certain noise with the knuckles and joints and that the same effect could be made with the toes. Finding we could make raps with our feet—first with one foot and then with both— we practiced until we could do this easily when the room was dark.[33]

The next year Margaret Fox Kane repudiated her confession.

Henry Slade, adept at slate writing, was another nineteenth-century practitioner who confessed. Yet he was endorsed by leading Austrian physicist J. C. F. Zöllner in his book *Transcendental Physics*. A group of scientists at the University of Pennsylvania investigated, and their observer in Europe reported adversely about Zöllner and his experts who had "endorsed" Slade. Zöllner was said to be of unsound mind, another was partly blind, a third had poor vision, while the fourth was old and did not see his associates' disabilities.

In 1882 some British men, including several scientists, formed the Society for Psychical Research with the hope of advancing the study of psychic phenomena such as spiritualism. Even in that year, a spiritualist was shown to be a fraud.[34]

Famous spiritualists profited before being exposed. Eusapia Paladino, an untutored Italian servant girl, was paid $125 per sitting when touring the United States. Professor D. S. Miller published his analysis of her art in 1910 in *Science*, and the *New York Times* editorialized on May 10, 1910: "But no one can read his trenchant analysis of her repeated and long continued conquests without feeling that the men of science have been her willing dupes and her abettors in a sort of conspiracy to mystify society."[35]

Florence Cook was investigated by Sir William Crookes who announced that she was genuine. However, Trevor Hall charges that she was Crookes's mistress and that he knew she was fraudulent.[36]

Marthe Béraud, also known as Eva C, was famous for her production of a seemingly material substance from her body, ectoplasm. Professor Charles Richet, a Nobel Prize winner and devotee of spiritualism, examined her and was enthusiastic; so was Baron Von Schrenck Notzing. Richet said that he had observed "a kind of liquid or pasty jelly" from her mouth or breast. When investigated by the Society for Psychical Research, London, 1920, the ectoplasm was apparently produced by regurgitating paper and fabric. In 1937 the *New York World Telegram*, in an exposé of voodoo in Harlem, described an ectoplasm box, manufactured in Chicago, wherein a smoky shape approximating a hooded human figure, floated upward.

Margery Crandon, also known as Mina Crandon, the wife of a distinguished Boston surgeon, was exposed by Harry Houdini. During the 1920s he joined with the *Scientific American*, offering a prize to any occult practitioner who could not be proved a fraud. He, following British nineteenth-century magician J. N. Maskelyne's lead, offered to do everything spiritualists accomplished. Once on board a ship with Theodore Roosevelt, Houdini showed Roosevelt how slate writing was done.

Houdini did accomplish enough of a duplication of spiritualist tricks that he was said to be a medium by some. He wrote:

> I once gave a séance while I was touring in England. It was a dark séance and just at the psychological moment a spirit came through the window and walked around on the wall and ceiling of the room and then out of another window. The explanation is simple. On the bill with me were two acrobats, hand to hand balancers. One took off his shoes and stockings and the other sneaked up to him. He pulled down the window and then did a hand-to-hand balance with his partner and walked around the room. He then went back to his seat, put on his shoes, and looked as innocent and meek as possible under the circumstances when the lights were turned on. I told everyone present that it was only a trick but as usual they insisted that I was a medium.[37]

Some spiritualists are not fraudulent but, rather, psychological aberrations such as multiple personalities. The Geneva shopkeeper Helene Smith could go into a trance and emerge as Marie Antoinette, a lady from Mars, or the daughter of a fourteenth-century Arab chieftain. A "guide" called Leopold more or less controlled some of her activities. The Swiss psychologist T. Flournoy made a thorough study and explained the control:

> He speaks for her in a way she would have no idea of doing, he dictates to her poems of which she would be incapable. He replied to her oral or mental questions, converses with her, and discusses various questions. Like a wise friend, a rational mentor, and as one seeing things from a higher plane, he gives her advice, counsel, orders, even sometimes directly opposite to her wishes and against which she rebels. He consoles her, exhorts her, soothes, encourages and reprimands her; he undertakes against her the defense of persons she does not like, and pleads the cause of those who are antipathetic to her. In a word, it would be impossible to

imagine a being more independent or more different from
Mlle. Smith herself, having a more personal character, an
individuality more marked, or a more certain actual existence.[38]

Flournoy carefully studied the alleged medium to decipher the origin and nature of her different personalities.
He found that when she was Marie Antoinette, she accepted cigarettes until informed that cigarettes were unknown in Marie Antoinette's time. She composed a Martian
language that proved to be related to the French Mrs.
Smith knew. The facts she related as an Arab daughter
came from a book she read, and the information was false.
The guide Leopold arose when Mrs. Smith as a child was
in danger of being mauled by a dog and a man rescued her.

In addition to the self-deception such as experienced by
Helene Smith, a realistic aura about spiritualism also arises
from the emotional reaction of witnesses. They are prone
to see outlines of their departed loved ones from almost
any kind of apparition. A competent observer sympathetic
to the occult has described the situation in his own experience:

> I was once at a spiritualistic séance where four of the five
> people present saw a [*sic*] object like a moon floating above
> the abdomen of the medium. They showed me, the fifth
> person present, exactly where it was and it was absolutely
> incomprehensible to them that I could see nothing of the
> sort. I know of three more cases where certain objects were
> seen in the clearest detail (in two of them by two persons,
> and in the third by one person) and could afterwards be
> proved to be non-existent. Two of these cases happened
> under my direct observation.[39]

Because every spiritualist cannot be as thoroughly
studied as was Helene Smith, some manifestations are
continually cited as genuine. Mrs. Piper, an American
medium during the late nineteenth century, was thus
certified by such luminaries as Sir Oliver Lodge, Professor

William James, and Professor N. S. Shaler, the geologist at Harvard University. Early in this century, Mrs. Pearl Curran of St. Louis became famous with her spirit personality, Patience Worth. The Reverend Arthur Ford was a Southerner who communicated with a drawl, but his spirit control, Fletcher, had a French-Canadian accent and could speak Japanese, Italian, French, Hindi, and classic Chinese; Ford and the real Fletcher had been boyhood friends. During the 1950s Morey Bernstein created a sensation with a Denver woman under hypnosis who took on the role of Bridey Murphy, a resident of Ireland in the early nineteenth century. Reporters from the *Chicago American* found that the facts of "Bridey Murphy's" childhood in Wisconsin could explain much of her personality under hypnosis.

The preponderance of female mediums needs explanation. One attractive theory is that mediumship is a way out of a drab, monotonous, lonely, and unhappy life. Such an idea could be tested through diligent and exhaustive interviews. Another theory about spiritualism has already had some verification. A group from the Toronto Society for Psychical Research, as well as one in England, invented characters and coaxed the imaginary individuals to produce raps and turn tables. Evidently, alleged spirits originate from within us.

Spiritualism had its greatest popularity during the nineteenth century, but a small revival has recently occurred. In California, for example, is Gavin Arthur, a grandson of the twenty-first president of the United States, who, besides claiming the existence of twelve rather than two sexual types, believes that he last lived in the thirteenth century. *Psychic News* invariably has a case, such as the medium Ethel Post-Parrish whose spirit guide is Silver Belle. Almost 100 people are said to have witnessed the materialization, and some "walked arm in arm with the spirit." Surfacing in 1975 was Gretchen Gottlieb, murdered in a German forest 100 years ago but reincarnated as Dolores Jay, the wife of a Methodist minister and amateur hypnotist in Virginia. Dr. Ian Stevenson, on the staff of the University of Virginia, claims that proof of reincarnation will soon be available; in 1975 he said that it would occur within four years. In 1974 he published the second edition of *Twenty Cases Suggestive of Reincarnation.* Seven of the cases of spontaneous reincarnation were in India, three in Ceylon, two in Brazil, seven among the Tlinit Indians of Southeast Alaska, and one was in a Druze community in Lebanon. His international census of cases numbers 600, with only a few in the United States and Canada, where cultures fostering belief in reincarnation are not dominant. He reported: "The idea that some portion of human personality survives physical death has persisted more strongly in Brazil perhaps than in any other country of the West. No less than 5% of the population of Brazil lists themselves formally as spiritualists, but there exists strong evidence that another 25% of the population are spiritualists although the census says Roman Catholic."[40] One of Dr. Stevenson's cases in the United States is a Russian-Jewish woman in Philadelphia who speaks Swedish and Norwegian when in a hypnotic trance and claims she is a peasant named Jensen Jacoby.

A well-known psychiatrist has published a case wherein he and one of his patients had been lovers involved in a religious massacre in the Pyrenees in 1244.[41] The less-formally educated also have their tales. A lady living near San Diego, California, who bet Britain's largest bookie that flying-saucer people would land on Earth in 1976, says she had been born several times on other worlds. Perhaps the best-known example is known as the Watseka Wonder, a girl who claimed she was another, deceased person; the examining physician's report is in Jeffrey Mishlove's *The Roots of Consciousness* (New York: Random House, 1975) as well as F. W. H. Myers, *The Human Personality and Its Survival of Bodily Death* (London: Longmans, Green, 1954). In 1976 the *National Observer* printed an account of speculations by Dr. Elisabeth Kubler-Ross, a psychiatrist, as well as one of Dr. Raymond Moody, a physician and author of *Life after Life*. The lady was quoted as convinced "beyond a shadow of a doubt there is life after death." The physician, on the other hand, said "what I've shown is not proof. I haven't collected a random sample or done a number of things that would make it 'scientific:'" The story also mentioned the work of Dr. Russell Noyes, a psychiatrist at the University of Iowa who published a study of 104 near deaths. He contends that the tales give insight into the dying process and say nothing conclusive about a hereafter. Nonetheless, the *Chicago Sunday Tribune* reprinted the article, May 23, 1976, on its first page using the headlines "Life After Death: Science Utters a Sheepish 'I Believe'" and "Life After Death—'No Doubt.'"

Another modern variation of spiritualism involves what are called out-of-body experiences. A Virginia businessman began having such experiences in 1958 and since then has been reported "out" hundreds of times.[42] He became a UFO believer and associates a few of his experiences with flying-saucer encounters. Others, such as Herbert B. Greenhouse, author of *The Astral Journey* (New York: Doubleday, 1975), make no such association. All cases of out-of-body experiences, however, may be due to organic brain damage. The medical term for seeing one's self outside the body is *autoscopic hallucination*, and this condition often accompanies epilepsy, brain tumors, and other pathological situations. Another interpretation is that the so-called out-of-body experiences are projections made to negate death: convinced of immortality, the subject tends to witness death as a spectator.

Another novelty is the so-called voice phenomena. In 1959 a Swedish film producer found on tape recordings sentences supposedly spoken by dead people.[43]

Unique, too, is *thoughtography*, practiced by an ex-hotel porter in Chicago. According to J. Eisenbud, professor of psychiatry at the Medical School in Denver, Ted Serios can produce recognizable images of distant objects by staring at the unexposed film in the camera.[44] In the bizarre class as well are levitations: "On December 13, 1868, at #5 Buckingham Gate, London, (Daniel Douglas) Home was reported to have opened a window in one room, apparently floated out of that window and appeared standing outside another window in another room."[45]

Most men and women touched by the bizarre occult must be satisfied with haunted houses and ghosts. A number of these are reported by D. Scott Rogo, an associate editor of *Psychic*.[46] In Chicago, Richard Crowe offers an escorted tour through a church and cemetery for the purpose of viewing at least a haunted house and, hopefully, a ghost. The University of California (Berkeley) was host to a ghost, according to a report by a visiting Japanese scholar. He encountered one in his room at the Faculty Club. Celebrated haunted houses of the past are described in detail by Charles Mackay.[47] However, seeing a ghost can be an everyday experience, a natural part of the grieving and mourning process. A group of researchers at the University of Minnesota's Department of Family. Social Science reported in 1976 that people who lose somebody important to them tend to perceive something like the ghost of the person who has died.

NOTES TO CHAPTER 7

1. Montague Summers, *Witchcraft and Black Magic* (London: Rider, 1945; reprint ed., Detroit, Mich.: Grand River Books, 1971), p. 72.
2. E. Lynn Linton, *Witch Stories* (London: Chapman and Hall, 1861; facsimile ed., New York: Barnes & Noble, 1972), pp. 4–5.
3. Paul Boyer and Stephen Nissenbaum, *Salem Possessed* (Cambridge, Mass.: Harvard University Press, 1974), p. 12.
4. Summers, *Witchcraft and Black Magic,* p. 32.
5. Burton H. Wolfe, *The Devil's Avenger* (New York: Pyramid Books, 1974), pp. 154–55.
6. In Nandor Fodor, *Encyclopaedia of Psychic Science* (New Hyde Park, N.Y.: University Books, 1966), p. 407.
7. Max Marwick, "Is Science a Form of Witchcraft?" *New Scientist* 63 (September 5, 1974):581.
8. Nicky Cruz, *Satan on the Loose* (New York: Signet, 1974), p. 17.
9. Ibid., p. 18.

10. *Chicago Sun-Times,* June 19, 1975.

11. John A. Keel, *Jadoo* (New York: Pyramid Books, 1972), pp. 192–95.

12. Charles Panati, *Supersenses* (New York: Quadrangle, 1974), p. 196.

13. Robert Darnton, *Mesmerism and the End of the Enlightenment in France* (Cambridge, Mass.: Harvard University Press, 1968), p. 52.

14. Panati, *Supersenses,* p. 41.

15. Wilson Van Dusen, *The Presence of Other Worlds* (New York: Harper and Row, 1974), p. 141.

16. Andrija Puharich, *Beyond Telepathy* (London: Darton, Longman and Todd, 1962), pp. 41–42.

17. Walter B. Gibson, *Hypnotism* (New York: Grosset and Dunlap, 1970), p. 45.

18. William A. Nolen, *Healing, A Doctor in Search of A Miracle* (New York: Random House, 1975).

19. Peter Gorner, "Faith Healing: Fake or Miracle?" *Chicago Tribune,* February 12, 1975.

20. *Newsweek,* April 29, 1974, p. 67.

21. Ibid.

22. Panati, *Supersenses,* pp. 91–95.

23. Ibid., pp. 95–99.

24. Darnton, *Mesmerism . . . France,* pp. 136, 146.

25. *Scientific American* 232 (January 1975):52–53.

26. Cyril Bibby, *Scientist Extraordinary* (New York: Pergamon Press, 1972), pp. 112–13.

27. J. J. Thomson, *Recollections and Reflections* (London: Macmillan, 1936), p. 147.

28. Robert Reid, *Marie Curie* (New York: Saturday Review/Dutton, 1974), p. 146.

29. A. T. Baird, *One Hundred Cases for Survival After Death* (New York: Bernard Ackerman, 1944), p. 207.

30. Eric Deeson, "Commonsense and Sir William Crookes," *New Scientist,* December 26, 1974, pp. 922–25.

31. Malcolm Jay Kottler, "Alfred Russel Wallace, The Origin of Man and Spiritualism," *Isis* 65 (March/June 1974):162–63.

32. Ibid., p. 164.

33. Herbert G. Jackson, Jr., *The Spirit Rappers* (New York: Doubleday, 1972), pp. 204–6. From THE SPIRIT RAPPERS, copyright © 1972 by Herbert G. Jackson, Jr. Reprinted by permission of Doubleday & Company, Inc.

34. Trevor H. Hall, *The Strange Case of Edmund Gurney* (London: Gerald Duckworth, 1964), p. 47.

35. Milbourne Christopher, *ESP, Seers and Psychics* (New York: Thomas Y. Crowell, 1970), pp. 188–204.

36. Trevor H. Hall, *The Spiritualists* (London: Gerald Duckworth, 1962; New York: Garret-Helix, 1963).

37. Harry Houdini, "A Magician Among the Spirits," in *The Case For and Against Psychical Belief*, ed. Carl Murchison (Worcester, Mass.: Clark University, 1927), pp. 315–65.

38. In D. H. Rawcliffe, *Illusions and Delusions of the Supernatural and the Occult* (New York: Dover, 1959), p. 181.

39. C. J. Jung, *Flying Saucers* (New York: Signet, 1969), p. 20.

40. Ian Stevenson, *Twenty Cases Suggestive of Reincarnation* (Charlottesville, Va.: University of Virginia Press, 1974), p. 181.

41. Colin Wilson, *The Occult* (New York: Random House, 1971), pp. 518ff.

42. Panati, *Supersenses*, p. 142.

43. Jan van Duren, "Voice Phenomena," in *Encyclopedia of the Unexplained*, ed. Richard Cavendish (New York: McGraw-Hill, 1974), pp. 267–68; also Sheila Ostrander and Lynn Schroeder, *Handbook of Psychic Discoveries* (New York: Berkley, 1974), pp. 223ff.

44. J. Eisenbud, *The World of Ted Serios* (New York: William Morrow, 1967; London: Jonathan Cape, 1968); also Max Toth, "Historical Notes Relating to Kirlian Photography," in *The Kirlian Aura*, ed. Stanley Krippner and Daniel Rubin (Garden City, N.Y.: Doubleday, 1974), p. 31; also Milbourne Christopher, *Mediums, Mystics and the Occult* (New York: Thomas Y. Crowell, 1975), pp. 111–21.

45. Owen S. Rachleff, *The Occult Conceit* (Chicago: Cowles-Regnery, 1971), p. 191.

46. D. Scott Rogo, *An Experience of Phantoms* (New York: Taplinger, 1974).

47. Charles Mackay, *Extraordinary Popular Delusions and the Madness of Crowds* (Boston: L. C. Page, 1932; Wells, Vt.: Fraser Publishing Co., 1969), pp. 593–618.

8 Show Time

At the beginning of the nineteenth century Dr. Thomas Beddoes at his Institute of Pneumatic Chemistry, Bristol, England, tested the idea that the breath of cows was beneficial to the health of human beings. He allowed the animals to remain in the bedchambers of the ill. His pupil for a short time was later the outstanding chemist Sir Humphry Davy. He, too, was a dramatic experimenter. When lecturing at the Royal Institution, his performance was in such demand that tickets were sold at inflated prices. When he was ill, periodic bulletins on his health were posted in the same manner as that of a political or entertainment personality today.

A commentator at the time science in the Western world began to prosper, the first historian of England's Royal Society was impressed with the sober deliberations of the scientists. As science developed, other avenues of activity took hold and one of the prominent ones today is dramatic presentation.

The tradition began with Galileo. His apocryphal dropping of two weights from the Leaning Tower at Pisa, though simple, was imaginative and flamboyant; likewise when he took his newly made telescope to the University of Bologna to convince others. Theatrical demonstration was used by Louis Pasteur in his anthrax experiment and by Marconi in showing the use of wireless telegraphy. Today, a small number of scientists dominate the so-called science news in the mass media, and for the most part the

116

men are colorful showmen at ease with the television and newspaper platforms.

Parapsychology joined the throng of theater some decades ago. Although gaining respectability in 1969 by becoming a division of the American Association for the Advancement of Science, it has branched into commercial as well as educational display. During February and March 1975, the California Museum of Science and Industry, Los Angeles, featured "Psi SEARCH," billed as "the first exhibition on the scientific inquiry into humans' psychic potential." The honorary chairman of the opening event, chemist Glenn Seaborg, proclaimed, "This Psi SEARCH Exhibition describes background and experiments in a manner to help the viewer learn and decide whether . . . [psi] qualifies as an area of science subject to verification by the scientific method." The psi section had fifteen experiments dealing with parapsychology; the SEARCH part contained testimonials as well as laudatory statements about the subject.

During the summer of 1968, Louise Huebner, designated as "Official Witch of Los Angeles" by the County Board of Supervisors led a group in the Hollywood Bowl in a ritual incantation to increase the sexual vitality of the city. During an August evening in 1974, New York had its first Psychic Sail on the marine and aviation ferryboat *Kennedy*. More than 500 paying customers had a variety of attractions, from an auric portraitist who drew in crayons to the so-called Chosen Chief of the Ancient Druid Order. On April 12 and 13, 1975, a Psychic Fair was held at McCormick Place, Chicago, with tickets of admission selling from $4.00 to $5.50. Viewers were treated to dozens of card readers, healers, numerologists, soothsayers, and parapsychologists. St. Paul, Minnesota, has its annual Gnosticon from July 23 to August 1, a festival organized by the publisher of occult books, Llewellyn. The Llewellyn retail outlet in St. Paul is the Gnostica Book Store. The company had sales of about $30,000 in 1961 but about a million dollars in 1976. The convention has a psychic fair and holds classes and workshops. The first World Congress of Sorcery in Bogota, Colombia, August 24–28, 1975, included a Haitian voodoo demonstration as well as a priest faith healer among a group of South American Indians.

Exhibits, shows and sales campaigns are also in local neighborhoods. In April 1975 the College of DuPage, Glen Ellyn, Illinois, had a Free Spirit Festival where more than thirty different groups concerned with parapsychology and religion reigned. In June 1975 the First Church of Sacred Metaphysics in Chicago's South Side held its twenty-second psychic festival featuring psychics and spiritualists. On June 23, 1974, an "Ancient Science Seminar" was held at the Oak Park Arms Hotel in the west Chicago suburb of Oak Park. Among the topics discussed were painless and knifeless surgery, graphology, and the great pyramid. In June 1975 the affluent Chicago suburb of Lincolnwood was host to a psychic exhibition with a ticket of admission selling for $5.00. During three days in September 1975, the Para Dimensional Conference at McCormick Place in Chicago dealt with handwriting analysis, pyramid power, psychic healing, numerology, Yoga, spiritualism, and psychic forecasting of business trends. In 1974 two entrepreneurs formed ESP Productions to book psychics into Chicagoland classes, lectures, and shopping-center fairs; by the end of 1977, they had a stable of more than 300.

Chicago is the center of the activity. The publisher of the *Midwest Psychic News* said so in 1976; and Brad Steiger, in *Psychic City: Chicago* (New York: Doubleday, 1976), lists the city as having 43 psychic and spiritual groups, 181 readers, 72 astrologers, 12 graphologists, 20 hypnotists, 16 psychic healers, 80 spiritualist churches, 21 retail outlets, and 8 psychic-related publications.

Parapsychology is not an all-inclusive term for the phenomena shown at fairs. In his article on the topic in *Encyclopedia of the Unexplained* (New York: McGraw-Hill, 1974), J. B. Rhine, the American godfather of the topic, defines parapsychology as "the science of 'psychic' abilities." He divides the subject into extrasensory perception

(ESP) covering clairvoyance, precognition, telepathy, and psychokinesis, the action of thought on moving, static, or living targets.

CLAIRVOYANCE

About one hundred years ago, Ambrose Bierce, the American literatus, defined a *clairvoyant* as a person, commonly a woman, who has the power of seeing that which is invisible to her patron—namely, that he is a blockhead. Those more favorably inclined to the phenomenon view clairvoyance as the condition when a mind can see and describe distant events, or at least those not in immediate perception. Examples are legion.

During the time of England's Queen Elizabeth, one scholar, John Dee, used a crystal ball to help his forecasting, perhaps as a guise for intelligence gathering in the queen's service. (His colleague in scrying Edward Kelley was far ahead of the times when he proposed wife-swapping with Dee.)

The scientist-mystic Emanuel Swedenborg offers a vivid case of clairvoyance. He was at a party in Amsterdam where he had a vision of the former czar of Russia, Peter III, who had been replaced by his wife, Catherine, being strangled to death in prison. Swedenborg asked the party attendants to note the date and time for checking when the news finally arrived in Amsterdam.[1]

In the United States in 1975 a fire in Shelton, Connecticut, of the Sponge Rubber Products Company factory was reputedly foretold by a self-styled clairvoyant. According to the arson investigation by the Federal Bureau of Investigation, however, his prescience was actually a plot to destroy the plant, collect millions in insurance money, and attempt to blame a radical political group.

The 1975 episode had the benefit of investigation, whereas in Swedenborg's time there was no effort to research the incident, nor was there such an effort for his description of a fire in Stockholm, described in the prior chapter. Philosopher Immanuel Kant was interested in Swedenborg's alleged ability, but the latter's reputation rather than serious study supported his contentions. Today Swedenborg's ability can also be judged in the light of his confession that he had extensive communication with inhabitants of other planets. For example, he said, "the inhabitants of the Moon are small, like children six or seven years old; at the same time, they have the strength of men like ourselves. Their voices roll like thunder, and the sound proceeds from the belly, because the Moon is in quite a different atmosphere from the other planets."

Louise E. Rhine, in her *Hidden Channels of the Mind,* reported a case with a happy ending. A young mother awoke from a dream about her baby being crushed by a falling chandelier at 4:35 A.M. As a precaution she removed the baby, and at the appointed hour the fixture hanging over the baby's crib fell. Gardner Murphy the psychologist recounted the story of the worker who had a dream about a broken scaffold. The next day he stayed on the ground and at noon the structure broke; several men were killed and many were injured. A physician with strong interests in extrasensory perception, commenting on both stories, claimed, "Scientifically, of course, such cases don't prove anything, because they can be called coincidence, unconscious self-deception or deliberate hoaxes."[2]

According to some entrepreneurs, clairvoyance can be learned. At least, directions for efficient crystal-ball gazing have been published. In his book *Crystal-Gazing and Spiritual Clairvoyance,* first issued in 1913, Dr. L. W. de Laurènce recommends attention to proper food, digestion, and sleep as well as calmness, patience, and perseverance. He cautions against using the developed powers for personal gain and gives a list of visions and their meanings. White clouds in the ball are supposed to be good and affirmative, while red, crimson, orange, and yellow lines spell danger, trouble, sickness, deception, grief, betrayal, slander, and loss.

PRECOGNITION

Precognition means knowing in advance. The next chapter treats such prediction as a technique from known patterns. In psychic phenomena, the prediction is "mysteriously" obtained and is a property of certain individuals. In cabarets and nightclubs, these people are known as psychics. Their predictions in all realms are sometimes published but very seldom checked for accuracy. Some of them earn a livelihood with their tales about the future. Occasionally a seer who takes no money and has made a startling forecast is publicized. Alan Vaughan is said to be the only person who wrote and registered that Robert Kennedy would be assassinated. His letter arrived at the Maimonides Dream Laboratory, Brooklyn, forty-eight hours before the actual event.[3]

In their *People's Almanac* (New York: Doubleday, 1975), David Wallechinsky and Irving Wallace have documented the successes and failures of predictions by some present-day psychics. There is a long list of wrong guesses but some specific correct ones are present as well.

In 1976 Alfred L. Webre and Phillip H. Liss started a consulting firm to deal in futures. Webre had taught economics at Yale University and Liss had been on the psychology faculty at Rutgers University. They told the *Village Voice*, April 2, 1976; "We believe that higher intelligent beings are signalling a peaceful political transformation of man. Our contention is that UFOs, Virgin Mary miracles, and the 1908 nuclear explosion in Tungus, Siberia, among others, have been deliberately designed by these beings as encoded messages." According to the newspaper, they are soliciting business from such companies as IBM, Dow, DuPont, and General Electric.

Dreams as precognition have long been recognized. In ancient Egypt the Pharaoh's dream of seven fat and seven lean years became the basis of government policy. In our time the public is swamped with books about prophetic dreams,[4] and some cling to Sigmund Freud's insight that the dreams are more a record of the past, particularly sexual repression. When the *Titanic* sank in 1912 on its maiden voyage, hundreds of people believed that they had forseen the tragedy in a dream. In 1932 when the infant Lindbergh son was kidnapped, two members of Harvard University's psychology clinic asked the public for their pertinent dreams to help solve the crime; about 1,300 responded, but only 7 had dreams in any way indicative of the outcome.

A scientific analysis of dreams as prophecy occurred shortly before the 1927 publication of J. W. Dunne's *An Experiment With Time*. The author thought that he had prophetic dreams, and the book recorded his long experience. In 1922 the British Society for Psychical Research experimented with Dunne's system of recording dreams immediately upon awakening. The tests were a failure, even with Dunne as the subject. After he died Dunne was revealed as a mystic visionary, rather than a hardheaded pilot and aircraft builder, who thought higher forces were revealing the future to him.

The need for special talent as a dreamer of the future or as a waking prophet has long been accepted. During the sixteenth century Michel de Nostredams, known as Nostradamus, became famous, and remained so, for his predictions, despite the fact that his literary style was "crabbed and obscure, archaic even for its period."[5] L. Sprague and Catherine de Camp studied the predictions of Nostradamus and found that only one of 996 in his book can in any way "support a belief in precognition."[6]

Interpretation has much to do with whether precognition is recognized. According to one tale, King Croesus of Lydia consulted an oracle about going to war against Persia, and the advice was

> When Croesus shall o'er Halys river go
> He will a mighty kingdom overthrow.

Croesus felt compelled to move, little realizing that the

couplet could also indicate his defeat, which did occur.

Fiction as precognition has also been contended. The two moons of Mars were described in the work of Jonathan Swift long before they were discovered. Author Gerald Heard gave specific details about the atomic processing installation at Oak Ridge, Tennessee, years ahead of its actual building. Other science fiction tales are touted as predictive. In the foreword to his *A Night to Remember* (New York: Holt, 1955), an account of the sinking of the *Titanic*, Walter Lord tells about a novel published in 1898 with an uncanny description reminiscent of the *Titanic*. Both the real and the imaginary ship were similar in size and said to be unsinkable.

Only recently has there been any attempt to analyze objectively and test scientifically the mass of anecdotes relating to precognition—as well as to the remainder of extrasensory perception. Eileen J. Garrett, a psychic who was repeatedly tested and examined, said: "If the whole, strange, mystifying psychic gift could be snatched out of the darkness of seance rooms and put into the capable, probing hands of science, everybody would feel much better about the subject and the world of science and philosophy would be enriched."[7]

Attempted scientific investigation of precognition has been done at Rhine's Foundation for Research on the Nature of Man, Durham, North Carolina, and the Psychical Research Foundation in the same city. Astronaut Edgar Mitchell's Institute of Noetic Sciences, the American Society for Psychical Research in New York City, the Division of Parapsychology at the University of Virginia, and the Maimonides Hospital in Brooklyn are also involved. The same group responsible for the scientist's statement against astrology issued in September 1975 and described in chapter 2 organized during the summer of 1976 to test the claims made by some of the practitioners of psychic and religious feats.

Precognition experiments have largely been checking ability to forecast, such as the random lighting of lamps.

In England, Professor G. N. M. Tyrell proceeded in this manner and found that his chief experimental subject guessed better than chance. At the Institute founded by the Rhines, studies in this area are conducted by Helmut Schmidt, a quantum physicist once employed by the Boeing Aircraft Company.

TELEPATHY

Despite the experiments, extrasensory perception of all kinds—including telepathy, where two minds apparently communicate without visible channels—has a host of critics to satisfy. For precognition only, Professor Robert Thouless said, "the future has not yet happened and therefore cannot produce any effects in the present."[8] A former president of the Greek Society of Psychical Research rejected precognition for the same reason.

That some people guess the future better than do others can be encompassed, minus parapsychology, in the omnipresent bell-shaped curve. Any large number of varying items, whether heights or weights of individuals or their problem-solving or future-recognizing abilities, apparently fit the curve, with a small number at either side of the large, average majority.

During the nineteenth century the foremost philosopher of science and physiology, Hermann von Helmholtz, emphasized, "Neither the testimony of all of the Fellows of the Royal Society nor even the evidence of my own senses would lead me to believe in the transmission of thought from one person to another independently of the recognized channels of sense."[9] Typical of the current critics is the 1951 statement of psychologist D. O. Hebb, then at McGill University, "Personally, I do not accept ESP for a moment, because it does not make sense. . . . ESP is not a fact, despite the behavioral evidence that has been reported. . . . My rejection . . . is—in a literal sense—prejudice."[10] When specifics of the rejection are included, the opinion follows the pattern in the remarks of Dr. George R. Price, formerly of the University of Minnesota: "My opinion concerning parapsychologists is that many of them are dependent on clerical and statistical errors and unintentional use of sensory clues and that all extra chance results not so explicable are dependent on deliberate fraud or mildly abnormal mental conditions."[11]

Since individual opinion, whatever the source, is comparable to the anecdotes generally given in support of ESP, a better indicator of the stance of scientists is in a poll. The British magazine *New Scientist* took such a sampling in 1973. Fifteen hundred of their readers responded, and one-quarter believed ESP to be "an established fact"; forty-two percent thought it was a likely possibility; twenty percent believed it was a province of academic psychology; and eighty-eight percent claimed that the investigation of ESP was a "legitimate scientific undertaking."

The critics of ESP invariably cite the frauds. In 1882 five young daughters of an English clergyman convinced investigators of their telepathic ability. Six years later they were observed using a code and a full confession followed.[12] Ilga K was a young Lithuanian peasant girl who had difficulties in reading. When, however, her teacher or mother had their eyes on the book, the girl read very well. The ESP interpretation was that the young lady had telepathic communication, but an official investigating body concluded that "Ilga's faculty was based upon auditory hyperacuity and that the mother and teacher provided her (consciously or unconsciously) with definite auditory and possibly optical aids."[13]

Vogt and Hyman compare the muscle reading of the so-called wonder horses of the early twentieth century to human mind readers. Clever Hans was a Russian trotting horse trained to solve arithmetical problems, spell and define words, and identify musical notes through perception of the unwitting signals given by spectators. Psychologist Oskar Pfungst solved the puzzle of Clever Hans in an experiment where he only knew half the answers to the questions put to the horse, whose response was likewise. J. B. Rhine and William McDougall examined a similar horse, Lady Wonder, in 1928, but Rhine concluded that the horse had telepathic powers. Human counterparts of the alleged horse mind-readers exist. Vogt and Hyman cite three who were prominent during the nineteenth century. During the 1920s a Moravian named Eugene de Rubini confused many people, including a committee of the Society of American Magicians. Finally, with the help of psychologists from the University of California, he was shown to operate as did Clever Hans.[14]

The supporters of telepathy as a reality have a large number of cases, at times from very credible witnesses. Meteorologist Horace G. Byers has written: "About three days before the birth of our first child my wife was in a highly nervous and sensitive condition. She awakened me by sitting up suddenly in bed and crying out 'Grandmother.' We at that time lived in Seattle, and my wife's grandmother, by whom she had been brought up, was in Chicago. I inquired what caused the excitement and was told that her grandmother had stood by the side of the bed, looking intently at her. Such a dream is perhaps nothing remarkable, but the fact remains that the next morning I received a telegram, saying that the grandmother had died the preceding night."[15]

Charles Panati describes many accounts of telepathy, with an unusual one being Robert Master's subject at his Foundation for Mind Research. A woman in a hypnotic state was apparently able to scan the mind of Masters.[16]

Lyall Watson's contribution is alleged telepathy in animals, studied also at Rhine's foundation by Walter J. Levy. According to Watson, the Soviets took newborn rabbits into a submarine and at the very moment they were killed, the mother rabbit, with electrodes implanted in her brain, had a sharp response. Watson also recounts the 1966 episode in the Soviet Union wherein a biophysicist and his actor friend, about 2,000 miles apart, were supposedly able to be in extrasensory communication: the actor deciphered what his friend was handling at a particular moment.[17]

Less-reputable telepathy stories abound in the realm of UFOs—unidentified flying objects. Several men and women have publicly proclaimed their telepathic contact with extraterrestrials. An unusual so-called contactee is a Mrs. Swan of South Berwick, Maine, who claims to have had messages from Affa, an inhabitant of the planet Uranus, Crill of the planet Jupiter, and others. She reported that Ponnar from Mercury wanted to leave the human race alone to stew in its own juice.[18]

UFO stories are usually not embraced by parapsychology buffs. It is probably other so-called psi material described by Sir Kelvin Spencer in the foreword he wrote for George W. Meek's *From Enigma to Science* (New York: Samuel Weiser, 1973). Sir Kelvin declared, "It is not unlikely that more than ninety pecent of paranormal literature is rubbish."

Critical analyses of results is part of the scientific tradition, and no one's work is exempt from the evaluation. In established parts of the discipline, the probing is done in scholarly journals, but in parapsychology much of the scene of activity is the theater of the street, the popular press. Jules Siegal in his article "Sixth Sense" in *Beyond Reason, Playboy's* book of psychic phenomena published in 1973, gives some of the usual criticism of Rhine and his followers. For one thing, unusual events such as a perfect hand at bridge do occur without any apparent reason. Then, fraud is forever a possibility, and cooperative hallucination may be taking place between researcher and subject.

The pragmatic response is the negative experiments. One done by the U.S. Air Force, where a random number device called Veritac was used, gave no better than chance ability to anyone. In his article in *Encyclopedia of the Unexplained,* J. B. Rhine gives other examples of failures: the French physiologist and Nobel-prize winner Charles Richet in his attempt to show clairvoyance at Cambridge University and the so-called Harvard experiments by G. H. Estabrooks. In his column in the October 1975 *Scientific American*, Martin Gardner describes the failure by scientist Russell Targ and others to demonstrate extrasensory perception with the help of machine analyses.

If the evidence is considered positive, explanations can take a variety of forms. Extrasensory perception can be viewed as a property of life, particularly in more complex organisms, and the ability follows the bell-shaped curve. That is, a small percentage of people can show the characteristic, while it must be wrenched out of others. Such a perspective does not really explain how clairvoyance, precognition, and telepathy work.

Another kind of theory would not assign ESP to any number, but rather show the trait to be an altered state of consciousness. Some drugs can bring about such a condition, while mystics achieve the state through other means. This view may be more intellectually satisfying than the first, but, like the first, does not really explain anything.

A third theory would be revolutionary and has no evidence of support. The contention would be that our conceptions of space and time are faulty. This is true theater rather than science because an idea in the latter discipline must be capable of having inferences to be tested and must be harmonious with great masses of data, whether or not the idea is revolutionary.

The theorists of parapsychology have concentrated on the last two types of ideas, providing entertainment but not understanding. In 1898 Dr. Richard Maurice Bucke published *Cosmic Consciousness*, purporting that a higher consciousness was latent in all people. Itzhak Bentov, a Czech-born U.S. citizen, promotes the contention that states of consciousness are like diffuse fields or probability waves, and "thus it becomes clear that there is a constant communication between all creation, since our fields intermingle."[19] William A. Tiller, professor of materials science at Stanford University, accepts the yogi philosophy of seven principles operating in man and claims different kinds of space-time frames for them. Moreover, "there is considered to be a level beyond those seven which shall be called Divine," that we can more or less forget about for a long time to come.[20] Stanley R. Dean, clinical professor of psychiatry at the University of Florida College of Medicine, told the 1972 meeting of the American Psychiatric Association several psychic aphorisms such as "thought fields survive death and are analogous to soul and spirit," and "The ultraconscious state transfigures the mind and reveals ultimate reality." Psychologist Lawrence Le Shan contends "time is without divisions, and past, present and future are illusory" and "space cannot prevent energy or information exchange between two individual objects, since their separateness and individuality are secondary to their unity and relatedness."[21]

In Robert E. Ornstein's collection of reports entitled *The Nature of Human Consciousness* (New York: Viking, 1974, p. 476), psychologist Charles T. Tart pleads "we need help from psychologists and biologists, as well as from physicists." In the same volume, psychologist Carl G. Jung (p. 451) has an answer in *synchronicity*, "the simultaneous occurrence of a certain (mental) state with one or more external events which appear as meaningful parallels to the momentary subjective state—and, in certain cases, vice versa."

Adrian Dobbs, a mathematician, postulated "psytrons," with properties similar to neutrinos, as being the carrier of ESP phenomena. Physicist Martin Ruderfer made a similar assumption, and astronomer Axel Firsoff suggested "mundons" as the carrier.[22] Philosophers intrigued with precognition have even published some essays on "backward causation."[23]

"Crazy" postulates are not forbidden in science. They are encouraged in the hope that one or more can lead to new insights. In the technique called *brainstorming*, used mainly in applied science and nonscience areas, ideas are generated without criticism, but the process necessarily continues on to test each idea. Then, too, physicist Niels Bohr once remarked at a meeting that the concept presented was not "crazy enough."

No one objects to "crazy" ideas. They appear in the traditional literature of science. D. F. Lawden in "Chemical Evolution and the Origin of Life" (*Nature* 202 [1964]: 412), suggested thinking protons and neutrons. Such ideas remain hidden in the literature until the consequences can be tested or comprehensiveness as a codifier can be assessed. This is where the theories about ESP are—hidden, because tests have not been made and strengths as a unifier have not been shown.

PSYCHOKINESIS

In the allied field of psychokinesis, wherein the mind affects the motion of an object, a theory has been investigated and more or less accepted. For poltergeist phenomena, at least, scientific investigation has given a reasonable answer.

The unexplained movement of matter can be approached with either a naturalistic or supernaturalistic frame of mind. If the latter, ideas similar to the "crazy" ones cited above can be given. However, the psychic researchers actually engaged in poltergeist work have stuck with the former approach. In 1955 G. W. Lambert speculated that the disturbances were caused by such agents as tides, earth tremors, underground rivers, squirrels, and termites. Today poltergeist phenomena are assigned to the unwitting energetic activity of adolescents. William G. Roll writes: "At the center of the turmoil—whether this be flights of glassware and crockery, levitations of furniture, or knocks and bangs—there is some living person. Often this is somebody at the age of puberty."[24]

In the many cases cited by Roll, the incidents occurred when a teenager was at home, but no one is ever pinned down with direct, cause-effect evidence. Psychic enthusiast Arthur Koestler described a situation in Bavaria in the same manner. When an eighteen-year-old girl was present, a telephone system broke down, neon ceiling lights went out, a light fixture swung, and hanging pictures fell to the floor. When the girl was dismissed from the job, the events ceased.[25]

A second type of psychokinesis, the conscious movement of matter by action at a distance, has been documented and demonstrated, but explanations, when available, are limited to fraud and showmanship. Lyall Watson describes some instances of such psychokinesis as though it were the unique ability of some performers. He tells about a Leningrad housewife able to make a magnetic needle spin and the Russian girl who separated the white and yolk of an egg.[26]

The most serious case of fraud in such psychokinesis was uncovered in 1973. The director of the Institute for Parapsychology in Durham, North Carolina, the laboratory of the Foundation for Research on the Nature of Man, headed by Joseph B. Rhine, admitted tampering with experimental apparatus to influence results. Walter J. Levy, Jr., was considered Rhine's "heir apparent."[27] In the March 1974 issue of *Journal of Parapsychology* Dr. Rhine wrote about the numerous cases of fraud and deceit by parapsychology experimenters. He gave no names, but in his own laboratory four of them "were caught 'red-handed' in having falsified their results, four others did not contest (i.e., tacitly admitted) the implication that something was wrong with their reports that seemed hard to explain and they did not try. In the case of the remaining four the evidence was more circumstantial, but it seemed to our staff that they were in much the same doubtful category as the other eight."

The psychokinesis marvel of our time, the Israeli psychic Uri Geller, is definitely a showman, and fraud has been charged. His prime supporter in the United States until they had a dispute about money, Andrija Puharich, trained as a physician, declared that Geller's powers come from extraterrestrial intelligence.

An account of Geller's escapades in the United States

and England reveal boasting by and some support of Geller together with a larger percentage of exposés, name-calling, and varieties of theater. The latter is most often in the Geller camp. In 1972 Geller spent six weeks at the Stanford Research Institute as a research subject. According to his supporters, he successfully predicted the throw of dice eight times in a row, guessed twelve times without error which one of ten aluminum cans contained objects seven times in a row, drew almost exact reproductions of simple pictures out of his view and taken from a locked safe, deflected a laboratory balance under a glass jar without touching it, and perturbed a device measuring magnetic fields. However, when contacted in 1974, a spokesman for the Institute said: "We still don't claim that Geller is a psychic. We still don't validate psychokinesis. In our laboratories he's never been able to break an object without touching it."[28]

Time magazine, dissatisfied with the procedures used at Stanford, criticized the work and berated Stanford Research Institute for "seriously investigating the so-called psychic powers of a questionable night club magician."[29] When Geller demonstrated before a group of *Time* editors, he was followed by professional magician James Randi who duplicated the feats. Appearing in Chicago in May 1975 to promote his book *My Story* (New York: Praeger, 1975), Geller was observed by magician David Copperfield who said: "He's terrific, and a fraud." In 1973 Geller's manager bet $100,000 to magician Milbourne Christopher's $10,000 that the magician would not be able to duplicate or explain Geller's feats. Christopher is still waiting for the chance to collect.

A summary of some of the work at Stanford was nonetheless printed in the British journal *Nature*. Their October 18, 1974, issue contained the report together with an editorial assessing significance. Of the three referees judging the Stanford paper, one advised against publication, one was guardedly in favor, and the third did not feel strongly either way. There was agreement that the experiments were weak in design and presentation. Two of the referees believed that the authors had not learned the lessons of past work in "this tricky and complicated area."

Perhaps the *Nature* report enhanced the position of Geller as a celebrity, entertainer, magician, or psychic. After his residence at the Stanford Institute, Geller and/or his managers always managed to mention the so-called scientific investigation as a "seal of approval." In 1974 he said, "Stanford has some things it is afraid to publish. Its new report has been submitted to *Nature* magazine, one of the top journals in the world. The story will be incredible when published."[30]

When Geller first appeared on English television, he was a sensation, and the *New Scientist* magazine invited him to participate in a few experiments under the supervision of a panel they had chosen. Geller accepted but delayed and finally rejected the offer.

In anticipation of the study, which never materialized, the *New Scientist* had sent Dr. Joseph Hanlon, a physicist, to the United States for three weeks to talk to the scientists at Stanford as well as others who had become involved with Geller. The magazine was not apparently bent on an exposé because their first report of the Stanford work had been highly favorable.

The October 17, 1974, issue of *New Scientist* contains in essence an uncovering of Geller the psychic as Geller the magician, cheater, and entertainer, originally a male model and stage performer in Israel. To the contention that magicians can duplicate his accomplishments, Geller replied, "Everything could be duplicated but it doesn't have to mean that I did it the way they did."[31]

Geller implies the paranormal, but for every event interpreted via the paranormal, Hanlon had an acceptable normal explanation. Geller's manager Puharich claimed teleportation for a camera case from New York to Israel, while Hanlon speculated that Geller could have simply purchased the article and altered it to fit the description. The key-bending exercises done by Geller may be the result of surreptitious preparation of the key when nobody was observing. Revealing the drawings in supposedly sealed envelopes can be done when an assistant has enough time to view them through a strong light, or rub alcohol on the envelopes to make them transparent, or even open and reseal them. Hanlon cited at least five people who claim to have seen Geller cheat.

Hanlon was struck by the "circus atmosphere" of the so-called Geller experiments at Stanford Research Institute. According to Hanlon, the videotapes of the work

> show that Geller constantly bounces up and down, touching everything in sight and running his hands through his hair. In the middle of a test, he frequently jumps up and flits about the room, stopping the test dead. Just as suddenly, he will go back to the test—or to a different one he abandoned earlier. He frequently asks for objects from outside the test room, to give him moral support: press clippings from past triumphs, pieces of metal coins, etc. And he will discuss at length what objects to choose and where to put them. He draws technicians and other observers into the experiment by asking them to help him concentrate, or to get other objects, or to pick a number.[32]

The theatrical nature of the events was enhanced by the very good press reaction. Geller has no need for a public relations person, voluntary or compensated. (The image-building of Madame Curie in America was expertly done, free of charge, by her American friend in the newspaper business.) Geller's appearance on television is invariably abetted by reports in magazines and the letter writers who react to the articles. The *New Scientist* had many letters in their November 7, November 28, and December 5, 1974, issues. On July 20, 1974, *Science News* in the United States reported on Geller's work at Birbeck College in London, and their August 3, 1974, issue contained reader response. The last one printed, from Robert Carroll of Hunter College, New York, suggested: "The exposing of such frauds should be left to those who are best equipped for it—

professional magicians who know what to look for. Scientists should stick to science." Despite such a recommendation, Reuter news service on May 5, 1975, reported that a group of French scientists say Geller is probably endowed with special powers. French scientist Albert Ducrocq is quoted as claiming that Geller is far from being a charlatan or trickster.

Perhaps somewhat of a compensation is the statement by two psychologists at the University of Otago, New Zealand, in the May 17, 1975, *New Zealand Listener*. In his book *The Magic of Uri Geller* (New York: Ballantine, 1975, p. 297), the Amazing Randi reports it to be "the most devastating summary of (Geller's) tricks that I have ever seen." Randi also quotes Professor J. W. Juritz of Cape Town, South Africa (p. 175): "No self-respecting physicist can accept the claims of Geller and continue to teach physics." Physicist Jack Sarfatti confesses in *Science News*, Dec. 6, 1975: "On the basis of further experience in the art of conjuring I wish to publicly retract my endorsement of Uri Geller's psychoenergetic authenticity."

NOTES TO CHAPTER 8

1. Wilson Van Dusen, *The Presence of Other Worlds* (New York: Harper and Row, 1974), p. 146.
2. Montague Ullman, "Can You Communicate With Others in Your Dreams?" in *The Psychic Scene*, ed. Martin Ebon (New York: New American Library, 1974), p. 17.
3. John Godwin, *Occult America* (New York: Doubleday, 1972), p. 37.
4. Cf. Alan Levy, *Interpret Your Dreams* (New York: Pyramid Books, 1962); Franklin D. Martini, *The Meaning of Your Dreams* (New York: Award Books, 1970); Elsie Sechrist, *Dreams—Your Magic Mirror* (New York: Cowles, 1968).
5. Richard Cavendish, ed., *Encyclopedia of the Unexplained* (New York: McGraw-Hill, 1974), p. 156.
6. L. Sprague de Camp and Catherine de Camp, *Spirits, Stars and Spells* (New York: Canaveral Press, 1966).
7. Owen S. Rachleff, *The Occult Conceit* (Chicago: Cowles-Regnery, 1971), p. 125.

8. Anthony Burgess, "Precognition," in *Beyond Reason* (Chicago: Playboy Press, 1973), p. 79.

9. Jules Siegel, "Sixth Sense," in *Beyond Reason* (Chicago: Playboy Press, 1973), pp. 163–64.

10. Ibid.

11. Ibid., p. 163.

12. C. E. M. Hansel, *ESP, A Scientific Evaluation* (New York: Scribner, 1966), p. 27.

13. D. H. Rawcliffe, *Illusions and Delusions of the Supernatural and the Occult* (New York: Dover, 1959), p. 41.

14. Evon Z. Vogt and Ray Hyman, *Water Witching U.S.A.* (Chicago: University of Chicago Press, 1959), pp. 92–105.

15. A. T. Baird, ed., *One Hundred Cases for Survival After Death* (New York: Bernard Ackerman, 1944), pp. 72–73.

16. Charles Panati, *Supersenses* (New York: Quadrangle, 1974), pp. 64–65.

17. Lyall Watson, *Supernature* (New York: Doubleday, 1973), pp. 255–61.

18. Robert Emenegger, *UFOs, Past Present and Future* (New York: Ballantine, 1974), pp. 55–62.

19. George W. Meek, *From Enigma to Science* (New York: Samuel Weiser, 1973), p. 90.

20. Ibid., p. 74.

21. Lawrence Le Shan, *The Medium, The Mystic and The Physicist* (New York: Viking, 1974), p. 86.

22. Alister Hardy, Robert Harvie, and Arthur Koestler, *The Challenge of Chance* (New York: Random House, 1974), p. 274.

23. Bob Brier, *Precognition and the Philosophy of Science* (New York: Humanities Press, 1974).

24. William G. Roll, *The Poltergeist* (New York: Signet, 1974), p. 144.

25. Hardy, Harvie, and Koestler, *The Challenge of Chance*, pp. 195–200.

26. Watson, *Supernature*, pp. 128–30.

27. *Scientific American* 231 (September 1974):68, 72.

28. *Chicago Tribune*, May 16, 1974.

29. Ibid.

30. Ibid.

31. *New Scientist*, October 17, 1974, p. 173 (this article first appeared in *New Scientist London*, the weekly review of Science and Technology); also Charles Panati, ed., *The Geller Papers* (Boston: Houghton Mifflin, 1976).

32. *New Scientist*, October 17, 1974, p. 180; also Milbourne Christopher, *Mediums, Mystics and The Occult* (New York: Thomas Y. Crowell, 1975), pp. 15–51.

9 Futurists

Foretelling the future through the use of established principles and trends rather than the mystery of precognition is a widespread activity among all classes of society. One need not be a scientist to engage in such forecasting. Every organization preparing a yearly budget has a plan for the future, and so does every person with goals. Moreover, prophets, false or otherwise, are very popular. At the January 1975 American Association for the Advancement of Science meeting in New York City, author Isaac Asimov, speaking on "The Science Fiction Writer as Prophet," drew an audience of 3,000 from the total registrants of 4,500.

Forecasters use causal relationships, well-accepted sequences, high positive correlations, and unquestioned tendencies to do their work. They do not generally cloak their operation with mystery if it is based upon the daily rise and set of the sun or the growth of an individual with time. Consequently, no one seriously doubts the prediction that next year the sun will rise in the east or the pronouncement about a boy becoming a man.

The scientific community prides itself on the quantitative predictions in the physical sciences and many other areas of knowledge seek a similar capability. Scholars in sociology, political science, and psychology seek to be in the same league with those who foresee the air temperature range tomorrow or the force on the underside of the larger piston in a hydraulic press when seven tons are added to the other side.

The predictions of the physical scientists are not that accurate to those disenchanted with the weatherman or those who seek to avoid the terror of earthquakes, volcanoes, and hurricanes. Meteorologists profess a high degree of excellence for their fresh forecasts; alternatives include the tingling in grandmother's toes, the depths to which perch swim, the fatty coat on bears, and the entertainment in the *Farmer's Almanac*. Earthquake prediction has lately become more viable, while the other natural disasters are being studied, with forecasting them still not in view.

Foretelling with the alleged help of science can also take on the aspects of a sensational feature story. A specious view of mechanisms for the theory of organic evolution may lead some to propose changed locomotion patterns because of the omnipresence of the automobile for all kinds of short travel. In the same vein, a wit could perceive future humans without much cerebral cortex because of the lack of present use. There have been circulated contentions that many many generations from now *homo sapiens* will have tiny legs, feelers growing from the forehead, and no teeth.

Perhaps nonscientists can be assigned to the brash forecasts, but scientists have also indulged in comparable projecting—and about their own discipline. At the end of the last century, several physicists proclaimed an end to major new theories—all of physics was known, and remaining was merely the exercise of finding numerical values more exactly. Yet within the period 1895–1950, three laboratory discoveries and two theories revolutionised the subject. Recently, biologist Bentley Glass has more or less repeated the forecast about the end of major discoveries in science. In the March 1975 issue of the *Bulletin of the American Academy of Arts and Science* physicist Victor Weisskopf claimed, "It is reasonable to predict that man will eventually understand all of nature scientifically."

Science is a dynamic, open system where one problem solved leads to several new ones. Reaching the moon, for example, brought some answers and a host of questions. If science does reach the point where problems do not exist, the discipline can no longer be called by the same name. It should then be a branch of an established dogma.

Using extrapolation from known tendencies can also be a dangerous activity. If, for example, the growth of a human being very early in life be projected for the remainder of a seventy-year period, weights and heights would be far out of line. Similarly, a physicist has shown that the number of Ph.D. degrees won by American physicists during the 1950s and 1960s could be extrapolated to every person in the United States having a Ph.D. in the subject by the middle of the twenty-third century.

Whether spurred by the alleged successes of the physical sciences or the drive to know beyond the present, futurists have exploded in number during the last half of the twentieth century. John McHale said: "One could mention here a vast number of government, civic and corporate institutions. . . . Even the prestigious and hitherto conservative group known as 'The American Institute of Planners' has had its second annual conference on 'The Next Fifty Years 1967–2017.' Almost every institution in American society now has its futures group whose concerns range from education for the future and museums of the future to plans for the construction of complete experimental cities."[1]

The World Future Society held its First General Assembly in 1971 and its second in 1975 in Washington, D.C., the seat of many future groups. The Office of Technology Assessment set up in 1973 as well as the Environmental Protection Agency, founded in 1969, attempt to foresee events. Long-range projections are almost routinely made by the Census Bureau, Bureau of Labor Statistics, the Agriculture Department, the Aviation Forecast Branch of the Federal Aviation Administration, the military branches, and the Federal Energy Administration.

Business engages with equal zeal in delineating the future. Being unable to detect the rising popularity in the United States of small cars or the oversupply of aerospace engineers, the planners now focus on several simultaneous descriptions of the future termed *scenarios,* each with a different set of beginning assumptions but having equal probability.

Quantitative methods are being attempted in many areas where numbers are generally absent. Olaf Helmer, Quinton professor of future research, University of Southern California, wrote:

> Delphi has come a long way in its brief history, and it has a long way to go. Since its invention about twenty years ago for the purpose of estimating the probable effects of a massive atomic bombing attack on the United States, and its subsequent application in the mid-sixties to technological forecasting, its use has proliferated in the United States and abroad. While its principal area of application has remained that of technological forecasting, it has been used in many other contexts in which judgmental information is indispensable. These include normative forecasts; the ascertainment of values and preferences; estimates concerning the quality of life; simulated and real decision making; and what may be called "inventive planning."[2]

Futurologists have tackled their problems with gusto and an air of certainty. Daniel Bell, professor of sociology at Columbia University, wrote an introduction to *The Year 2000* by Herman Kahn and Anthony Wiener (New York: Macmillan, 1967). He compared present-day efforts with earlier twentieth-century attempts and claimed: "What is striking about these volumes is their fanciful character, the personal and even prejudiced judgments, the airy and even comical tone, as if the idea of speculating about the future had a somewhat absurd but pleasant quality—in effect, a lack of seriousness." Kahn and Wiener forecast societies free of major wars, totalitarian movements, and depressions. They were concerned about the huge amount of leisure time to be created by automation. In an interview with *Women's Wear Daily*, Tuesday, May 27, 1975, Kahn said that the average family in the United States in the year 2000 will live like a physician's family lived in 1960. "There will be clean air and clean water everywhere, . . . we'll live much farther out, much more rural and isolated, but also have a small apartment in the city. . . . Twenty-five years from now, the average guy will earn the equivalent of $25,000 from one job. . . ." In 1976, with William Brown and Leon Martel, he expanded his vision in the book *The Next 200 Years: A Scenario for America and the World* (New York: William Morrow): population is seen to be stabilized and energy and food problems will have been conquered.

Extremists among the futurists are in two opposing camps with prejudice, basic predispositions, and errors giving them their respective stance. One is the undue optimist, painting a rosy picture of things to come. The other is the pessimist, laden with doomsday prophecies.

The popularity of the sad future may be the result of marketplace considerations. Hollywood found tales of disaster to be profitable at the box office. Books may have been produced for the same reason. There are, however, alleged scientific bases for the predictions.

The second law of thermodynamics has long been used as a rationale for pessimistic forecasts. First postulated about one hundred years ago as a generalization for heat engines, the second law of thermodynamics has been extrapolated to the entire universe, and its prediction of ever-increasing unavailable energy, *entropy,* has been extended to the entire observable region. The heat death of the universe entails our world being at low temperature at some indefinite time in the future.

The vagueness of the time element can be only moderated. The distant future of maximum entropy encompasses more than a few or even a hundred or a thousand human generations. With such an interval, the efficacy of the law becomes suspect.

Other bases for doomsday predictions are likewise questionable. One is the Malthusian doctrine that human population will expand beyond the capability of the land to support life. Books have been published noting the date of the onset of starvation as 1975 or 1984. It is almost similar to the date of the end of the world postulated by the religious sect Jehovah's Witnesses. Their first collapse date was in 1914. Readers of the church's bimonthly publication, *Awake*, were told in 1966 and again in 1968 that a mathematical formula pointed toward an end in the autumn of 1975. In 1960 von Foerster, Mora, and Amiot published in *Science* their "Doomsday: Friday, 13 November, A.D. 2026," replete with mathematical formulas and based on the assumption of a huge world population on that date.

Lesser-known scientific principles can also be employed to predict doom. In astronomy, a relationship about stars called the R-H diagram proclaims the eventual change of our sun to a large, cool star enveloping the planets. Life on earth would end—in the millions of years required for the transformation. Or the rise in carbon dioxide content of the atmosphere should promote pronounced global warming, to the detriment of life. Or species do not last forever.

Professor Reid Bryson of the University of Wisconsin suggests that interglacial conditions, as are now on earth, can change to full glacial conditions and an attendant very low crop yield and food crisis within only 100 years. He bases his prediction on pollen in sediment cores from lakes in the northeastern United States. He has cores containing pollen samples of the last 9,000 years, and current pollen are like that found due to ancient vulcanism. Man-made pollution appears to be the current cause.

Two scientists, John Gribben and Stephen Plagemann, in their *Jupiter Effect* (New York: Walker, 1974) have, as described in chapter 2, a closer doomsday date. In 1982 all nine planets of the solar system will be aligned on the same side of the sun. Their gravitational pull may cause huge storms on the sun, which could alter wind directions on the earth, change its rotation, and produce earthquakes. A review of the book in the November–December 1974 issue of the *American Scientist* decribed it as "a commercial commodity of the crassest kind. The authors are clearly after the large cult and astrology market and the many Californians genuinely fearful of earthquakes." The reviewer claimed that "each link in the chain of "solid scientific reasoning" can be attacked, but it is easier to look at the earthquake record."[3] He did, and showed such anomalies as times of low sunspot activity in this century coincided with a larger number of major earthquakes.

Another definitive criticism was published by a Belgian astronomer in a 1975 issue of *Icarus*, the science journal dealing with the solar system. He showed that the four major planets are not aligned in 1982; that the combined planetary tidal bulge on the sun would be 2.7 million times smaller than the tides raised on the earth by the moon; that the evidence shows that seismicity and solar activity are independent. The two American scientists replied that "the exact tidal mechanism . . . looks less plausible than it did when we wrote our book."

The fault of the single-factor prohecies of doom is the simplistic assumption that one factor can be an accurate gauge of complex earth activity. As described in chapter 1, during the nineteenth century the British and others should have learned the lesson of the erroneous attempts to find a weather indicator in atmospheric pressure changes. The weather glass or barometer was used to signal the future weather pattern. Many living rooms still have such a toy as a piece of furniture, but meteorologists have been alerted for several decades that great numbers of factors are involved with the weather.

Doomsday prophecies are still abundant when all relevant factors are considered by the futurologists. In 1974 the president of France claimed "the great curves that describe the future in our times all lead to catastrophe."

Astronomer Fred Hoyle, who has no hesitancy about re-marking on a variety of subjects in his astronomy books, wrote in a book published in 1975: "When one contem-plates the huge human populations that have grown with startling suddenness during the last century or so, when one contemplates the excessive modern pressure on natural resources, it is hard to summon much confidence in a future extending more than a few decades. Devastating crises, one feels, must overtake the human species within a hundred years at most. We are living today, not on the brink of social disaster, as we often tend to think, but actually *within* the disaster itself."[4] Interviewed about the year 2000 by the *Washington Star* in 1975, author Isaac Asimov reported "I anticipate in the course of the next 25 years, there will be a kind of famine psychology sur-rounding earth's population. I think the great, big, fat problem of the next 25 years is getting enough food."

At the 1976 Baja conference sponsored by the Charles F. Kettering Foundation and the Wright-Ingraham Insti-tute, the twenty participants considering the interrelated problems of population, food production, land use, climate, and environmental quality concluded: "Famine, social un-rest and possible political chaos may not be far away. . . . By the year 2000 the problems in food production, storage, transportation and distribution will make today's problems appear as child's play."

Those who cry disaster for the United States only are just as articulate. Professor George H. Ramsey of the Georgia Institute of Technology, after a three-year study of U.S. environmental problems, claimed that we are becoming deficient in energy, resources, and food, while decaying with our pollution and economic dislocations. Alvin Toffler, author of *Future Shock*, in his *Eco-Spasm Report* (New York: Bantam, 1975) lists Watergate, Viet-nam, unemployment, inflation, the energy crisis, and several other events as symptoms of our being at the brink of disaster.

The extreme pessimists gained respectability in 1972

when an international study group called The Club of Rome publicized their *Limits To Growth* (New York: Universe Books, 1972). The book is the outline of a project on the future of mankind wherein a computer model of world growth was used. The authors admitted shortcomings, imperfections, oversimplifications, but nonetheless stated explicit conclusions: "If the present growth trends in world population, industrialization, pollution, food production, and resource depletion continue unchanged, the limits to growth on this planet will be reached sometime within the next one hundred years. The most probable result will be a rather sudden and uncontrollable decline in both population and industrial capacity."

The prediction was assaulted for presenting pollution as a single variable without definition, for assuming the world capacity to absorb pollution was four times the present value, for failing to consider market forces, and for a host of other issues. Perhaps the commentary of a special task force of the World Bank in September 1972 summed up the criticism: "Many of the assumptions fed into the models were 'extremely pessimistic' and 'not scientifically established.' Use of data was often 'careless and casual.' Extrapolations were made 'heavily and dogmatically.' (They) had 'allowed for' current uncertainty about limits of resources simply by multiplying all proved reserves by five, a procedure 'patently absurd.'"

The second report to the Club of Rome, *Mankind At the Turning Point* (New York: Dutton, 1974), although breaking down the earth into ten regions, was equally pessimistic. The only way to avoid catastrophe, they claimed, was immediate population control in the poor countries and generosity in the rich ones.

The response to the doomsday prophecies could be adverse criticism, acceptance with an effort to achieve the measures needed to avoid catastrophe, acceptance with the adoption of a personal life-style needed for a stable world community, or rejection for a variety of reasons. In the first category the editor of *Nature*, John Maddox, called the first Club of Rome report "sinister," and economist Gunnar Myrdal labeled it "pretentious nonsense." Professor Victor Hicken's *The World Is Coming To An End!* (New Rochelle, N.Y.: Arlington House, 1975) examines the 1960s prophets of political, social, and ecological doom. Frederick J. Wells in *The Long-Run Availability of Phosphorus: A Case Study in Mineral Resource Analysis* (Baltimore, Md.: Johns Hopkins University Press, 1976) shows that a prediction that phosphorus supplies, vital for life, would be very low within 100 years was off by a factor of 1,000 because of a decimal-place error. In category two are world federalists of many kinds, each with miniscule power today. The third kind of response is found in the communes and back-to-nature movements such as the Lindisfarne Association in Southampton, Long Island, New York. In the state of Washington there is another kind of reaction called "Alternatives for Washington," where thousands of citizens study and discuss interlinked problems and solutions, a kind of participatory democracy that appears to be a plus, whether or not the doomsday forecasters are pseudoscientists.

Nobel-prize-winner Linus Pauling's reaction may be unique. At the celebration of the one hundredth anniversary of the founding of the American Chemical Society, New York, April 1976, he predicted that within twenty-five to fifty years "there will occur the greatest catastrophe in the history of the world." Then he quickly added that he expected the human race to survive, and by 2076 it should have solved its problems.

Rejection of pessimistic prophesies need not be out of hand. Those saturated with optimism about the future can ignore the predictions on the basis of their own predilections, sometimes based upon a study of history. They can cite the experts who declared that man would never fly in a heavier-than-air craft or never travel in space. They can point to the dire forecasts of the early twentieth century about the approach of human starvation or the end of war because nitrogen fertilizer deposits in Chile were being depleted. Science and technology found answers to such dilemmas, and as the argument goes, there is justification for technological optimism.

The extreme-optimism view of the future was given by engineer-physicist Boris Pregel in 1941: "We can look forward to unlimited cheap power and fuel, an indefinite supply of raw materials, comfort for all with the minimum of labor—those things that should remove the causes of poverty, envy and greed, make wars unthinkable and usher in a golden age for human beings."[5] Historian L. S. Stavrianos wrote in his *Promise of the Coming Dark Age* (San Francisco: Freeman, 1976): "*Homo sapiens* is on the way to becoming *homo humanus.*" Astronomer Robert Jastrow used the same crystal ball when writing: ". . . there is only one forward path, the path to unending technological expansion. . . . Whatever setbacks occur, we shall go forward to ever more magnificent achievements."[6]

Physical scientists with their extended view of time and space are particularly prone to extreme optimism. At the end of the nineteenth century the Russian space pioneer Constantin Tsiolkovskii foresaw man colonizing the entire solar system. Now, high-energy physicist Gerard O'Neill of Princeton University proposes the construction of space cities composed of immense rotating aluminum cylinders. He imagines one million people in such an environment by the end of the century. He said at a conference on the colonization of space at Princeton, May 1974: "By 2074 more than 90 percent of the human population could be living in space colonies, with a virtually unlimited clean source of energy for everyday use, an abundance and variety of food and material goods, freedom to travel and independence from large-scale governments. The Earth could become a worldwide park, free of industry, slowly recovering by natural means from the near death-blow it received from the industrial revolution: A beautiful place to visit for a vacation." Scientist Edward S. Gilfillan, Jr., in his *Migration to the Stars* (New York: Robert B. Luce, 1975), wrote a more extended, albeit comparable, scenario based on interstellar travel. Astronomer Carl Sagan, in his moments as a seer, has other types of visions: "Cybernetics, molecular biology, and neurophysiology together will some day very likely be able to create artificial intelligent beings which hardly differ from men, except for being significantly more advanced. Such beings would be capable of self-improvement, and probably would be much longer-lived than conventional human beings."[7]

Kindly critics may feel compelled to excuse the physical scientists because they think in terms of thousands and millions of years. Theoretical physicist Freeman J. Dyson in 1966 showed how to take the planet Jupiter apart—in 40,000 years. During the summer of 1975 the National Aeronautics and Space Administration sponsored a seminar from which scientists reported: "No fundamental, insuperable limitation to the ability of Mars to support terrestrial life has been unequivocally identified." They talked in terms of 100,000 years to make the planet habitable.

Kindly critics may pass over the forecasts of the extremists as entertainment, but no such rationalization can be set up for those who follow a similar path in sociology, politics, and economics. Iranian-born F. M. Esfandiary in his 1970 book *Optimism One: The Emerging Radicalism* (New York: W. W. Norton) presents the first through his description of pretechnological society more replete with conformity, alienation, and violence. However, the result in economics can be disastrous. For example, the Harvard ABC curves were devised shortly after World War I. One curve, A, represented stock prices as an index of speculation, another was a measure of dollar volume through checks drawn on bank deposits, and the C curve showed the money market as indicated by short-term commercial loans. The three curves supposedly moved in sequence. The interpreters of the curves were too optimistic and failed to forecast the great depression of 1929. Who can say now that the economics department of McGraw-Hill publications were realistic in assessing the prospects for American business for 1988? They assumed no major war, reasonably full employment, and inflation at a 4 percent rate. Among the forecasts were over 125 percent growth rate for chemicals, plastics, electric utilities, instruments, and electrical machinery; a rise of 34 percent in real family income; a rise of 84 percent in constant dollars in business capital expenditures; and a rise in output per man-hour.[8]

Perhaps a way to encourage more caution among the futurists is to apply a little-known New York City statute aimed at fortune tellers. The City's code of criminal justice prohibits the acceptance of payment for predicting the future, so as "to prevent the ignorant and the gullible as well as the curious from being ensnared by the guiles and fantasies of those who profess to 'crystal gaze' as to the course of future events."

NOTES TO CHAPTER 9

1. John McHale, *The Future of Future* (New York: Braziller, 1969), pp. 258–59.
2. Olaf Helmer, foreword to *The Delphi Method*, ed. Harold A. Linstone and Murray A. Turoff (Reading, Mass.: Addison-Wesley, 1975).
3. Don L. Anderson, *American Scientist* 62 (November/December 1975): 721.
4. Fred Hoyle, *Highlights of Astronomy* (San Francisco: Freeman, 1975), p. 137.
5. McHale, *The Future of Future*, p. 244.
6. Robert Jastrow, introduction to Adrian Berry, *The Next Ten Thousand Years* (New York: Saturday Review/Dutton, 1974), p. 6.
7. I. S. Shklovskii and Carl Sagan, *Intelligent Life in the Universe* (New York: Dell, 1974).
8. *Business Week,* January 13, 1975, p. 22.

10 Detection

A dip or complete immersion in pseudoscience may appear to be a harmless activity. Everyone knows otherwise-normal people who are sold on astrology or believe in the wonderful world to come wrought by science and technology. However, appearances are deceiving. The effects of pseudoscience can be catastrophic. For one, death can ensue. Late in 1934 the manager of a bookshop in Charing Cross Road, London, told a newspaper reporter: "In the past twenty years two of the assistants in our occult book department have committed suicide. We only allow assistants to stay in that department for three months. They read the books in their spare time, and in the past few years several have become mentally unbalanced."[1] Richard Cavendish in *The Powers of Evil* (New York: Putnam, 1975, p. 3–4) tells several odd stories. In 1969 six people in Switzerland were found guilty of beating a girl to death to try to drive the devil out of her. In 1970 in Yorkshire, England, a man of fifty-four was frightened enough by talk of black magic and the devil that he jumped from a window and died from the injuries. In 1973 a Polish man in England died choking on a piece of garlic he had put in his mouth before going to sleep as a protection against vampires. Martin Ebon's collection, *The Satan Trap* (New York: Doubleday, 1976), shows other dangers from the occult.

In January 1976 a part-time clairvoyant in Adelaide, Australia, produced hysteria and exodus of families after he announced his vision of an earthquake and tidal wave for Monday, January 19. None occurred. In February Mrs. Irmgard Lincoln, a psychic, held a news conference in Washington, D.C., to announce that the Martians were coming. "We will have them here on the 4th of July, very definitely," she said.

John W. Miner, former chief of the Medicolegal section of the Los Angeles County district attorney's office, claims that medical quackery kills. He estimates that each year in the United States it takes more lives than do all crimes.

Illness can also occur. Dr. Irving M. Rosen, training director of the Clevelend Psychiatric Clinic, told the *Chicago Tribune* on April 19, 1975, that mystical experiences reported by saints, drug users, and the mentally ill are often similar. Dr. Rosen used self-image, willpower, reality judgment, time sense, emotional state, and awareness of surroundings as criteria. However, Dr. Rosen did indicate that some varieties of mystical experience are unrelated to mental illness.

Economic considerations are also involved. The American Medical Association estimates that each year Americans spend more than two billion dollars on health fads and frauds. This is more money than is used each year in the United States for health education and medical research combined.

The danger of pseudoscience to the scientific enterprise was described by the editor of *Science*, Philip H. Abelson, in his June 21, 1974, editorial. He wrote: "The danger . . . is that uncritical and undiscriminating minds may accept imaginative speculation as fact." Some readers did not agree. In the November 8, 1974, issue some responses were printed. One called the phenomena "milestones of mental development in our students that we should welcome rather than deplore." Another offered, "I think it is a great mistake to suppose that what Abelson calls 'pseudoscience' poses any threat to the integrity of science. A greater threat may lie in those scientists who are too eager to restrict its boundaries." A third, a physical scientist well known for his interest in parapsychology, urged greater funding for research on the ideas.

Martin Gardner, author of *Fads and Fallacies in the Name of Science,* popular since its publication in 1952, has pointed out another danger of pseudoscience. He wrote in his "Mathematical Games" column in the *Scientific American,* April 1975: "Important advances in science have been crowded out of newspapers, magazines, radio and television to make room for reports on poltergeists, demon possession, psychic healing, prehistoric visits to the earth by astronauts from other worlds, the vanishing of ships and planes in the Bermuda Triangle, the emotional life of plants, the primal scream and so on ad nauseam."

If the millennium of adequate science and engineering coverage by the mass media did occur, the popularity of pseudoscience would not necessarily be abated, for well-trained and accomplished scientists have been avid believers and promoters of pseudoscience. Psychologist Edwin G. Boring in his introduction to C. E. M. Hansel's *ESP, A Scientific Evaluation* (New York: Scribner's, 1966), reported: "Among the notable believers in ESP in the last century, Hansel mentions Augustus DeMorgan (mathematician and logician), Alfred Russel Wallace (naturalist and independent inventor of the theory of evolution), Sir William Crookes (physicist famed for early research in radioactivity), Henry Sidgwick (philosopher and ethicist,), Sir William Fletcher Barrett (physicist, known for his studies of magnetism, heat, sound, and vision), Sir Oliver Lodge (physicist known for his investigations of electromagnetic phenomena) and many others." In our time, psychoanalyst C. J. Jung was a lifelong believer in ESP, physicist Wolfgang Pauli took some of Jung's reflections seriously, and physicists Pascual Jordan and Juergen Petzhold are some of the several physical scientists convinced of the reality of parapsychology. On December 24, 1974, The *National Enquirer* reported Jordan as saying: "I accept as positive fact that some persons have the power to transmit their thoughts and read the thoughts of others, and some people have the power to produce recorded spirit voices on tape without trickery." Professor Brian Josephson, 1973 Nobel-prize recipient in physics, is quoted in poltergeist and automatic-writing exponent Matthew Manning's book *The Link* (New York: Holt, Rinehart and Winston, 1975, p. 16): "We are on the verge of discoveries which may be extremely important for physics. We are dealing here with a new kind of energy . . . psychic phenomena are mysterious, but they are no more mysterious than a lot of things in physics already. In times past, 'respectable' scientists would have nothing to do with psychical phenomena; many of them still won't. I think that the 'respectable' scientists may find they have missed the boat!" English physicist John G. Taylor published *Superminds* (New York: Viking, 1975), a sympathetic portrayal of Uri Geller and numerous psychic phenomena.

Some pioneer scientists, too, were engrossed in pseudoscience. According to critic Theodore Roszak, "Copernicus very nearly resorted to pagan sun worship as a means of supporting his heliocentric theory. . . . Kepler's astronomy emerges from a search for the Pythagorean music of the spheres. Newton was a life-long alchemist."[2] Newton defended his theory of universal gravitation against the charge that the idea was mystical. Attraction between objects at a distance without an apparent connection was said to be occult. C. S. Lewis has shown that many important sixteenth-century thinkers, supposed heralds of modern civilization, believed in spiritualism, magic, witchcraft, and numerology.[3] Frances Yates has suggested that science flourished only in those communities with a strong tradition of mysticism.[4]

From the standpoint of education, the occult and some pseudoscience are dangerous because they negate the confidence of the scientific enterprise in human reason. A scientific investigator takes on his work with the unwitting assumption that he, together with others, is capable of solving the problem. Sometimes several generations pass before the solution is attained, but the idea that some day the understanding will come through human reason is not forsaken.

Perhaps the most compelling reason for distinguishing between science and pseudoscience is not as clear to scientists as to administrators. They must allocate resources to research and need to know where results or blind alleys may result. Men, money, and materials cannot be squandered.

There are many characteristics of science one may apply in order to distinguish it from pseudoscience. Likewise, the latter has properties making detection a less than arduous task. At least a charge such as that leveled at Newton's gravitation concept by some of his contemporaries —that it was occult—can be more adequately investigated.

Every recognized science has a data base—a mass of information to be classified, understood, explained, and shown to lead to new revelations. The material must also be in the public domain, available to all competent investigators. Astronomy, for example, is the realm of planets, stars, galaxies, and related matter; biology deals with living materials, and historical geology is concerned with the development of the earth with time. What is the subject matter of magic or psychic healing? Is it fraud or the physics of sleight of hand? The facts of any science are not hearsay, unsubstantiated gossip, or private illumination. Yet parapsychology is laden with singular confessions. An investigator in modern psychic research wrote:

> The basic materials from which psychical research starts are stories which people tell of extraordinary and unexpected things having happened to them; of dreams that have afterwards been fulfilled, of convictions they know who has rung them up on the telephone before they have lifted it up, of having seen people, either living or dead, at places where they could not have been, and so on. Such stories do not form a very good basis for a scientific study of the paranormal since their value or evidence depends on the reliability of people telling them and on the circumstances in which they are told, whether, for example, soon after or long after the event.[5]

There is no data base in a number of fads, cults, and superstitions posing as science. The followers of Maharishi Mahesh Yogi push transcendental meditation, a kind of mental and physical relaxation, but also claim much for the science of creative intelligence. Their Maharishi International University, Fairfield, Iowa, established in 1974, offers many subjects in the light of the science of creative intelligence. What is the latter? According to Demetri Kanellakos of Stanford Research Institute, a member of the international resource faculty, the science of creative intelligence is an analysis and synthesis on how all things work in nature. It aims to show how certain principles govern all natural phenomena and are paralleled by the operation of the human mind. The Maharishi said, "During Transcendental Meditation, the whole nervous system pulsates between deep rest and activity. This natural process within the individual is just an image of the natural process of expansion and contraction in the physical universe."[6] This kind of analogy was the basis of alchemy, and the latter is no longer considered a science by serious thinkers. Nonetheless, some scientists continue to endorse the science of creative intelligence, although Nobel-prize-winner Melvin Calvin, who has addressed one of the science of creative intelligence symposia, claims the use of his name is "perilously close to false advertising." Transcendental meditation has plenty of testimonials and support from other sources and does not really need the scientists. For example, on May 24, 1972, the Illinois House of Representatives resolved "that the State of Illinois give all possible cooperation to the new Center for the teaching of the Science of Creative Intelligence to be founded in Chicago, Illinois."

Transcendental meditation and its science of creative intelligence has a wide variety of competing fads. One is the Arica Institute, named after a town in Chile by its founder, son of a Bolivian army general. An important Arica goal is to unite body and mind and get people to "think with their entire bodies." The development is supposed to proceed through vigorous exercises with emphasis on breathing, meditation, and chants. Another package presented for self-awareness is the system of Bhagwan Shree Rajneesh of India, advertised to do what Yoga, Christianity, primal therapy, bioenergetics, Gestalt therapy, body awareness, and group encounter cannot do separately. The United States has a few entries in these roads to nirvana. One is a technique of deep massage developed by Ida P. Rolf and now certified by the Rolf Institute of Structural Integration. Their purpose is to loosen the connecting tissue covering the muscles of the body and correct the imbalances due to falls, bad posture, tension, and emotional trauma.

American medicine has always had manipulators. Chiropractic, the art and science of spine manipulation, calls itself the world's largest nondrug healing profession, and also unlike the others, the U.S. Congress has sanctioned chiropractic treatments under Medicare. Moreover, chiropractic schools require two years of college for entrance and have a four-year curriculum resembling that of medical schools, except for the omission of pharmacology and surgery. All chiropractors call the misarrangement of bones *subluxations*, but some claim to treat a wide range of disorders while others limit themselves to muscle, nerve, and bone-related ailments.

Chiropractic was started at the end of the nineteenth century. Earlier the United States saw the origin of such medical schools of thought as Thomsonism, homeopathy, and naturopathy, but during the twentieth century with the growth of science there also came into being many pseudosciences without a data base.

The idea that there exists another space-time continuum has been used to bring fraud, hoax, illusion, delusion, and hallucination to the status of science. Sir Arthur Conan Doyle, the famous author of Sherlock Holmes tales, promoted a photograph of two young girls playing with humanoid figures, a few inches high, as genuine evidence for the existence of fairies and elves.[7] The enthusiasts for UFOs cite the sudden appearance and disappearance of tall, dark men as well as the instant transference of men and materials from one part of the earth to another.[8] A French author writing in the same vein describes the reappearance in the flesh of Joan of Arc, long after she had been burned.[9] All of these claims are alien to the precepts of modern science, and even distorting the theory of relativity cannot give a rationale to the contention that space harbors small, strange, or reincarnated humanoids.

A science has to have a subject matter; it cannot be based on a convoluted, shortsighted, or arbitrary point of view about the nature of parts of the universe. Nor can some one else's subject matter be confiscated with an erroneous concept. Many health and food faddists adopt medicine and nutrition as their own and push for the ingestion of sunflower seeds or vitamin E as the magic potion. Former playwright and screen writer Robert Ardrey wrote books and made a film arguing that men evolved as a fighting animal, making aggression and defense of territory an uppermost motivation; anthropologists are skeptical.

If every erroneous idea of scientists were to be labeled pseudoscience, accepted and established science would be a tiny dot in a huge book of foolish and misguided attempts at understanding nature. Pioneers and moderns alike have many more aborted concepts, some circulated for decades, than ones that are finally corroborated. The wrong idea becomes pseudoscience only when continually supported in the face of much evidence against it. Followers of Lysenko in the U.S.S.R. can be so labeled because inheritance of acquired characteristics cannot be demonstrated and a biology based upon such an error is a pseudobiology. The followers of Madame Blavatsky and the originators of theosophy can be called pseudoscientists, among other names, because the ideas they hold cannot be substantiated.

Another vital reason pushes theosophy out of the arcana of legitimate science. Theosophy has no subject matter, like many of the others described, but theosophy is also a secret organization, and secrecy is not a part of the scientific enterprise. The data base must be open to all qualified investigators.

The polymath Leonardo Da Vinci conducted some of his scientific work in secret and balked at open communication: he had a unique, backward handwriting. When modern science began to flourish, however, lack of secrecy became more established. Now any investigator who does secret work is outside the community of science.

Another secret organization, the Rosicrucians, may have their origin in the alchemy of the early seventeenth century. In 1614 there was published at Cassel, Germany, a pamphlet entitled "The Discovery of the Fraternity of the Meritorious Order of the Rosy Cross," and in 1615 another pamphlet, "The Confession of the Rosicrucian Fraternity." An authority on the early history of the sect believes that it was founded in Nuremberg by a Lutheran alchemist.[10] According to Gerald Bailey, editor of the *Rosicrucian Digest*, the Rosicrucians "unite into one livable philosophy, metaphysical idealism and such practical sciences as physics, chemistry, biology, physiology and psychology." According to their literature, issued from San Jose, California, Rosicrucians were in America long ago. In 1801 the order went underground and 108 years later emerged and began building the society more openly. The Rosicrucians have a secret ritual room in their lodge halls and wear gold crosses with loops at their top called ankhs, Egyptian symbols of immortality. Each year they hold an annual rite in the Great Pyramid of Cheops in Egypt. One of their most infamous adherents is Sirhan Sirhan, the assassin of Robert F. Kennedy; but they also boast of Ben Franklin and Thomas Jefferson as members.

Secrecy and lack of subject matter exclude some pseudosciences from the arcana of science. Unfortunately, the scientific enterprise still contains those who draw moral lessons from nature, an attribute long discarded by progressive disciplines. Physics and chemistry do not find ethical instruction for mankind in the way one chemical reacts with another. Yet during the early renaissance, bestiaries, pointing out morals through animal behavior, were popular books. One story was about the ant-lion, a union of both organisms and unable to eat either meat or seeds; it perished by starvation, as would every double-minded man who tried to follow both God and the devil. Another tale told about the popular Roman prelate who during early Christianity set out to travel to Britain to convert the natives. After a few days' travel, while he rested, a locust alighted on him; and *locusta* in Latin means "stop." He took this as a sign from God to stop and return to Rome, where he was soon elected Pope. In one of the most famous bestiaries, *Physiologus,* the panther's habit of sleeping for three days after eating and then awakening to emit a rare perfume attracting men was said to represent Christ's descent into hell, with the perfume being the teachings of the church.

The relation of man to nature as viewed by modern science has been drawn, albeit extremely, by philosopher-mathematician-essayist Bertrand Russell. He wrote in his *Scientific Outlook,* published during the 1930s:

> Even more purposeless, more void of meaning is the world which Science presents for our belief. Amid such a world, if anywhere, our ideals must henceforward find a home. That man is the product of causes which had no prevision of the end they were achieving; that his origin, his hopes and fears, his loves and his beliefs, are but the outcome of accidental collocations of atoms; that no fire, no heroism, no intensity of thought and feeling, can preserve an individual life beyond the grave; that all the labors of the ages, all the devotion, all the inspiration, all the noonday brightness of human genius are destined to extinction in the vast death of the solar system and that the whole temple of man's achievement must inevitably be buried beneath the debris of a universe in ruins.[11]

The pseudoscience of alchemy had as one of its basic precepts the moral uplifting of man through the study of metal transmutations to gold. Reaching a moral acme for man was the real goal of those who sought the philosopher's stone and the elixir of life. Lee Stavenhagen reports:

Throughout the Latin literature on the subject, the alchemical process is treated symbolically. The base matter, of course, was man, corrupted by sin; the elixir was the cleansing power of the holy spirit; and so on. Consequently, the ultimate obtainable by the Great Work was an *imitatio*, an approach to perfection as symbolized by alchemical gold, which, it should be noted, was generally held to be something different from the gold of natural origin. The focus in Latin is always on the alchemist himself, however exotic and unfailing his secret repertoire of processes may be. European alchemical literature overflows with delightful legends of adepts who attained magical longevity by virtue of their chemical accomplishments. The successful practitioner was typically revered as an ancient man whose physical well being, in addition to his wealth, marked outwardly the nobility of spirit from inward transmutation.[12]

In many pseudo- and occult sciences, the focus is on the individual rather than nature. The response to an event or catastrophe in African witchcraft is the question of who rather than what. The questions are Who did it? Who cast a spell? Who was the witch? The procedure prevents coming to grips with evidence.

During medieval times in Europe a similar kind of approach to evidence was invoked. A person accused of a crime could be judged simply by the chance of his choosing the correct of two identical-appearing packages, but only one contained a cross. Another technique of discrimination was to see whether a hot iron could be held.

Obtaining so-called evidence via an ordeal is as reprehensible as avoiding the truth. Charles Mackay in his *Extraordinary Popular Delusions and the Madness of Crowds* (Wells, Vt.: Fraser, 1969) relates how Mesmer refused to accept the verdict of eminent oculists that a lady Mesmer had treated was not cured of blindness. Mesmer instead proclaimed a conspiracy against him.

The godfather of hypnotism also had no recourse to a procedure which is a prime characteristic of science—experimentation. This activity, which is almost synonymous with modern science, is rarely if ever a feature of pseudo-science. To be sure, alchemists had laboratories and did try working with materials under their control; they did experiment. Likewise, parapsychology makes an effort at experimentation.

A sympathetic investigator of parapsychology wrote:

> In the experimental sciences, experiment is not merely a method of confirming what takes place; it is above all the method of testing and guiding theoretical advance. If a theoretical possibility is suggested by observation or by a preliminary experiment, the experimentalist asks: "How can I devise an experiment to find out whether this is true or false?" This was not how most of the early psychical researchers thought; they accumulated anecdotes and based theories on them but did not take the further step of devising experiments to see whether the theories were true or false. They do not seem generally to have realized that the essential requirement of a fruitful scientific theory is that it should lead to observable consequences that can in principle be tested by experiment.[13]

In the strictist sense an experiment is done when the investigator has all pertinent factors under his control in a contrived situation, and the significance of each is tested one or at most two at a time. Galileo was such an experimenter, according to the apocryphal tale about his dropping weights from the Leaning Tower of Pisa. In his judgment, the weight of a falling object had no connection to its speed of downward descent. He could vary other factors, if he wished, such as height, time of day, temperature, and whatever else he thought to be important. During the early nineteenth century English chemist Humphry Davy was an experimenter when he found the cause of acid and base formation during the decomposition of water through an electric current. His was a longer activity wherein he tested a larger number of significant factors as possible causes. He finally found the air of Britain with its content of seawater to be responsible.

The word *experiment* has been loosely used in science for the experience that is really empiricism. This verification procedure is with minimum recourse to theory and seeks a practical result. A person with a score of keys before a locked door has an empirical experience if he discards tiny and oversize keys as being inappropriate and then tries to open the door with the other keys. A paint manufacturer who tests the quality of paint by examining painted strips of metal is similarly given to minimum recourse to theory and is seeking a practical result. The work of the alchemists and parapsychologists is also better viewed as empiricism.

Experiment or empiricism is not as vital as the presence of any kind of verification. Testing of ideas through logic, experiment, empiricism, observation, field studies, case studies, statistical analyses, or even trial and error gives an area of knowledge a foot in the door of legitimate science. Hypotheses and verification are the core of procedure in science, and the pseudosciences are herein woefully deficient. Moreover, the sciences with great certainty have quantitative verification, and numbers and mathematics are not in the armament of the mystic, the occultist, and the psychic.

Legitimate science has an open, public data base and workers engaged in hypotheses-building and idea-testing, whether or not in a laboratory. The last activity, verification, proceeds with the understanding that a competent investigator is able to repeat any reported result; replication is expected. Parapsychology has no such constraint. Thouless reports:

> There is one other requirement of tests of ESP about which there has been much controversy and some misunderstanding. This is the condition of "repeatability." In an ordinary physical experiment, such as that of determining the acceleration due to gravity at the earth's surface, we have only to specify how the experiment is to be set up to be sure that anyone carrying it out will (within the limits of error of his

observations) get the same result. Such an experiment is completely repeatable. No experiment in parapsychology is repeatable in that sense; one can specify the conditions in which one has oneself obtained a successful ESP result without any strong conviction that everyone else who tries will get the same result.[14]

A celebrated recent case of lack of replication was exposed at the American Association for the Advancement of Science meeting, New York, January 1975. A polygraph, or lie detector, operator, Cleve Backster, in 1967 had reported measuring an electrical response in a philodendron when he only thought of burning a leaf or actually dumping a pan of brine shrimp into boiling water. At the meeting, a panel of two plant physiologists and three animal physiologists disputed the claim. Attempts to reproduce the results at Cornell University as well as at a laboratory in San Antonio set up specifically for the purpose, failed. In more than 200 trials, philodendron plants did not respond to brine shrimp being dumped into boiling water. Backster was also a member of the panel and said that he never repeated his experiment because he had not yet "finalized" the procedure. He charged that the shrimp and flowers used by others were guarded and sensed "hostile feelings" of the experimenters. In Backster's terms, there was a "consciousness interlock contamination" of test plants as well as a stressful laboratory environment.

In 1811 James P. Tupper's book in England, *An Essay on the Probability of Sensation in Vegetables,* attempted to establish by analogy physiological similarities between plants and animals. The author concluded that plants, like animals, have nervous systems, require sleep, possess will, and are subject to and experience irritability. The book went through three editions. A generation later, a founder of modern psychology, Gustav Theodor Fechner, wrote *Nanna* or *The Soul Life of Plants* and wrote that plants "participate in the cosmic soul life, and, indeed, have their own souls."

The Soviet Union also had its "talking plant" episode. In 1970 Professor Ivan Isidorovich Gunar made his discovery, but in 1974 he revised his opinion and made the comment, "Pseudoscience is profitable not only to its priests. In all ages, mysticism and 'miracles' have helped bourgeois society to divert people from real social problems."[15]

Perhaps the Soviets learned the lesson of their Lysenko fiasco. After World War II competent biologists in that country failed to duplicate the laboratory work offered by Lysenko in partial defense of his thesis that acquired characteristics were inherited. Lysenkoism was given government sanction and support while his antagonists were sent to Siberia or given technician jobs.

At the start of the Lysenko affair, criteria to distinguish between science and pseudoscience were first being published in the United States. In 1949 analyst of science Robert Merton wrote in his *Social Theory and Social Structure* (New York: The Free Press) the four norms or rules of science. He said that each was not unique to science, but together they were peculiar to the discipline. Merton listed *universalism*, implying that only logical structure and quality determine merit of a contribution, with age, sex, religion, politics and training of the investigator being disregarded; *organized skepticism* requires that all science be judged critically, regardless of the eminence or experience of the scientist; *communality* gives the scientific enterprise the openness that make data and conclusions public rather than secret; *disinterestedness* means the pursuit of science is not for prestige, power, or financial gain but only for the cause of understanding.

Merton's norms are a mixture of characteristics of science and scientists. A focusing on the individual can be done. The American Medical Association's department of investigations has compiled the profile of a medical quack and many of the following are appropriate for the pseudoscientist: (1) He uses a special or "secret" formula or machine that he claims can cure a disease; (2) he promises a quick or easy cure; (3) he advertises, using "case histories" or testimonials to impress people; (4) refusing to accept the tried and proven methods of medical research and proof, he clamors constantly for "medical investigation" and recognition; (5) he contends that medical men are persecuting him or are afraid of his competition; (6) he contends that his method of treatment is better than surgery, x-rays, or drugs.

Martin Gardner's criteria in his *In the Name of Science* (New York: G. P. Putnam's Sons, 1952) are solely about the individual. He wrote about the pseudoscientist in the 1957 paperback version entitled *Fads and Fallacies in the Name of Science* (New York: Dover, pp. 12–14): "1. He considers himself a genius. 2. He regards his colleagues, without exception, as ignorant blockheads. 3. He believes himself unjustly persecuted and discriminated against. 4. He has strong compulsions to focus his attacks on the greatest scientists and the best established theories. 5. He often has a tendency to write in a complex jargon."

Personal characteristics are more difficult to apply and each singly may describe an established scientist. That he considers himself a genius is true of many present and past able scientific workers. The often quoted remark of Harvard mathematician George Birkhoff is appropriate. When told by a Mexican physicist of the hope that the United States would continue to send savants of his stature, Birkhoff replied, "In the States, I am the only one of my stature."

Viewing colleagues as blockheads appears to be a professional-jealousy activity, although to think of all in the same category is unique. It is conceivable that an established scientist in a pique of anger due to politics or disillusion could react in such a manner.

Claims as an injured party are widespread and other associated attributes described by Gardner need to be invoked. The pseudoscientist not only identifies himself as unjustly persecuted but also believes that he is a martyr in the sense of Galileo.

Established plant physiologists, like the majority of other

established personnel, whatever the discipline, have not always been open to new ideas. [At the beginning of the twentieth century Sir Jagadis Chandra Bose spoke to the Royal Society about plant responses, and Sir John Burdon Sanderson, "the grand old man" of British physiology, claimed it was absolutely impossible to have an electric response from plants. Bose's paper was not published, but in 1920 he was made a fellow of the Royal Society.[16]]

Pseudoscientists seize upon episodes of this nature to present themselves as parties wronged by the dogmatic and inertia-ridden powers. Sir Bose did not complain publicly about his treatment, but several twentieth-century people on the fringes of science have compared themselves to the well-known, misunderstood pioneers. At the American Association for the Advancement of Science meeting, San Francisco, February 1974, Immanuel Velikovsky, at the session devoted to analyzing his theories, compared himself to Giordano Bruno, the Copernican martyr. Velikovsky had been shabbily treated, and perhaps his remarks were justified on that account—but not on the basis of the solidity of his position. (He was outraged to have his theory be placed in the same category with palmistry, astrology, and scientology.) The widow of Wilhelm Reich, in her biography of him (New York: St. Martin's Press, 1969, p. xxi), wrote: "He felt that his discoveries put him in a class with Galileo or Giordano Bruno, and he took his very real persecutions as the inevitable fate of every great discoverer. . . . In his later years, he undoubtedly began to identify more and more with Christ whose true message he thought, was distorted by his disciples, and he feared the same would happen to his work."

The paranoid pseudoscientist will more likely than not attack the greatest scientists. The revolutionists who would like to introduce the idea that the earth has been visited by astronauts from other planets are consistent in their attack on archaeologists. The best known, Erich von Däniken, never misses an opportunity to cast aspersion upon the ability and wisdom of archaeologists and anthropologists.

The complex jargon of pseudoscientists is typified in such a phrase as "conscious interlock contamination." However, they as well as normal scientists invent their own more understandable vocabulary. Velikovsky shuns the ordinary word *prediction* for his own "advance claim."

Perhaps Gardner's five criteria collectively, just as Merton's together, characterize the pseudoscientist. There may not be one single description suitable for the entire group, although some individuals are struck by the "warm and human" nature of the pseudoscientists. The physicist who was the *New Scientist*'s chief investigator of Uri Geller said he could not help but like Geller. Similarly, many are drawn to Immanuel Velikovsky as a man of warmth and charm. On the other hand, in 1952 Gardner claimed (pp. 31–32) "Dr. Velikovsky is an almost perfect textbook example of the pseudoscientist—self-taught in the subjects about which he does most of his speculation, working in isolation from fellow scientists, motivated by a strong compulsion to defend dogmas held for other than scientific reasons, and with an unshakable conviction in the revolutionary value of his work and the blindness of his critics."

Detection of pseudoscience and pseudoscientists may be a simple matter in most cases, but the record is clear that the label can be misleading, erroneous, and libelous. In 1948 two Nobel prize winners in physiology and medicine, Drs. E. D. Adrian and Sir Henry Dale, testified in a South African court against the claims of the muscle manipulating technique of F. Matthias Alexander. Dale said it was "intensely dangerous quackery" and ought to be made "criminal." The judge concurred with "in its claims to cure, the system constitutes dangerous quackery." Yet the ethologist Nikolaas Tinbergen in his 1973 Nobel prize acceptance speech recommended the Alexander technique for autistic children.

Physical scientists have long made a *bon mot* of Lord Kelvin's claim that description and manipulation with numbers makes a subject certain. Sociologists, historians, political scientists, and economists listened and acted for their disciplines. During the early twentieth century, Canadian Stephen Leacock wrote a humorous essay deriding the introduction of quantitative methods into the social sciences. Now, however, econometrics is an established study, and quantitative methods are encouraged in practically all social sciences.

During the late sixteenth and early seventeenth centuries, Francis Bacon, a herald for modern science, helped introduce a questionable feature of science. (Bacon did only one semiscientific exercise during his lifetime. He thought that snow could be used to preserve fowl; accordingly, one day he stuffed a dead chicken with snow. From this he caught a chill and died soon thereafter.) Much of his writing was superb public relations for the fledgling scientific enterprise. However, he described a procedure no one ever uses and may have been a factor in the growth of the pseudosciences emphasizing collecting intangibles.

Bacon illustrated his method using the phenomenon of heat. He would have investigators first compose a table of affirmations; they would select from the carefully arranged facts collected in natural history all those instances where heat is exhibited. He mentioned twenty-seven such as meteors, flames, pepper, and the rays of the sun. The second task would be construction of a table of negatives, or where heat is absent. Since this would be an infinite task, the list would be restricted to those comparable to the first table; thus, mention would be made of heavenly bodies, such as the sun, not having heat. The third assortment composed would be a table of digressions, or where heat is present in various degrees. The three tables would be used cautiously with "indulgence of understanding" to arrive at a "first vintage."

Undoubtedly, the collection of flora, fauna, and minerals abounding on the earth began long before Francis Bacon and exists now as legitimate objects for study. Bacon may only be in part responsible for adjudging the exercise to be a scientific one and for wanting collections of diverse phenomena including human frailties. He wrote about forming "a history and tables of discovery for anger, shame, fear, etc."

At the beginning of the twentieth century Dr. Duncan MacDougall did trials to pinpoint the human soul; indeed he believed that he could show its tangible nature. He weighed one tubercular volunteer at the moment of death and found a loss of three-quarters of an ounce. He could not determine the exact moment of death for his next subject, but during eighteen minutes between the man's last breath and the time he finally established death, more than one and one-half ounces of weight loss was recorded. He found other weight losses, discarding some instances as untrustworthy. To cap his work, he tried to measure the weight of soul substance with dying dogs. Finding none he concluded that dogs had no soul substance.

Currently another Englishman is making a table more in the Baconian tradition about human religious experiences. Sir Alister Hardy, a marine biologist as well as a past president of the British Society for Psychical Research, is in charge of the Religious Experience Research Unit. He wants to build up a body of knowledge about man's religious experience to show that it is as fundamental as sex. He said, "we hope it may lead to an experimental approach to religion."

The only way to be on the safe side is to be completely open for all who wish to present ideas, however they may be finally judged. Censorship should only occur where death or illness will obviously ensue. Otherwise, the marketplace for concepts should be available to all. In the 1970s in Germany, the authorities at Ravensburg Polytechnic placed obstacles in the way of a physicist lecturing on his "Introduction to Parapsychology and Paraphysics." This should serve as an example of the wrong way to approach the occult and pseudosciences. Likewise, in 1977 an assistant professor of geology at the University of North Carolina, David M. Stewart, charged, and the university denied, that his failure to secure tenure was related to his making public a psychic's prediction that within a year an earthquake would take place in Wilmington, North Carolina. It did not.

The chance always exists that a pseudoscience can be the midwife for the birth of a science. Alchemy may be so viewed in relation to chemistry, and astrology can be thought of as an origin of astronomy. A historian of psychology has said, "it is almost correct to say that scientific psychology was born of phrenology, out of wedlock with science."[17] After food faddists pointed to skim milk, brewer's yeast, wheat germ, and blackstrap molasses as wonder foods, the scientific study of nutrition arose.

Moreover, what is labeled pseudoscience in one country may not be so elsewhere. Authorities in the U.S.S.R. once called cybernetics a pseudoscience, and followers of classical genetics were termed fascists.

Squelching pseudo- and occult science does not remove their root causes; therefore, such a wrong effort merely drives the tendencies underground. Whether or not the basic causes can be eradicated, if such is desired, is also questionable.

According to some, the occult sciences derive their sustenance from natural tendencies. D. H. Rawcliffe is one of many who supports "The urge toward mysticism, the occult and the supernatural is fundamental in human nature; to whatever degree of sophistication the individual may attain, he can seldom quite free himself from it."[18] Albert Einstein is credited with: "The most beautiful and most profound emotion we can experience is the sensation of the mystical. It is the source of all true science."

It may be that the natural tendency stems from fear. Science does not pretend to have all the answers, and, minus a guide for an anomalous event, the average person with a nonscientific frame of mind turns to an answer giver. The occult is one such purveyor.

Perhaps the tendency appeals to those disillusioned with the apparent failure of traditional value and systems. Seeking beliefs and ideals, the individual is beckoned by the occult and pseudosciences. The latter also serve as vehicles for outsiders, those whom the establishment has not or cannot absorb.

Perhaps the natural tendency is a by-product of adolescent rebellion. Younger people are the customers for the multitude of paperbacks about flying saucers, magic, and witchcraft.

Old and young, however, are subject to the profit-making that results from pseudoscience. Were there no money to be made in the occult and borderland sciences, a large percentage of them would die from lack of sustenance. Remaining would be those catering to the individuals who need certainty and ego-building, and the ones surviving as entertainment.

NOTES TO CHAPTER 10

1. Quoted in Montague Summers, *Witchcraft and Black Magic* (1945; republished ed., Detroit, Mich.: Grand River Books, 1971), pp. 180–81.
2. Theodore Roszak, "The Monster and the Titan, Science, Knowledge and Gnosis," *Daedalus* 103 (Summer 1974):28.
3. C. S. Lewis, "New Learning and New Ignorance," in his *Introduction to English Literature in the Sixteenth Century* (New York: Oxford University Press, 1954), pp. 1–65.
4. Frances Yates, *Rosicrucian Enlightenment* (London: Routledge, 1972).
5. Robert Thouless, *From Anecdote to Experiment in Psychical Research* (London: Routledge and Kegan Paul, 1972), p. 11.
6. In Constance Holden, "Maharishi International University: 'Science of Creative Intelligence,'" *Science* 187 (March 28, 1975):1176–80.
7. Sir Arthur Conan Doyle, *The Coming of the Fairies* (London: Hodder & Stoughton, 1922).
8. F. W. Holiday, *Creatures from the Inner Sphere* (New York: Popular Library, 1973), pp. 219–20; and Brinsley LePoer Trench, *Mysterious Visitors* (New York: Stein and Day, 1973), pp. 50–52, 55.
9. Robert Charroux, *Legacy of the Gods* (New York: Berkley, 1974), p. 162.
10. H. Stanley Redgrove, *Alchemy: Ancient and Modern* (New York: Barnes & Noble, 1973), pp. 62–65.
11. Quoted in Morris Goran, *Science and Anti-Science* (Ann Arbor, Mich.: Ann Arbor Science Publishers, 1974), chap. 3.
12. Lee Stavenhagen, ed., *A Testament of Alchemy* (Hanover, N.H.: University Press of New England, 1974), pp. 65–66.

13. Thouless, *From Anecdote to Experiment,* p. 14.
14. Ibid., p. 53.
15. *Newsweek,* September 16, 1974, p. 53.
16. "Ariadne," *New Scientist* 65 (March 6, 1975):616.
17. Edwin G. Boring, *A History of Experimental Psychology* (New York: Harper & Row, 1929), p. 55.
18. D. H. Rawcliffe, *Illusions and Delusions of the Supernatural and the Occult* (New York: Dover, 1959), p. 8.

Selected Bibliography

Baroja, Julio Caro. *The World of the Witches*. Chicago: University of Chicago Press, 1965.

Bell, A. H., ed. *Practical Dowsing*. London: G. Bell, 1965.

Blair, Lawrence. *Rhythms of Vision*. New York: Schocken, 1976.

Bonewits, P. E. I. *Real Magic*. New York: Coward, McCann & Geoghegan, 1971.

Burckhardt, Titus. *Alchemy*. Baltimore, Md.: Penguin, 1971.

Burland, C. A. *The Arts of the Alchemist*. New York: Macmillan, 1968.

Burr, Harold Saxton. *The Fields of Life*. New York: Ballantine, 1972.

Cammell, Charles R. *Aleister Crowley: The Man, The Magic, The Poet*. New Hyde Park, N.Y.: University Books, 1962.

Cantor, G. N. "Phrenology in Early Nineteenth-Century Edinburgh: An Historiographical Discussion." *Annals of Science* 32 (1975).

Cavendish, Richard, ed. *Encyclopedia of the Unexplained*. New York: McGraw-Hill, 1974.

———. *The Powers of Evil*. New York: G. P. Putnam's Sons, 1975.

Christopher, Milbourne. *ESP, Seers and Psychics*. New York: Thomas Y. Crowell, 1970.

———. *Mediums, Mystics and the Occult*. New York: Thomas Y. Crowell, 1975.

Cohen, Daniel. *ESP, The Search Beyond the Senses*. New York: Harcourt Brace Jovanovich, 1973.

———. *The Far Side of Consciousness*. New York: Dodd Mead, 1974.

Cohn, Norman. *Europe's Inner Demons.* New York: Basic Books, 1975.

Crookall, Robert. *Out-of-the-Body Experiences.* New Hyde Park, N.Y.: University Books, 1970.

Crowley, Aleister. *The Book of Thoth.* New York: Lancer Books, 1971.

Cruz, Nicky. *Satan on the Loose.* Old Tappan, N.J.: Fleming H. Revell, 1973; New York: Signet, 1974.

Davies, John D. *Phrenology, Fad and Science.* New Haven, Conn.: Yale University Press, 1955.

Dean, Stanley R., M.D., ed. *Psychiatry and Mysticism.* Chicago: Nelson-Hall, 1975.

de Camp, L. Sprague. *Lost Continents. The Atlantis Theme.* New York: Dover, 1970; New York: Ballantine, 1975.

De Givry, Grillot. *Witchcraft, Magic & Alchemy.* Boston: Houghton Mifflin, 1931; New York: Dover, 1971.

de Guistino, David. *Conquest of Mind, Phrenology and Victorian Social Thought.* London: Croom Helm, 1975.

Delano, Rev. Kenneth J. *Astrology, Fact or Fiction.* Huntington, Ind.: Our Sunday Visitor, Inc., 1973.

Doane, Doris Chase, and Keyes, King. *How to Read Tarot Cards.* New York: Funk and Wagnalls, 1968.

Donnelly, Ignatius. *Atlantis: The Antediluvian World.* London: Sidgwick and Jackson, 1950.

Douglas, Alfred. *The Oracle of Change.* Hammondsworth, England: Penguin, 1972.

————. *The Tarot: The Origins, Meaning and Uses of the Cards.* London: Victor Gollancz, 1973.

Ducasse, C. J. *The Belief in a Life After Death.* Springfield, Ill.: Charles C. Thomas, 1961.

Ebon, Martin, ed. *The Psychic Scene.* New York: Signet, 1974.

————. *Reincarnation in the Twentieth Century.* New York: Signet, 1967.

————. *The Satan Trap.* New York: Doubleday, 1976.

Ehrenwald, Jan. *The ESP Experience: A Psychiatric Validation,* New York: Basic Books, 1978.

Eisenbud, J. *Psi and Psychoanalysis*. New York: Grune and Stratton, 1970.

――――. *The World of Ted Serios*. New York: William Morrow, 1967; London: Jonathan Cope, 1968.

Eisler, Robert. *The Royal Art of Astrology*. London: Herbert Joseph, 1946.

Evans, Christopher. *Cults of Unreason*. New York: Farrar, Straus and Giroux, 1973.

Fuller, John. *Arigo, Surgeon of the Rusty Knife*. New York: Thomas Y. Crowell, 1974.

Gallant, Roy A. *Astrology, Sense or Nonsense*. Garden City, N.Y.: Doubleday, 1974.

Gardner, Martin. *In the Name of Science*. New York: G. P. Putnam, 1952.

Garrison, Omar. *The Hidden Story of Scientology*. New York: Citadel Press, 1974.

Gauquelin, Michel. *The Scientific Basis of Astrology*. New York: Stein and Day, 1969.

Geller, Uri. *My Story*. New York: Praeger, 1975.

Gibson, Walter B. and Litzka R. *The Complete Illustrated Book of Divination and Prophecy*. New York: Doubleday, 1973.

Godwin, John. *Occult America*. New York: Doubleday, 1972.

Goldsmith, Donald, ed. *Scientists Confront Velikovsky*. Ithaca, N.Y.: Cornell University Press, 1977.

Green, Celia. *Out-of-the-Body Experiences*. New York: Ballantine, 1973.

Hall, Trevor H. *The Spiritualists*. London: Gerald Duckworth, 1962; New York: Garret-Helix, 1963.

――――. *The Strange Case of Edmund Gurney*. London: Gerald Duckworth, 1964.

Hammond, David. *The Search for Psychic Power*. New York: Bantam, 1975.

Hansel, C. E. M. *ESP: A Scientific Evaluation*. New York: Scribner, 1966.

Houdini, Harry. *A Magician Among the Spirits*. New York: Harper, 1924.

Hughes, P. *Witchcraft.* Baltimore, Md.: Penguin, 1967.

Jackson, Herbert G., Jr. *The Spirit Rappers.* New York: Doubleday, 1972.

Jerome, Lawrence E. *Astrology Disproved.* Buffalo, N.Y.: Prometheus, 1977.

Johnson, Vera Scott, and Wommack, Thomas. *The Secrets of Numbers.* New York: Dial, 1973; and Berkley, 1974.

Kaplan, Stuart R. *Tarot Classic.* New York: Grosset and Dunlap, 1972.

Keene, M. Lamar. *The Psychic Mafia.* New York: St. Martin's Press, 1976.

Knight, David C. *The ESP Reader.* New York: Grosset and Dunlap, 1968.

Koestler, Arthur. *The Roots of Coincidence.* New York: Random House, 1972.

Kottler, Malcolm Jay. "Alfred Russel Wallace, The Origin of Man and Spiritualism." *Isis* 65 (March/June 1974).

Krippner, Stanley, and Rubin, Daniel, eds. *The Kirlian Aura.* Garden City, N.Y.: Doubleday, 1974.

Krippner, S. *Song of the Siren.* New York: Harper and Row, 1975.

Landsburg, Alan. *In Search of Magic and Witchcraft.* New York: Bantam, 1976.

————. *In Search of Strange Phenomena.* New York: Bantam, 1977.

LaVey, Anton Szandor. *The Satanic Bible.* New York: Avon, 1969.

Leek, Sybil. *Phrenology.* New York: Macmillan, 1970.

Le Shan, Lawrence. *The Medium, the Mystic and the Physicist.* New York: Viking, 1974.

Levi, Eliphas. *The History of Magic.* London: Rider, 1913.

Lindsay, Jack. *Origins of Astrology.* New York: Barnes & Noble, 1971.

Luce, Gay Gaer. *Biological Rhythms in Human and Animal Physiology.* New York: Dover, 1971.

Lyons, Arthur. *The Second Coming, Satanism in America*. New York: Dodd Mead, 1970.

Mackay, Charles. *Extraordinary Popular Delusions and the Madness of Crowds*. Boston: L. C. Page, 1932; Wells, Vt.: Fraser Publishing Co., 1969.

MacNeice, Louis. *Astrology*. New York: Doubleday, 1964.

Malko, George. *Scientology, The Now Religion*. New York: Dell, 1970.

Mann, W. Edward. *Orgone, Reich and Eros*. New York: Simon and Schuster, 1973.

Maple, Eric. *The Dark World of Witches*. South Brunswick and New York: A. S. Barnes, 1962.

Michelet, Jules. *Satanism and Witchcraft*. Secaucus, N.J.: Lyle Stuart, 1939; New York: Dell, 1972.

Mishlove, Jeffrey. *The Roots of Consciousness*. New York: Random House, 1975.

Monroe, Robert. *Journeys Out-of-the-Body*. New York: Doubleday, 1972.

Moore, R. Laurence. *In Search of White Crows: Spiritualism, Parapsychology, and American Culture*, New York: Oxford University Press, 1977.

Moss, Thelma. *The Probability of the Impossible*. Los Angeles, Calif.: J. P. Tarcher, 1974.

Muck, Otto. *The Secret of Atlantis*, New York: New York Times, 1978.

Muldoon, Sylvan, and Carrington, Hereword. *The Projection of the Astral Body*. New York: Samuel Weiser, 1970.

Murchison, Carl, ed. *The Case For and Against Psychical Belief*. Worcester, Mass.: Clark University, 1927; New York: Arno Press, 1975.

Murray, Margaret. *The Witch-Cult in Western Europe*. London: Oxford University Press, 1921.

Myers, W. H. *Human Personality and Its Survival of Bodily Death*. New York: Longmans Green, 1954.

Nolen, William A. *Healing, A Doctor in Search of A Miracle*. New York: Random House, 1975.

Ostrander, Sheila, and Schroeder, Lynn. *Psychic Discoveries Behind the Iron Curtain*. Englewood Cliffs, N.J.: Prentice-Hall, 1970; New York: Bantam, 1971.

————. *Handbook of Psychic Discoveries*. New York: Berkley, 1974.

Owen, A. R. G. *Can We Explain the Poltergeist?*. New York: Taplinger, 1964.

————. *Psychic Mysteries of the North*. New York: Harper & Row, 1975.

Panati, Charles. *Supersenses*. New York: Quadrangle, 1974.

————, ed. *The Geller Papers*. Boston: Houghton Mifflin, 1976.

Parrinder, Geoffrey. *Witchcraft: European and African*. London: Faber and Faber, 1963.

Pauwels, Louis, and Bergier, Jacques. *The Morning of the Magicians*. New York: Stein and Day, 1964.

Penseè editors. *Velikovsky Reconsidered*. Garden City, N.Y.: Doubleday, 1976.

Playboy editors. *Beyond Reason, Playboy's Book of Psychic Phenomena*. Chicago: Playboy Press, 1973.

Podmore, Frank. *The Newer Spiritualism*. London: T. Fisher Unwin, 1910; New York: Arno Press, 1975.

Pratt, J. G. *ESP Research Today*. Metuchen, N.J.: Scarecrow Press, 1973.

————. *Parapsychology: An Insider's View of ESP*. New York: E. P. Dutton, 1966.

Price, Harry. *Fifty Years of Psychical Research*. New York: Longmans Green, 1939; and Arno Press, 1975.

Puharich, Andrija. *Beyond Telepathy*. London: Darton, Longman and Todd, 1962; Garden City, N.Y.: Doubleday, 1973.

————. *Uri: The Journal of the Mystery of Uri Geller*. Garden City, N.Y.: Doubleday, 1974.

Rachleff, Owen S. *The Occult Conceit*. Chicago: Cowles-Regnery, 1971.

————. *The Secrets of Superstitions*. Garden City, N.Y.: Doubleday, 1976.

Randi, James. *The Magic of Uri Geller.* New York: Ballantine, 1975.

Rao, K. R. *Experimental Parapsychology: A Review and Interpretation.* Springfield, Ill.: Charles C. Thomas, 1966.

Rawcliffe, D. H. *Illusions and Delusions of the Supernatural and Occult.* New York: Dover, 1959.

Redgrove, H. Stanley. *Alchemy: Ancient and Modern.* 2d rev. ed., 1922. Reprint. New York: Barnes & Noble, 1973.

Rhine, J. B. *New World of the Mind.* New York: William Sloane, 1953.

———. *The Reach of the Mind.* New York: William Sloane, 1971.

———, ed. *Progress in Parapsychology.* Durham, N.C.: The Parapsychology Press, 1971.

Rhine, J. B., and Pratt, J. G. *Parapsychology: Frontier Science of the Mind.* Springfield, Ill.: Charles C. Thomas, 1962.

Rhine, L. E. *Mind Over Matter.* New York: Macmillan, 1970.

Roberts, Jane. *The Seth Material.* Englewood Cliffs, N.J.: Prentice-Hall, 1970.

Rogo, D. Scott. *Parapsychology: A Century of Inquiry.* New York: Taplinger, 1975.

Roll, William G. *The Poltergeist.* New York: Signet, 1974.

Rose, Louis. *Faith Healing.* Middlesex, England: Penguin, 1971.

Roszak, Theodore. *Unfinished Animal.* New York: Harper & Row, 1975.

Scholem, Gershom. *On the Kabbalah and Its Symbolism.* New York: Schocken, 1965.

Seabrook, William. *Witchcraft: Its Power in the World Today.* New York: Harcourt Brace, 1940.

Seligmann, Kurt. *The Mirror of Magic.* New York: Pantheon, 1948.

Shadowitz, Albert, and Walsh, Peter. *The Dark Side of Knowledge: Exploring the Occult.* Reading, Mass.: Addison-Wesley, 1976.

Shapin, Steven. "Phrenological Knowledge and Early Nineteenth-

Century Edinburgh." *Annals of Science* 32 (1975).

Shealy, C. Norman, M.D. *Occult Medicine Can Save Your Life.* New York: Dial, 1975.

Shumaker, Wayne. *The Occult Sciences in the Renaissance.* Berkeley, Calif.: University of California Press, 1972.

Smith, Richard Furnald. *Prelude to Science.* New York: Scribner, 1975.

Smith, Susy. *Ghosts Around the House.* New York: World, 1970.

Starkey, Marion. *The Devil in Massachusetts.* New York: Alfred A. Knopf, 1949.

Stavenhagen, Lee, ed. *A Testament of Alchemy.* Hanover, N.H.: University Press of New England, 1974.

Stearn, Jess. *Edgar Cayce—The Sleeping Prophet.* New York: Doubleday, 1967; and Bantam, 1968.

Steiger, Brad. *A Roadmap of Time.* Englewood Cliffs, N.J.: Prentice-Hall, 1975.

Stemman, Roy. *Spirits and Spirit Worlds.* Garden City, N.Y.: Doubleday, 1976.

Stelter, Alfred. *Psi Healing.* New York: Bantam, 1976.

Stevenson, Ian. *Twenty Cases Suggestive of Reincarnation.* Charlottesville, Va.: University of Virginia Press, 1974.

Summers, Montague. *The History of Witchcraft and Demonology.* New Hyde Park, N.Y.: University Books, 1956.

Targ, Russell, and Puthoff, Harold. *Mind-Reach: Scientists Look at Psychic Ability.* New York: Delacorte, 1977.

Tart, Charles, ed. *Altered States of Consciousness.* New York: John Wiley, 1969.

Taylor, John G. *Superminds.* New York: Viking, 1975.

Temkin, Owsei. "Gall and the Phrenological Movement." *Bulletin of the History of Medicine* 21 (May-June 1947).

Thommen, George. *Biorhythm, Is This Your Day?* New York: Crown, 1964.

Thouless, Robert. *From Anecdote to Experiment in Psychical Research.* London: Routledge and Kegan Paul, 1972.

Tompkins, Peter. *Secrets of the Great Pyramid*. New York: Harper and Row, 1971.

Toth, Max, and Nielsen, Greg. *Pyramid Power*. New York: Freeway Press, 1974.

Ullman, Montague; Krippner, Stanley; and Vaughan, Alan. *Dream Telepathy*. New York: Macmillan, 1973.

Velikovsky, Immanuel. *Worlds in Collision*. New York: Doubleday, 1950.

Velikovsky and Establishment Science. Glassboro, N.J.: Krones Press, 1977.

Vogt, Evon A., and Hyman, Ray. *Water Witching U.S.A.* Chicago: University of Chicago Press, 1959.

von Däniken, Erich. *Chariots of the Gods?* New York: Bantam, 1971.

————. *Miracles of the Gods*. New York: Delacorte, 1975.

Wallis, Roy. *The Road to Total Freedom: A Sociological Analysis of Scientology*. New York: Columbia University Press, 1977.

Watson, Lyall. *Supernature*. New York: Doubleday, 1973.

————. *The Romeo Error*. Garden City, N.Y.: Doubleday, 1973.

Webb, James. *The Occult Underground*. LaSalle, Ill.: Open Court Publishing, 1974.

Weiner, Herbert. *9½ Mystics: The Kabbala Today*. New York: Holt, Reinhart and Winston, 1969.

West, John Anthony, and Toonder, Jan Gerhard. *The Case for Astrology*. New York: Coward-McCann, 1970; Baltimore, Md.: Penguin, 1973.

White, John, ed. *Psychic Exploration: A Challenge to Science*. New York: G. P. Putnam's Sons, 1974.

White, John, and Krippner, Stanley, eds. *Future Science: Life Energies and the Physics of Paranormal Phenomena*. New York: Anchor/Doubleday, 1977.

White, Stewart Edward. *The Unobstructed Universe*. New York: E. P. Dutton, 1940.

Wilhelm, Richard. *The I Ching or Book of Changes*. Princeton, N.J.: Princeton University Press, 1950.

Wilson, Colin. *The Occult*. New York: Random House, 1971.

Wolman, Benjamin B., ed. *Handbook of Parapsychology*. New York: Van Nostrand Reinhold, 1978.

Worrall, Olga and Ambrose. *The Gift of Healing*. New York: Harper and Row, 1965.

Index